KILLER WEED

Marijuana Grow Ops, Media, and Justice

Killer Weed illustrates how and why marijuana grow ops have been portrayed by law enforcement and the media as a criminal activity of epic proportions and how their regulation is changing civil society, municipal authority, and the criminal justice system. In their study on which the book is based, Susan C. Boyd and Connie I. Carter collected and analysed more than 2500 newspaper articles published in national, provincial, and local newspapers in British Columbia from 1995 to 2009, focusing on the origins and impact of the discourse surrounding grow ops. The authors demonstrate that when it comes to marijuana cultivation, the media frequently exhibit similar perspectives and draw on the same spokespeople, especially representatives from law enforcement.

Killer Weed also looks at civil responses to illegal drug production and sales. Boyd and Carter explore the intersections between criminal justice, civil society, and the regulation by insurance companies and public utilities of marijuana grow ops and the people who operate them. Through an examination of court challenges, reports, and legal and civil initiatives, the book contextualizes and supplements the coverage of marijuana grow ops offered by newspaper reporting. It concludes with a critical analysis of the current Canadian approach to the control of drugs in light of the contemporary global movement to legalize and regulate marijuana.

SUSAN C. BOYD is a professor in the Faculty of Human and Social Development at the University of Victoria.

CONNIE I. CARTER is a senior policy analyst for the Canadian Drug Policy Coalition.

SUSAN C. BOYD AND CONNIE I. CARTER

Killer Weed

Marijuana Grow Ops, Media, and Justice

UNIVERSITY OF TORONTO PRESS
Toronto Buffalo London

ISBN 978-1-4426-4367-3 (cloth)
ISBN 978-1-4426-1214-3 (paper)

∞

Printed on acid-free, 100% post-consumer recycled paper with
vegetable-based inks.

Library and Archives Canada Cataloguing in Publication

Boyd, Susan C., 1953–, author
Killer weed : marijuana grow ops, media, and justice
Susan C. Boyd and Connie Carter.

Includes bibliographical references and index.
ISBN 978-1-4426-4367-3 (bound). – ISBN 978-1-4426-1214-3 (pbk.)

1. Marijuana – Government policy – Canada – History – 21st century.
2. Marijuana – Law and legislation – Canada. 3. Drug control – Canada –
History – 21st century. I. Carter, Connie, author II. Title.

HV5840.C3B69 2014   362.29'5097109051   C2013-906190-8

This book has been published with the help of a grant from the Canadian
Federation for the Humanities and Social Sciences, through the Awards to
Scholarly Publications Program, using funds provided by the Social Sciences
and Humanities Research Council of Canada.

University of Toronto Press acknowledges the financial assistance to its
publishing program of the Canada Council for the Arts and the Ontario
Arts Council.

Canada Council   Conseil des Arts
for the Arts   du Canada

ONTARIO ARTS COUNCIL
CONSEIL DES ARTS DE L'ONTARIO
50 YEARS OF ONTARIO GOVERNMENT SUPPORT OF THE ARTS
50 ANS DE SOUTIEN DU GOUVERNEMENT DE L'ONTARIO AUX ARTS

University of Toronto Press acknowledges the financial support of the
Government of Canada through the Canada Book Fund for its publishing
activities.

Contents

vi   Contents

Tables and Figures

Table

Figures

Acknowledgments

We would like to thank everyone at University of Toronto Press for their interest and support in making the publication of this book possible, including Virgil Duff and Doug Hildebrand.

We would also like to thank the Social Science and Humanities Research Council of Canada for funding this research project. It could not have come to fruition without their support. Several people lent support for this project. We would like to thank Jade Boyd for reading and providing detailed and discerning comments on the first draft of the book and the anonymous reviewers provided by University of Toronto Press. We would also like to thank Micheal Vonn, John Conroy, Rielle Capler, and Philippe Lucas, for their insightful comments on small sections of Chapter 5, and Andrew Ivsins for his statistical analysis of reports and studies. However, any errors or mistakes in these pages are of our own making. Finally, we would both like to thank our families for all of their support over the years we worked on the book.

Some of the material in Chapter Five was previously published in an article in *Critical Studies in Media Communications*. We are grateful for their permission to reprint the material in this book.

KILLER WEED

Marijuana Grow Ops, Media, and Justice

Introduction: Marijuana Grow Ops – Setting the Scene

In 2004, the *Vancouver Sun* quoted Commissioner Giuliano Zaccardelli of the Royal Canadian Mounted Police (RCMP), who explained that in Canada most marijuana-growing houses are not "ma-and-pa" operations, but dangerous organized crime businesses:

> "We are not just talking about a simple crime," he said, "... these grow operations are related to the murders that take place in our streets, to the serious harm that happens to the fabric of this nation." The RCMP estimates annual Canadian marijuana production to be between 960–2,400 metric [sic] tonnes.[1]

In the same article:

> Public Safety Minister Anne McLellan said Tuesday the government is committed to eradicating marijuana growing operations, and that people who smoke pot are "stupid." "I see grow-ops as one of the single biggest problems we face in our communities – they do represent a serious threat to public safety," McLellan told Canada's first national conference on the illicit operations.[2]

Two years earlier, in 2002, a House of Commons committee report recommended that the possession of small amounts of cannabis be decriminalized. Then came a report from the Senate Special Committee on Illegal Drugs that recommended the legalization of cannabis and criticized prohibitionist arguments, which according to the report had allowed Parliament to "impose severe prison sentences for simple possession of cannabis, to grant extraordinary police powers, and to permit wide-ranging policy procedures in terms of shadowing, searching, and the collection of evidence." Moreover, the report points out that the "implementation of prohibition in Canada was accompanied by a marked trampling of the fundamental civil liberties of Canadians, as well as blind acceptance of the police representation of cannabis users."[3] Neither of these well-researched proposals written by Canadian members of Parliament and Senators were evident in 2004, when both the (Liberal) public safety minister and the RCMP commissioner were calling for harsher laws to eliminate marijuana grow ops, identified by them as "the single biggest problem we face in our communities" threatening the "fabric of the nation."

Canadians who consumed marijuana, almost half of the Canadian population, were called "stupid" by former Public Safety Minister Anne McLellan.[4] This dramatic shift in the political environment was reinforced with the election of the Conservative Party in 2006. The minority Conservative government pushed for more law-and-order initiatives, including harsher penalties for producing and selling marijuana. In 2007, this government created a new National Anti-Drug Strategy, and it now supports punitive sanctions for marijuana possession, trafficking, cultivation, and importing and exporting. Bill C-26 (2007), reintroduced as Bill C-15 in 2009, attempted to amend the Canadian Controlled Drugs and Substances Act (CDSA), by introducing mandatory minimum sentences for drug offences for marijuana cultivation and trafficking. This Bill was reintroduced in 2010 (as S-10) and again in September 2011, as part of the omnibus crime bill, the Safe Streets and Communities Act, passed into law on 13 March 2012. The Act is made up of many different bills that amend (to name only a few) the Criminal Records Act, International Transfer of Offenders Act, and Canadian Human Rights Act. In relation to the CDSA, the Safe Streets and Communities Act increases the maximum penalty for the production of cannabis from 7 years to 14 years. The Act creates a complex system of escalating mandatory minimum penalties determined by the following: the amount of cannabis (or other criminalized drugs) involved, the nature of the crime and aggravating factors such as being near a school or where youth congregate or in the presence of youth, having been convicted of a drug crime within the past 10 years, acting for the benefit of organized crime, or using or threatening to use weapons. Mandatory minimum penalties would apply if production of the drug constituted a potential security, health, or safety concern such as if the accused used property belonging to a third party, the production constituted a potential public safety hazard in a residential area or to children who were either on or near the site, or the accused placed or set a trap. Legal experts argue that the Criminal Code of Canada definition of criminal organizations is so broad that "many low-income drug users" who collectively produce, sell, or buy small amounts of criminalized drugs, including marijuana, to mitigate the cost and to support their use will be at risk for arrest and imprisonment.[5] Furthermore, the "location factors" such as being near a school or where youth congregate are vague and could be "applied to almost any location" in a community.[6]

The Safe Streets and Communities Act applies to drug production, trafficking, possession for the purpose of trafficking, and importing and exporting. Specific to amendments to the CDSA and cannabis production are some of the following increases in mandatory minimum penalties: imprisonment for 6 months if the number of plants produced is more than five and less than 201 and the production is for the purpose of trafficking; however, the minimum penalties increase to imprisonment for a term of up to 3 years depending on the set of broadly defined aggravating factors that may apply.

In November 2012, Canada's mandatory minimum sentences for some drug offences came into effect. In the same month, across the border, two US states voted in referendums to abolish the prohibition of cannabis and legally regulate and tax it. Adults in Colorado can now legally grow up to six marijuana plants in their home and possess one ounce of cannabis for personal use; legal dispensaries will be set up so that consumers can buy cannabis. Adults in the State of Washington can now possess one ounce of marijuana; licences will be issued to farmers to grow cannabis, stand-alone stores will be set up to sell marijuana to consumers, and the state has applied a 25 per cent sales tax to the sale of marijuana.[7] Furthermore, to date, 17 US states and the District of Columbia have lessened penalties for possession of marijuana.

In contrast, in 2012, Canada's drug laws became harsher when the Safe Streets and Communities Act came into effect – enacted even though critics had shown clearly that Canadian drug laws were already severe, and that a century of drug prohibition has not stemmed the consumption of marijuana.[8] There was no need to enact mandatory minimum sentencing for drug offences. Forty-four per cent of adults who participated in a recent national survey reported using cannabis at least once in their lifetimes.[9] Rates for youth were even higher: 61 per cent of youth surveyed had used cannabis at least once in their lifetimes.[10] Nevertheless, cannabis remains illegal for recreational users, which means that over 60 per cent of youth and 44 per cent of adults in Canada have broken federal law and engaged in a criminal activity. In Canada, marijuana grown outside of designated medical marijuana sites is illegally produced. Outside of designated medical marijuana users (and recreational users in the states of Washington and Colorado), it appears that US marijuana users buy their drug of choice from the illegal market, grow it themselves, or obtain it from a friend.[11] The situation in Canada is similar. One might ask if our drug laws are justifiable and even feasible given that so many Canadian adults and youth have used cannabis. Since the 1960s, marijuana continues to be Canada's most popular criminalized drug or plant. One might also ask why we continue to criminalize marijuana when harsh laws and enforcement have consistently failed to stem consumption.

In this book, we take for granted that social problems are socially constructed, and we ask the questions: Why is the production and selling of marijuana seen as a social problem? How is marijuana production and selling framed by news media, vocal spokespeople, law enforcement agents, and other groups? What are the many ways in which regulation and prohibition of marijuana shapes the actions taken by national, provincial, and municipal governments? How do these programs, policies, and laws in turn extend the authoritarian agendas of police and politicians? What effects do the multitude of forms of regulation have on civil liberties?

This project is made more urgent by recent developments in drug policy at the level of the Canadian federal government. Rather than seek to understand why Canadians favour marijuana over a host of available legal and illegal drugs, or how Canada could lessen penalties for marijuana possession as other Western countries like Portugal and, as noted above, 17 US states and the District of Columbia have done, the Conservative federal government, in 2009, introduced their "Drugs Not 4 Me" anti-marijuana campaign aimed at Canadian young people.[12] Reminiscent of Nancy Reagan's "Just Say No" abstinence campaign in the United States in the 1980s, "Drugs Not 4 Me" urges Canadian youth to "say no." Bus ads and government websites feature materials from the campaign, and one of the advertisements has appeared on television and in movie theatres.

In this advertisement video, a white, male, blond-haired youth at a suburban house party is offered marijuana by other young people, who are depicted as being from diverse non-white ethnicities/races. He hesitates before taking the offered joint, and the film cuts to a "gateway" scenario where he is shown fighting with his mother, taking ecstasy, and falling asleep at school. Cutting back to the present, the boy says "No" to the youth offering him marijuana and walks away. The video stresses key themes in dominant drug discourses, namely, that one-time use is potentially dangerous, drug use is a gateway to personal and social chaos, and drug use is racialized. Here, the young man's whiteness is represented as innocence, at the same time as racialized "Others" are represented as threats to suburban space and its white residents and visitors. There is no discussion of legal drugs such as alcohol, tobacco, or prescription drugs on the "Drugs Not 4 Me" website or ads. Nor is there any mention of Canada's federal medical marijuana program. Since 2001, the Medical Marihuana (sic) Access Regulations (MMAR), administered by Health Canada, provide a legal exemption for cannabis use for patients with serious medical conditions or terminal illnesses.[13]

Also absent from the Canadian government's website is information about general public support for marijuana reform.[14] Numerous surveys show that Canadians favour cannabis reform and a lessening of penalties. A 2012 Ipsos Reid poll found that 66 per cent of Canadians favour the decriminalization of possession of small amounts of cannabis, and an October 2012 Angus Reid poll found that 75 per cent of British Columbians support the decriminalization or legalization of marijuana.[15] Yet, since the late 1990s, Canadian newspaper journalists, police, RCMP, municipal and provincial task forces, and a number of politicians have identified marijuana grow ops as a new and dangerous criminal activity of "epidemic" proportions. This book illuminates the theoretical/conceptual distinction in media reporting – between use and users, and between users and producers. Our primary focus is on media representations of marijuana grow ops; we also explore claims about users, marijuana, and production as they are often combined to underscore specific themes or claims about the evils of illegal drugs.

Newspaper articles routinely refer to the "scourge" of residential growing operations and call for harsh new laws and other regulatory mechanisms such as municipal bylaws. Media reports typically suggest that residential and other forms of marijuana production constitute a major social problem and a key causal factor in drug consumption, organized crime, and violence. Law enforcement spokespeople and media reports describe marijuana grow ops as dangerous, sophisticated, large, extensive, and linked to organized crime. These claims commonly appear in the three major newspapers in British Columbia, and one national newspaper, the *Globe and Mail*.

This book illuminates how marijuana grow ops emerged as a social problem in Canada and how the regulation of marijuana grow ops is radically changing civil society and the power of criminal justice systems and municipalities. To define civil society, we draw on Michael Burawoy's articulation of this concept; he includes those associations, movements, and publics outside the economy and the state. This realm of social activity comprises but is not necessarily limited to political parties, faith and religious communities, print media, and the variety of voluntary organizations such as recreational and interest-based associations, populist and right-wing groups, and charity and social justice–oriented groups.[16] As an example, newspaper reporting has focused on recent efforts in some municipalities in British Columbia to regulate residential grow ops; these efforts trouble the important boundaries between the application of municipal bylaws and the enforcement of the Criminal Code of Canada. Several municipalities, including Surrey, BC, have implemented multipartner initiatives that draw on a hybrid of regulatory mechanisms. These include municipal residential electrical inspections, information from electric power suppliers, and the participation of fire departments, local police, and RCMP detachments. This collection of individuals and groups has compelled residents suspected (but not proven) of operating grow ops to undergo electrical inspections under the auspices of municipal bylaws. Residents are expected to open their homes for inspection by these multipartner teams (RCMP, BC Hydro, etc.) – and pay for the inspections, whether a grow op is found on their premises or not. These efforts pose serious questions about the public accountability of such multipartner initiatives, as well as the de facto extension of the enforcement of Canada's Criminal Code to municipalities, including fire departments. At the same time, these municipal programs represent a larger trend towards the proliferation of enforcement strategies targeted at the production of cannabis. Newspaper reporting typically, although not exclusively, focuses on the "successes" of these initiatives and praises the multipartner nature of these forms of regulation. This same reporting gives little consideration to a wider debate about the implications of these initiatives, instead choosing to report them as an unquestionably legitimate move towards eradication of residential growing operations.

Our analysis of marijuana grow ops emerges from a larger three-year study, "The Media, Methamphetamine, and Marijuana Grow-op Project." Under the direction of the lead author, we collected and analysed 15 years (1995–2009) of newspaper articles in national, provincial, and local newspapers in British Columbia with a focus on how social problems were contextualized and how discourse and systems of meaning were produced. In British Columbia, the *Province* and the *Vancouver Sun* are two of three major daily newspapers owned during our study period by Canwest Media Works. The *Province* is a tabloid newspaper that uses large banner headlines and colour photographs to illustrate its news stories. It has a weekly readership of about 860,000 people. The website for the *Province* claims that the newspaper "will take on a burning BC problem, such as crystal meth or stolen cars, and drive home what needs to be done to tackle the problem."[17] The other two publications featured in our analysis are the national newspaper, the *Globe and Mail*, and British Columbia's other major daily, the Victoria *Times Colonist*, the latter of which was recently sold to Glacier Media. Given the selection of three BC-based newspapers in our sample, the *Province*, the *Vancouver Sun*, and the *Times Colonist*, much of our focus in this book is on news reportage in British Columbia. We were particularly interested in analysing reportage in these papers because Vancouver, BC, has been labelled the "pot capital" of Canada. In addition, many civil initiatives to regulate marijuana grow ops emerged in British Columbia, and local reportage of these events has been extensive. Of course, these newspapers also reported on news from other provinces and national concerns; the *Globe and Mail* provided a national perspective in its reporting. Chapter 2 specifically highlights reportage of events in Alberta, and other chapters examine both federal and provincial concerns related to marijuana grow-ops. The final sample included 2,524 articles published from 1995 to 2009 in the *Globe and Mail*, the *Province*, the *Vancouver Sun*, and the *Times Colonist*; the Appendix to this book provides a more detailed description of our analysis.

One key finding of our study is that although there are key differences between the four newspapers, when it comes to the topic of marijuana cultivation, all four tend to exhibit similar perspectives and draw on the same spokespeople. Another key finding is the way in which themes overlap in these news stories. The majority of these articles draw on law enforcement spokespeople, and they consistently over-lap concerns about the presence of dangerous equipment, possibility of fire, mould, theft of electricity, electrocution, presence of weapons, the possibility of violence because of burglaries and turf wars between organized crime groups, and risk to children found in grow-ops. For example, 1,303 articles (52%) in our study sample were primarily about law enforcement and marijuana grow-ops, but law enforcement is mentioned in many other articles about other subject areas such as weapons, organized crime, municipal programs, and children. The analysis that follows draws on examples representative of these overall findings. Rather than confine our analysis only to print media text, we include news photos and headlines as similarly potent cultural products.

This book also looks beyond media representation: throughout these pages we acknowledge the interplay among cultural, social, and political spheres, media and symbolic representation, and the interlocking nature of representation and the law. Little research highlights civil responses to illegal drug production and selling. For example, little critical attention has been given to the Safety Standards Amendment Act, which is a BC-based legislative and civil initiative to identify and remove marijuana grow ops. There has been little critical media coverage of this Act. In 2006, the Liberal government in the Province of British Columbia introduced and passed the Safety Standards Amendment Act, legislation that allows the province's electricity producers to disclose electricity consumption information to municipal governments. The purpose of this amendment was to help identify clandestine residential cannabis-growing operations, on the assumption that an unusually large consumption of electricity could indicate the presence of hydroponic equipment used for the indoor cultivation of cannabis. This legislation permits the disclosure of this information to safety authorities for the purposes of inspections. In addition, the amendment permits local governments to disclose electrical consumption information to police.

To address the absence of critical analysis of civil responses, we look outside the lens of criminal justice to understand the intersection among criminal justice, civil society, and corporate regulation (i.e., by insurance companies, BC Hydro) of marijuana grow ops and the people who operate them. Thus, in this book we go beyond newspaper reporting to illuminate how legal, political, and civil initiatives emerge. Through an examination of court challenges, reports, and legal and civil initiatives, we contextualize and supplement the coverage of marijuana grow ops offered by newspaper reporting.

In this introductory chapter, we provide a theoretical framework to understand our media analysis of representations of marijuana grow ops over a 15-year span.

Theoretical Perspectives on Media and Crime Studies

To analyse media representations of marijuana grow ops, we drew from critical and feminist researchers. Our theoretical framework is interdisciplinary, drawing on social construction theory and cultural criminology perspectives. We draw on feminist theories to help us explore the social construction of knowledge. For example, in Canada, feminist scholars such as Yasmin Jawani, Sherene Razack, and Sunera Thobani, to name a few, contribute to our understanding of media representations of crime and nation building and the intersection of race, gender, and class.[18] This body of theoretical work offers rich perspectives for exploring how individuals deemed to be outside of normative frameworks make rhetorical claims about drug use and how dominant forms of expertise are constructed.[19] Feminist scholars, in particular, have demonstrated how drug policy is gendered, racialized, and class based and have highlighted the intersection of the regulation of women, reproduction, mothering, and the war on drugs.[20] Cultural criminology is an important part of our approach to the news media because it provides a lens to understand the social, cultural, and political factors that shape media representations of marijuana production. These include the media's uncritical acceptance of the expansion of criminal justice practices and policies in Western nations; the continuous interplay of "moral entrepreneurship, moral innovation and transgression" that characterizes media reporting; and the proliferation of media representations of crime and deviance linked to the use and production of illegal drugs.[21]

Both feminist and cultural criminology scholars are influenced by the scholarship on social constructionist approaches to social problems. This scholarship illustrates how social problems are constructed through strategies of visual and textual representation. Social constructionist analyses draw our attention to the institutionally based claims makers who shape our understanding of "social problems" such as marijuana grow ops. Not only do these vocal claims makers help to define the nature of "social problems," but also they offer solutions that often accord with institutional priorities and concerns.[22] This scholarship draws our attention to how claims about "social problems" can be contradictory, particularly when claims makers offer competing narratives of the origins and solutions to social problems.[23] In the case of marijuana cultivation, institutionally based claims makers including the RCMP, the US Drug Enforcement Administration (DEA), and public health officials may not only compete with each other to define this social "problem," but also be challenged by others including spokespeople from groups supporting drug policy reform, marijuana compassion clubs, and academics.

Since the 1970s, critical and feminist researchers have looked closely at news and representations of crime, justice, law, and culture.[24] Their analyses encouraged other researchers to examine news stories and photographs as cultural products and to see law and order as an important and popular news category.[25] These researchers argue that "crime, deviance, and control exist as socially and culturally constructed phenomena, rather than as random events in the 'natural' world."[26] Every day, newspapers, radio, and Internet sites communicate the opinions of key claims makers. News reports help shape and circulate emerging "truth claims" about social issues such as marijuana grow ops. As McMullan observes, "truth claims are anchored in discourse and discursive formations that produce particular ways of organizing thinking, talking and doing in regard to selected topics."[27] Researchers have also drawn our attention to how key institutional claims makers can mobilize the media to get their concerns on the public agenda.[28] Police, in particular, work in conjunction with the media to promote images of crime that support the goals of policing work. News outlets are the primary means by which police communicate with the public, and these same media outlets are heavily reliant on police for information about crime given that reporters rarely witness directly the events they report. News stories disproportionately emphasize the beginning stages of a criminal justice process (i.e., discovery of a crime, arrests), and as a result, police are often the key or only spokespeople who appear in news stories about crime.[29] The political economy of news media, including decreasing news budgets, the growth of low-cost "infotainment," and the lack of investigative reporting, mean that police have become the primary definers of crime and policing issues.[30] In Canada, cutbacks to public broadcasters and the dominance of corporate media, standardized editorial policies, and limiting codes of practice of professional journalism contribute to this situation.[31] As a result, news media can easily operate as conduits for police perspectives and ideologies on crime. Researchers examining the relationship between the media and police have found that police frame their work to strengthen their position as legitimate sources of information on crime. Researchers have also found that police sometimes use news media outlets to "construct crime waves" to secure resources or highlight a positive public profile.[32] Because of their reliance on police information, news media outlets can be wary of undermining their relationship with police by publishing negative stories about policing behaviour. Scholars have noted the increasing reliance by police on corporate communication strategies and media relations officers to convey policing messages.[33] As Chermak and Weiss suggest, "police organizations have increasingly acknowledged that news media provide key opportunities to do legitimation work and news generally are part of the 'policing apparatus' of society."[34] Journalists frame their stories to give them intelligible narratives accessible to wide ranges of audience members, and it follows, therefore, that organizations presenting concrete narratives of crimes will have considerable power to influence (although not determine) political debate and the public policy agenda.[35] By examining law-and-order discourse about crime and its aftermath, we can begin to understand what groups exercise power through the representation of issues and ideas in some ways and not others.[36]

A number of other theorists brought our attention to news media representations of illegal drugs.[37] Reinarman and Levine's research, in particular, argued that US news media offer narrow representations of drugs, drug use, selling, and criminal justice responses, and they attempt to shape public opinion about crime, especially drug crime.[38] A 2013 study of representations of marijuana in Canadian print media (1997–2007) suggests that representations of marijuana use are "normalized for social elites" such as popular male musicians and celebrities; however, poor and racialized people are "Othered."[39] The authors of this study also note that print media representations of marijuana use are gendered; women's marijuana use is depicted as the exception, and women charged with trafficking are framed as either naive or, conversely, "evil."[40] The authors assert that print media framing is often shaped by the perceived privilege, social status, gender, and ethnicity of the individuals depicted in these stories; for example, poor and racialized men's marijuana use is often linked to violence.[41]

Print media and other texts introduce and contextualize social "problems" and present ideas about drugs, including the production of marijuana, the nature of addiction, morality, criminality, the drug user, trafficker, and producer, organized crime, the effectiveness of treatment, law enforcement, criminal justice, and punishment. Moreover, media stories provide an opportunity to analyse how the intersections of race/ethnicity, gender, class, and culture shape media discourse and drug policy. Throughout the pages of this book, we discuss how Canadian media, law enforcement agents, and central spokespeople link marijuana grow ops to outlaws, racialized gangs, and organized crime that threaten public safety. Small-scale "mom-and-pop" growers are represented as relics of a bygone and gentler era, now replaced by primarily violent male and racialized criminals.

News Photographs, Headlines, and Truth Claims

In analysing media representations of marijuana grow ops, we must keep in mind that newspaper text and pictures work together as a site in the "production of meaning and truth-claims."[42] Drawing from Fraser and Moore's analysis of "illegal drugs discourse," we are interested in making clear how a "particular understanding of order is in operation" via text and photographs related to marijuana grow ops.[43] We also want to understand the significance of the use of photographs in newspapers because images in news media are viewed as "facts" that "speak for themselves."[44] As Stuart Hall suggests, photos have ideological significance because they "can *enhance*, *locate*, or *specify* the ideological theme, once it has been produced, by a sort of reciprocal mirror-effect."[45] Applying Hall's exploration of news media allows us to see how representations of marijuana "grow operations" are fetishized in photos "refracting the ideological theme at another level" – a theme that we come to recognize and understand, in this case, as the "truth" of marijuana grow ops.[46] Photographs of the effects of marijuana production also help to naturalize political claims by seeming to offer incontrovertible physical evidence of these claims. In this context, the visuals, that is, photographs used to illustrate and accompany newspaper stories, provide a particularly effective shorthand form of discourse that evokes for the reader the three most familiar stories about drug production:

1 Its supposed threats to public safety
2 Its tendency to threaten otherwise safe communities
3 Its association with particular criminal types.

Throughout this book, we include and describe some photos that accompanied newspaper stories. In addition, we provide headlines in boxes to illustrate how they, too, are a shorthand form of visual and textual claims about marijuana grow ops.

Our analysis does not claim that news reports are determinant in their shaping of public opinion or of drug policy. As Doyle suggests in his analysis of crime in the media, we cannot know how diverse audiences may interpret discourses related to the production of marijuana. Nor can we hold Canadian newspapers solely responsible for changes to Canada's drug laws. As Jenkins points out, "media factors alone cannot provide a complete answer" to why some drugs become the focus of societal concern.[47] Indeed, scholars such as Marcel Martel observe that a variety of interest and professional groups, as well as political cultures, have all played a part in shaping Canada's drug policy regimes.[48] But, as we indicated above, newspapers produce and circulate institutionally based "truth claims" about drugs, their production, and sale that reflect the perspectives of a limited number of claims makers, including key groups like policing organizations. Given the dominance of these claims in media reporting, they are, therefore, deserving of a fuller scholarly examination. We contend that the discursive shaping of the "problem" of marijuana grow ops deserves an in-depth analysis that can elucidate major claims and speculate on the role that media reporting can have in shaping public responses to drug production, selling, and use. Our basic thesis is that media reporting *constructs* as much as it *reflects* the "truth" of marijuana cultivation.

In this book, we draw on the analysis of critical and feminist researchers described above. However, our theoretical framework and analysis differs because we are looking at *both media representations of marijuana grow ops and criminal law and civil initiatives.* We are interested in how civil initiatives are taken up in Canada to regulate marijuana grow ops and how they inform and intersect with criminal law initiatives. Our interdisciplinary approach, which includes attention to visual representation, cultural practices and counter discourses, media narratives, and analysis of criminal and civil initiatives, provides a unique theoretical framework to examine marijuana grow ops or, more accurately, the sites of indoor and outdoor cultivation of marijuana. In this book, we refer to such a site as a "marijuana grow op," a term commonly used by the media, police/RCMP, and key claims makers. However, we would like to make clear that many people who grow marijuana refer to this activity as growing, cultivating, and tending marijuana gardens. The term *marijuana grow op* usually refers to illegal growing and does not accurately reflect, for example, those people who are legally growing medical marijuana in Canada. Numerous news articles link marijuana grow ops with organized crime. In this book, we refer to organized crime as "systematic criminal activity for money or power."[49]

Marijuana Use, Arrest Rates, and Convictions in Canada

Marijuana scholars Grinspoon and Bakalar point out that "marijuana, cannabis, or hemp is one of the oldest psychoactive plants" known and was used for medicinal purposes for thousands of years in China, Africa, and India.[50] The plant contains over 460 compounds, tetrahydrocannabinol (THC) being only one of them; the fibre of the plant has long been used to produce cloth, rope, oil, and other products. In the mid-nineteenth century, the plant became popular in the West; many patent medicines contained marijuana, and doctors prescribed it to their patients and wrote about its healing qualities. Since the mid-1960s, although illegal, cannabis has been popular for recreational purposes by youth and the not so youthful in Canada and other countries.

An abundance of social science research acknowledges the positive effects of consuming marijuana. The early 1894 British *Indian Hemp Drugs Commission Report*, the US 1944 *LaGuardia Committee Report*, the Canadian 1972 *Le Dain Final Report* and 2002 *Senate Special Report* (to name just a few) acknowledge the positive experiences of marijuana users. The 1972 Le Dain Commission's *Interim Report* found that marijuana is used "simply because of the pleasure of the experience."[51] Contemporary recreational marijuana users in Canada continue to consume the plant because of its pleasurable effects.[52] Drug use surveys demonstrate that cannabis is popular in Canada and around the world (see discussion below). It has also been long acknowledged that marijuana has medicinal qualities that provide relief for a number of serous illnesses such as chronic pain, glaucoma, AIDS-related symptoms, seizures from epilepsy, and arthritis.[53] In addition, the plant is consumed by Rastafarians and other groups in and outside of Jamaica who believe that cannabis is a sacrament and a blessed substance.

Although cannabis is more benign than alcohol and tobacco, like all drugs, there are some health risks for chronic users (influenced by frequency and quantity of use).[54] Because cannabis is not injected, it is most often smoked or consumed orally, the risks associated with injection cocaine, heroin, and amphetamine use (i.e., HIV and Hepatitis C infections) are absent.[55] Unlike with other legal and illegal drugs, there is no evidence that cannabis use increases mortality.[56] Overall, the negative public health impacts of cannabis use are low compared with other illegal and legal drugs such as opioids or alcohol. Unlike opioids and alcohol, the risk of overdose from cannabis "is difficult, if not impossible,"[57] as is the risk of cannabis-related accidents compared with alcohol-related accidents.[58]

As we discuss in more length in chapter 1, as part of Canada's drug prohibition efforts, marijuana was criminalized in 1922 with no parliamentary debate, and as a consequence, the plant was no longer available in a legal form for medicinal or recreational use. At that time, it was not a popular recreational drug as it is today; in fact, following criminalization, there were no arrests for marijuana-related offences for the next 10 years.[59] It was not until the 1960s, when marijuana became popular among middle-class youth and the counterculture movement, that marijuana use and arrest rates rose in Canada. Scholars and users of marijuana note that since the 1960s its widespread use has become a normalized activity in Canada and other Western countries; it is the most popular criminalized drug/plant worldwide.[60]

Canada is the only country to provide a federal medical marijuana program (other countries have enacted state and provincial, and even city medical marijuana legislation and programs); although it is limited in scope (as we discuss more fully in chapter 5), it recognizes marijuana's medicinal value. Nevertheless, in Canada, it remains a criminal offence to possess, sell, cultivate, import, and export marijuana for recreational purposes. As mentioned at the beginning of this chapter, in 2004, 44 per cent of adults who participated in a national drug survey reported having used marijuana once in their lifetimes.[61] The 2006 Vancouver Youth Drug Survey found that youth between the ages of 14 and 25 reported that in the year prior, almost 70 per cent had tried marijuana (56% had tried tobacco).[62] The 2004 Canadian Addiction Survey reports that 22 per cent of young men and 10 per cent of young women, aged 15 to 24, use cannabis on a daily basis.[63] Although adolescent cannabis use in British Columbia experienced a downward trend over the past 10 years, by age 18, 50 per cent of high school students had tried marijuana.[64] Close to 5 per cent of students reported having smoked one to two marijuana joints the previous Saturday, and 3 per cent reported having smoked five joints or more.[65] In the most recent McCreary Centre study of adolescent health in British Columbia, the proportion of students who had ever tried marijuana has decreased from 37 per cent in 2003 to 30 per cent in 2008.[66] Another recent BC-based study found that 46 per cent of youth had tried marijuana.[67] However, marijuana remains illegal for recreational users.[68]

In 2011, the number of drug offences that fell under the authority of the Canadian Controlled Drugs and Substances Act was at its highest, continuing a steady upward trend since the early 1990s.[69] The war on drugs in Canada increasingly focuses on cannabis. In 2011, there were 113,345 drug offences in Canada (a 4.3% increase from 2010).[70] In 2011, cannabis offences accounted for 69 per cent of all drug offences. Simple possession accounted for 70 per cent of all drug offences, and of these, 54 per cent were for cannabis possession – an increase of 7 per cent since 2010.[71] In terms of the total cannabis possession offences in 2011, 14 per cent are to women. For trafficking, production, and distribution offences in 2011, 16.8 per cent of these charges are to women.[72] In 2012, there were 109,455 drug offences in Canada, a 4.5 per cent decrease from 2011; however, 52 per cent were for cannabis possession offences.[73]

In 2010, there were 109,222 drug offences reported by the police in Canada, and cannabis offences accounted for 69 per cent of all drug offences – an increase of 10.2 per cent since 2009. Fifty-two per cent of all drug offences in 2010 were for cannabis possession.[74] Although key media spokespeople suggest that we need to crack down on drug traffickers and cultivators, in 2010 and 2011, possession of cannabis still comprised over half of all drug offences.[75] Between 2009 and 2011, drug offences rose 15.7 per cent even though the overall crime rate has been decreasing for 30 years; since the 1970s, the steady increase in drug offences has been driven by cannabis offences.[76]

Men are far more likely to be represented in police-reported incidents of cannabis possession.[77] In 2011, for example, the rate of these incidents was 57 per 100,000 population for women and 342 for men. Despite these differences, incidents of cannabis possession grew at a faster rate between 2009 and 2011 – 33 per cent more women as compared with 21 per cent more men were reported to be in possession of cannabis. The rate of incidents of cannabis production, distribution, or trafficking was 13 per cent for women and 66 per cent for men, although between 2009 and 2011 the rates of these crimes declined for both women and men.[78]

Since the early 1980s, BC drug offence rates have been among the highest in Canada, and Vancouver and Victoria have reported some of the highest statistics for drug offences in metropolitan areas.[79] But, Brennan and Dauvergne point out that crime rates for drug offences do not accurately reflect the actual numbers of people engaged in lawbreaking and suggest that increases in drug offences often reflect police practices such as increased attention to particular categories of crime.[80] A 2013 study in British Columbia found that charges for cannabis possession vary considerably between police departments and between municipal police and RCMP detachments in the province. The RCMP are responsible for an overwhelming majority of the charges in British Columbia. This study also suggests that charges for possession of cannabis in British Columbia have doubled between 2005 and 2011 despite low public support for the imposition of a criminal conviction for this offence.[81]

Data from Canadian federal criminal court caseloads in 2006–07 indicate that more than half (55%) of all adult cases involving drug-related charges resulted in a guilty charge. In 2005, the Correctional Service of Canada identified 5,588 drug offenders under federal supervision (prison, probation, and parole), about 26 per cent of the total federal offender population.[82] Of these drug offenders, 2,654 were serving time in federal prisons, representing 22.6 per cent of the total federal prison population. Over half of the total number of adults convicted of drug trafficking during this period were sentenced to prison, on average for 278 days. Although the 2005 report by the Correctional Service of Canada does not break down cannabis offences, 9 per cent (1,053) of the federal prison population was serving sentences for drug trafficking, 1.1 per cent (133 people) for importation, and 1.4 per cent (158 people) for cultivation/manufacturing. Most surprising, given the law-and-order rhetoric about lenient sentencing and police profiling of high-level traffickers, 17 per cent (1,991 people) of those sentenced to prison were serving sentences for possession of illegal drugs.[83]

An earlier 2000 review of drug offenders by the Correctional Service of Canada demonstrates that there has been a steady rise in drug offenders being sentenced to prison. For example, in 2000, only 11 per cent of those serving sentences for drug offences in federal prison were charged with possession of an illegal drug; in 2005, 17 per cent were serving sentences for possession of an illegal drug. Similarly, in 2000, 0.7 per cent were serving sentences for cultivation/manufacturing, and in 2005, 1.4 per cent were serving sentences for the same offence. These statistics do not include provincial prisons, which hold the bulk of Canadian prisoners serving 2 years or less.[84] Critics note that the provinces will bear the brunt of court and prison costs because of the expected increases in prison time for people convicted under the new provisions for mandatory sentencing for some drug offences set out in the Safe Streets and Communities Act.[85] Canada's federal and provincial prisons are already overcrowded, and it is feared that the expected increase in the prison population stemming from the Safe Streets and Communities Act will lead to unsafe prison conditions and, as we discuss in chapters 3 and 4, further overrepresentation of Aboriginal and marginalized people in prison.[86]

In Canada, there has been a steady increase over the past 30 years of women charged with criminal activity. In 2009, women accounted for one-fifth (22%) of all adults charged with a criminal offence, up from 15 per cent in 1979.[87] In 2009, adult women were incarcerated at a lower rate than men, except for offences of drug possession, prostitution, and disturbing the peace.[88] A recent study reports on data collected between 2008 and 2011 on women in BC's provincial prisons. Of the women willing to participate in the research (336 participants), 22.9 per cent were incarcerated for drug charges and another 33 per cent were incarcerated for breach of conditions, which could also have been linked to drug charges.[89] In 2009, one of the most common offences for adult women was administration of justice violations, such as failure to appear in court or to follow a court order, breach of probation, etc. – the rate per 100,000 was double the rate for female youth. Women and female youth in 2009 were more likely than their male counterparts to be charged with an administration of justice violation.[90] Twenty per cent of all charges against adult women in 2009 were for administration of justice violations.[91]

The number of existent pre-court diversion programs and alternative measures affect how many drug offences proceed to court. In addition, lack of evidence, stays, withdrawals, dismissed or discharged cases, and pre-charge screening by the Crown, which occurs in British Columbia, will also affect the percentage of guilty findings. In 2006–07, over half of all federal drug-related court cases were stayed, withdrawn, dismissed, or discharged.[92] The proportions of cases stayed, withdrawn, dismissed, or discharged are not indications that the criminal justice system does not work; rather, they can indicate that the justice system uses alternatives to prison sentencing and reserves this option for the most heinous crimes.[93] However, after November 2013, under the provisions of the Safe Streets and Communities Act, conditional sentencing will no longer be an option for drug offences described earlier in this chapter that carry a mandatory minimum sentence.[94]

Cannabis offences have steadily increased since the early 1990s; however, we can see that from 2000 to 2011 there has been a decrease in cannabis production/cultivation charges – from a high in 2000 of 9,062 offences, to 5,691 offences in 2008, and a slight increase in the years 2009 (6,219 incidents) and 2010 (7,091 incidents), to a decrease in 2011 (5,247),[95] and a small increase in 2012 (5,557). It is not possible to interpret why police-reported cannabis production offences decreased over this period. There are many factors such as the special civil initiatives launched by many municipalities in British Columbia and elsewhere, or more cultivation in other locales such as the United States or other parts of Canada. In addition, police may charge marijuana-growing operators with a trafficking violation because it carries a harsher penalty than cannabis production alone; unfortunately, Canada's available

Table 1.1 Arrests for Cannabis Possession and Cannabis Production, 1998–2012

	Possession			Production		
Year	Actual incidents	Rate per 100,000	Change from previous year (%)	Actual incidents	Rate per 100,000	Change from previous year (%)
1998	34,419	114.13	–	7,561	25.07	–
1999	39,594	130.23	14.11	9,007	29.62	18.15
2000	45,407	147.96	13.61	9,062	29.53	−0.30
2001	47,720	153.84	3.97	8,403	27.09	−8.26
2002	49,647	158.35	2.93	8,113	25.88	−4.47
2003	41,295	130.52	−17.57	8,601	27.18	5.02
2004	47,957	150.14	15.03	8,327	26.07	−4.08
2005	43,208	134.00	−10.75	6,949	21.55	−17.34
2006	43,942	134.89	0.66	6,550	20.11	−6.68
2007	47,355	143.81	6.61	6,504	19.75	−1.79
2008	50,408	151.29	5.20	5,691	17.08	−13.52
2009	49,151	145.72	−3.68	6,219	18.44	7.96
2010	56,853	166.60	14.33	7,094	20.79	12.74
2011	61,764	179.11	7.51	5,247	15.22	−26.8
2012	57,429	164.65	−8.08	5,557	15.93	4.7

Source: Statistics Canada 2013a. Cansim Table 252-0051 – Incident-based crime statistics, by detailed violations, annual. Retrieved: 7 Oct. 2013 from http://www5.statcan.gc.ca/cansim/a05.

justice statistics do not indicate how many of the total cannabis-trafficking offences also included a marijuana grow op. Nevertheless, the category of police-reported cannabis production cases has steadily grown since 1977, with a slight decrease between 2001 and 2008, and again in 2011.[96] Table 1.1, drawn from 2013 Statistics Canada data, illustrates the cases of both cannabis possession and cannabis production reported by the police from 1998 to 2012. These data suggest that, in Canada, it is difficult to obtain an accurate statistical measure of the actual size of the underground marijuana-cultivation industry. We cannot rely on police-reported incidents of crime to estimate the size of this economy as these data can be influenced by police practices that focus on drug offences when time, resources, and priorities permit.[97] Although scholars have attempted to measure the size of the industry based on "founded" cases reported to police, these measures remain speculative, as we will discuss below.

From the numbers provided in Table 1.1 and Figure 1.1, it is clear that simple possession of cannabis rather than cannabis production make up the bulk of police-reported marijuana incidents. But, despite this evidence, media reports and law enforcement spokespeople still claim that cannabis production/trafficking is a major threat to social order. Moreover, it is clear now that the war on drugs in Canada is most significantly a war on cannabis users, just as it is in the United States – where possession charges are even higher, and 80 per cent of all drug charges in the United States are for possession and of those for cannabis, 88 per cent are for possession.[98]

Figure 1.1 Cannabis Incidents Reported by Police, 2012.

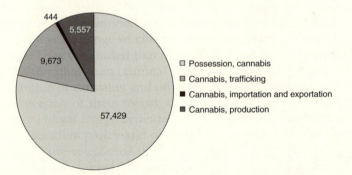

Indoor and Outdoor Cultivation of Marijuana

Before moving on to examine the scholarship on marijuana grow ops, this section provides a brief description of indoor and outdoor marijuana-cultivation sites. In the news sources that we examined, a marijuana grow op appears to be any site where cannabis plants are grown. However, we argue in this book that the term *marijuana grow op* is a contentious term, as discussed above: it is usually reserved for illegal indoor sites and equated with criminality. The term *grow op* renders invisible legal medical marijuana gardens and those people who grow plants at home or cultivate marijuana outdoors in small gardens. For the purposes of this book, we use both the conventional term *marijuana grow op* and the term *garden*. Grow ops can range in size from one plant upwards. Since the upswing in marijuana use in the 1960s in North America, people have grown plants for personal use and for distribution to others. Over the years, domestic growing of marijuana has expanded in North America and other Western countries. In the past 10 to 20 years, the number of grow ops has increased, although, as we indicated above, no one really knows how many grow ops exist. Grow ops are also likely quite diverse in terms of size, location, and use of technology.

Marijuana plants can be grown in both outdoor and indoor settings. Outdoor settings might include backyards, clearings, and forested areas. Indoor settings could include anything from a couple of plants on a kitchen windowsill, to more plants grown in a converted closet or room in a house, to several hundred or even thousands of plants in basements, warehouses, and other facilities. Where available natural light is not sufficient, marijuana gardeners can use equipment and other materials that include potting soil, trays, fertilizers, lights, and fans to regulate humidity. Depending on the size and location of a grow op, gardeners might use a generator to supply electricity for the equipment and to keep the indoor site warm. Cultivators might also use hydroponic techniques for growing cannabis. Hydroponic growing uses a soil-less technique whereby plants are grown in a nutrient-rich water solution, or in a soil-less growing medium like bark. These techniques have long been used by gardeners to grow vegetables, fruit, and decorative houseplants indoors. The US National Space and Aeronautics Administration, for example, has been experimenting with hydroponic methods of growing food for lengthy periods of space travel.[99] Whereas early marijuana growers in North America favoured outdoor gardens, police surveillance and urban growing has led to a shift in growing practices, and indoor grow ops seem to be more prevalent in some areas.

Scholarship on Marijuana Cultivation

Scholarship on marijuana includes an increasing number of non-peer–reviewed but credible articles on cannabis policy, although studies that focus solely on cultivation are few. The UN Office of Drugs and Crime produces annual bulletins on crop monitoring throughout the world.[100] Other international studies have focused on estimating the size of in-door crops and comparing legal frameworks for either the regulation or prohibition of both possession and cultivation of marijuana.[101]

As noted above, scholarly considerations of cultivation policies are few; however, scholarly interest is growing. Decorte, Potter, and Bouchard report that in most industrialized countries there is a sub-cultural scene centred on the drug and plant itself.[102] Although this culture emerged in the 1960s, it is now much more widespread and includes cannabis clubs, societies, 4:20 gatherings, campaigns and reform groups, websites, cultivation competitions, books, and maga-zines. Decorte et al. refer to the cultural scene as "cannabis culture." This term is already used widely in British Columbia and has long been the title of a Canadian-based magazine that is now only avail-able online.[103] This scene consists not only of recreational use of cannabis, but the trading of information on how to grow marijuana plants. Advice on cultivating marijuana is widely available in maga-zines, books, and at plant-growing competitions akin to other types of agricultural fairs. Decorte et al. observe that unlike cannabis, there is no celebration of the aesthetic pleasures of cultivating plants like coca and poppies for the production of cocaine and heroin.[104] Decorte et al. also observe that the cultural significance of cannabis as a plant is further reaffirmed by the recognition of its medical and industrial uses (such as hemp products), as well as the ecological and spiritual benefits of cannabis cultivation, all of which contribute to the rever-ence of the plant.[105] In this book, we assert that cannabis cultivation is far more diverse than what conventional media, municipal, or police claims and reports present. Our findings suggest that in direct contrast to the discussion above, police, municipal, and media reports in and outside of Canada emphasize the link between marijuana growing and organized crime and criminal groups. In addition, newspaper reports rely heavily on police organizations for information about marijuana grow ops.

Several scholarly attempts have been made to estimate the size of this underground economy. A study conducted in the United States by Caputo and Ostrom found that tax revenues from a regulated cannabis market would range in the billions of dollars.[106] Another economic analysis of outdoor cannabis cultivation in New Zealand by Wilkins and Casswell argued that police claims about the extent of organized crime's involvement in these activities were likely overstated.[107] A further report by these authors estimates the amount of cannabis seized by police in New Zealand and suggests that it ranges from 26 per cent to 31 per cent of the total crop, a higher rate than for countries such as the United States and Canada. This high rate of seizure might be accounted for by several factors: most cannabis consumed in New Zealand is home-grown rather than imported and thus, theoretically, more visible to police action; in addition, their estimates are based on cannabis plantations rather than border seizures, and outdoor plant cultivators are more susceptible to police seizure. New Zealand ranks very low on a worldwide scale of corruption.[108] They ask if an expanded police program would effectively eliminate the cultivation of cannabis but caution against this assumption for several reasons. Increased enforcement might precipitate a change to indoor cultivation making grow ops harder to detect; the price of cannabis could increase also increasing the motivation for growing cannabis; and the increased price of marijuana could improve the viability of an import market in New Zealand.[109]

Other scholarly research has focused on the experiences, motivations, and interests of cannabis cultivators. A small study of home-based growers in the United Kingdom done for the Rowntree Foundation found that home cultivation in England and Wales has increased steeply in the 1990s because of improvements in technology.[110] However, the Rowntree Foundation researchers note that the actual yield is "highly variable." Like Weisheit's 1990 and 1991 US research, the Rowntree study suggests that growers are not a homogeneous group in terms of motivations, cultivation techniques, or approaches to markets.

Hough et al. found that the distinction between drug producers and drug users is particularly blurred in the case of cannabis. This finding has implications for any policy based on a "sharp distinction between cannabis users, on the one hand, and suppliers, on the other."[111] These researchers note that growers in their sample began to cultivate marijuana at home to improve its quality, to save money, and as a way to avoid the illegal market and contact with drug sellers.[112]

Weisheit's 1990 study of outdoor marijuana growers in Illinois suggests that cultivators are heterogeneous groups of individuals crosscut by differences of motivation and levels of profitability. As he says of his group of interviewees, they are:

> not disenfranchised Americans who seek to make a social statement by their activities. Neither are they a lost generation of youth for whom marijuana growing is a short-term acting-out behaviour. Instead they are middle-aged citizens who quietly engaged in growing for its monetary and aesthetic rewards. Most growers are employed active members of the community whose income from marijuana supplements their legitimate income rather than replacing it.[113]

Weisheit characterizes growers in his study in three ways: *hustlers* who grow marijuana for the business challenge and who would likely be involved in other large-scale businesses if not marijuana; *communal growers* who begin as users and graduate to cultivation as part of their overall interest in marijuana – these growers are the ones most likely to give away marijuana to others; and *pragmatists* who begin growing marijuana because of economic necessity. This latter group grows marijuana to manage difficult economic times rather than to simply make money. Weisheit found that although growers tended to fear violence from individuals who might steal their crops, on the whole, they were non-violent themselves.

Hafley and Tewksbury examined outdoor marijuana cultivation in rural Kentucky in the early 1990s through interviews with growers.[114] Like researchers such as Weisheit, they note that cannabis production in the United States is on the rise as a result of a number of factors including an early agreement in the 1970s that allowed the United States to spray the herbicide paraquat on Mexican marijuana crops. They point out that, in 1992, the federal government spent $13 billion on drug eradication, interdiction, education, prosecutions, and imprisonment (the majority of this funding earmarked for cannabis) which had two important effects on domestic cannabis production: it led to increased profits as well as enhancements in the organization needed to support cultivation and distribution.[115] These authors found that rural marijuana cultivation is organized around family and community ties that protect growers from detection by law enforcement. Cultivation is also driven by economic necessity and used to support family. Networks of growers appear to be well established stretching back to the 1970s and tend to draw on kin and close friends for help planting and harvesting marijuana. Although possession of weapons is common, these authors found that weapons are used to protect crops rather than endanger law enforcement officials. We also note that in rural Kentucky, owning a weapon is not unusual. The United States has the highest gun ownership rates of all Western nations.[116] The authors offer a picture of marijuana cultivation that stresses both its potential profitability and its challenges, including the cost of seeds, security to guard outdoor crops, labour, and costs of bribes to local law enforcement.[117]

Potter's study of cannabis cultivation in the United Kingdom found that domestic production has risen to become a significant percentage of the overall cannabis consumed in that country. Potter's study pushes beyond Weisheit's interest in the motivations of growers to examine the relationships between growers and the "wider cannabis market."[118] Potter speculates that widespread use of advanced growing techniques and cheaper equipment has led to a larger domestic supply of this drug. Growers of this domestic supply fall into two categories: co-operative producers and large-scale producers focused on exporting their product. The former tend to be less organized, less hierarchical, and smaller in scale. Commercial or large-size growers are more likely to be involved in organized crime and, overall, produce more marijuana but with fewer people than co-op growers.[119] Co-op growers are more likely to produce cannabis for their own use or the use of friends, though some have larger-scale operations producing supplies for medical use. Among this latter group, motivations for growing cannabis are various but not usually financial in nature.

Potter studied commercial growers, including those who conduct business on a small scale with from one to five plants. He found that these growers are using the limited profits from marijuana cultivation to supplement their incomes. But, his examination of large-scale commercial operations found that financial motivations were often paramount. As the size of an operation grew, growers were more likely to use strong-arm tactics to avoid law enforcement. Whether large or small, many of these commercial growers maintained relationships with other cultivators, sellers, and equipment suppliers. Some commercial growers used a co-op model with up to 20 members growing small amounts of cannabis each. In this way, individual growers could lower their risk of receiving a custodial sentence if caught. These grower groups worked together to sell their product and rarely employed violence.[120] In sum, Potter found that many people grow cannabis, but that operations vary considerably in terms of their size, motivations for growing, and connections with others who cultivate and distribute cannabis.

Hakkarainen and Perala's 2011 qualitative study consisting of 38 face-to-face interviews with growers, a Web survey (1,298 growers), and a media analysis in Finland, found similar results. They discovered that their growers were mostly engaged in small-scale cultivation, with from one to 10 plants. Their interviewees challenged prohibitionist drug policy and mainstream values and saw themselves as situated between the mainstream and the criminal underworld; they had no ties to organized crime and grew cannabis for personal use and to share with small groups of friends.[121]

Decorte's study of growers, which included 89 face-to-face interviews with participants in Belgium and 659 Web-based surveys, found that the majority of growers were a diverse group of small-scale growers (70% grew 20 or fewer plants, 27% grew five or fewer plants).[122] They were not motivated solely by profit; in fact, most never sold their plants. Rather, they grew cannabis for a variety of reasons: because it was cheaper than buying it on the illegal market, out of curiosity, because of the pleasures of growing, and to guarantee a source of organic cannabis and milder strains than those found in the coffee shops in the Netherlands. Over 50 per cent of the interviewees and survey respondents in this study grew their cannabis in outdoor settings.

In 2012, Hammersvik, Sandberg, and Pedersen published their findings from a year of ethnographic fieldwork with 45 cannabis growers (10 large-scale growers and 35 small-scale growers). They found five mechanisms that deter small-scale growers from transitioning into large-scale growing: (1) Large-scale growing entails more organization, employees, money, and a "higher risk of detection." (2) Large-scale operations are expensive to run. (3) Large-scale growers need access to distribution channels and skills to participate in the black market. (4) Advanced "horticulture skills" are required. (5) "Small-scale growers are embedded in the 'cannabis culture,' which emphasizes anti-commercialism, anti-violence and ecological and community values."[123] The authors suggest that "within the framework of continued

prohibition" repressive laws are more likely to affect small-scale growers rather than large-scale growers and that governments could "join
forces" with small-scale growers "in their fight against crime and large-
scale operators."[124]

Other studies have shed some light on marijuana cultivation by examining how cannabis users obtain their supply. In the United States,
Caulkins and Pacula's 2006 study drew on data from the National
Household Survey on Drug Abuse to estimate the sources of marijuana.
Based on data from 8,339 respondents who reported using marijuana
in the previous 12 months, they found that only 1 per cent had grown
it themselves, another 2 per cent had traded it, while 39.2 per cent had
bought it, and 57.8 per cent got it for free from friends or others. These
authors estimate the number of purchases of cannabis in the previous 12 months and suggest that the number exceeds 401 million in the
United States. Caulkins and Pacula's findings indicate that "marijuana
acquisition among the general population is almost the antithesis of
the images of anonymous drive-through street markets for cocaine
or heroin that play a prominent role in media depictions of drug
selling."[125]

In Canada, a growing body of research on Canadian cannabis drug
laws and policy has focused almost exclusively on issues related to
possession and, more recently, on medical cannabis policy and judicial decisions.[126] In 2004, economist Stephen Easton developed a math-
ematical model to determine the size of BC's underground cannabis
cultivation trade, and he concluded that it is a robust and growing form
of economic activity. He argued that this trade could be legalized to
realize significant potential tax revenues.[127]

Martin Bouchard has studied extensively the Province of Quebec's
marijuana-cultivation industry.[128] His work includes a detailed model
for estimating the size of the underground economy in Quebec that
combines qualitative and quantitative measures, including interviews
with growers. One of Bouchard's findings is that growing marijuana
is likely not as successful as police often claim it is. He suggests that
police estimates of the size of Canada's crop as well as estimates of
the amount or value of each plant seized are also likely exaggerated,
and he draws on a more conservative model to estimate the size and
value of Quebec's crop. The growers he spoke with generated much
less marijuana per plant than most police estimates; because of vari-
ables like weather, seed quality, soil conditions, indoor versus outdoor

operations, or humidity and light, grow ops have upwards of a 25 per cent to 35 per cent plant loss per crop.[129] Even using a more conservative model than police, Bouchard estimates that a significant portion of Quebec's crop is likely exported to other Canadian provinces or the United States. This trend has been noted elsewhere in Canada.[130]

In other work, Bouchard and Holly Nguyen examined youth participation in marijuana cultivation. They drew on a school-based sample of adolescents from an economically depressed part of Quebec and asked them about their drug use, involvement in other crimes, and level of involvement in cannabis production.[131] What they found echoes other studies like Weisheit's of adult growers – that youthful cannabis growers are a diverse group with diverse motivations and levels of commitment and involvement in cannabis growing.[132]

Little research and few peer-reviewed articles exist on the specifics of marijuana cultivation in British Columbia. In 2011, Kalacska and Bouchard published their findings about outdoor cannabis growing in Vancouver Island and BC's Gulf Islands. They estimate the size of outdoor cannabis production in these locations in British Columbia by comparing aerial police detection data and analysis of airborne hyperspectral imagery. They conclude that cannabis is the "number-one cash-crop in the region under study."[133]

In 2012, another study was published estimating the size of BC's cannabis industry. Werb et al. assert that, "85% of the cannabis market in BC is controlled by organized crime."[134] The researchers attempt to estimate the size of the industry by using an econometric analysis of the cannabis industry that includes expenditure estimates, frequency of cannabis use, quantity of cannabis used, and price of cannabis in British Columbia. They propose that BC residents spend approximately Can$407 million a year on cannabis and conclude that given the size of the industry, alternative regulatory models are needed that could take advantage of the potential tax revenues on the sale of this product.[135]

A 2006 peer-reviewed study by Malm and Tita examines policing strategies in British Columbia, most notably, "Green Teams" – specialized teams of police officers established to eradicate marijuana cultivation within a municipality.[136] Using spatial measures, they found that generally municipalities that employed the use of police-based Green Teams had a decline in marijuana cultivation. However, it appears that the authors' analysis is drawn from "suspected" cases brought to the attention of the police (although they do not clarify specifically which numbers they are drawing from in the article) rather than actual "founded" cases of marijuana production.[137] Their interpretation of results could be quite different if based on "founded" cases. Caution must be exercised about this study, however, as it is based solely on police activities, and the RCMP funded the research for this project, although this is not mentioned in the article. Malm and Tita's study and the RCMP-funded research papers in the next paragraphs focus on improving police regulation of marijuana production. Their research is quite distinct from the scholarly research findings discussed above which focus on the diversity and complexity of cultivators.

Several unpublished RCMP-funded research papers have been written on marijuana cultivation in British Columbia. In the following sections, we examine these reports quite closely because newspaper reports, key claims makers, municipalities, and the RCMP in Canada have referenced them extensively in and outside of our study period. Because these reports have been so widely referenced, they have the potential to inform policy changes including punitive changes to the law, increased policing, and enactment of municipal strategies to reduce marijuana production. These papers were not published in scholarly professional journals or books; thus, they have not undergone peer review (read: by established scholars in the field). The lead author of many of these papers is Dr Darryl Plecas, who holds the position of RCMP university research chair in crime reduction. One of these papers, written in 2002 by Plecas, Dandurand, Chin, and Segger, is based on BC police files from January 1997 to 31 December 2000 of "alleged" and "founded" marijuana cultivation cases. The second paper, written in 2005 by Plecas, Malm, and Kinney, examines alleged marijuana cultivation cases in British Columbia from 1997 to 2003.[138] The 2005 work draws on the earlier study from 2002. The RCMP has also funded a 2002 paper on marijuana trafficking[139] and a 2001 paper on sentencing for marijuana cultivation in British Columbia, Alberta, and the State of Washington.[140] All of these papers assert that marijuana grow ops are epidemic; a growing problem in British Columbia; "large," "sophisticated," and connected to organized crime; and that they pose a significant risk to residential neighbourhoods (fire hazards, violence, etc.). Yet, surprisingly, their data seem to contradict these claims.

In their 2002 paper, Plecas et al. suggest that the number of alleged marijuana-cultivation incidents coming to the attention of the police in

British Columbia between 1997 and 2000 increased on average 48 per cent per year. However, our analysis of their data suggests that the average increase in actual "founded" case over that period is 31 per cent. Plecas et al. state that there was an increase of 222 per cent between 1997 and 2000 in alleged cultivation incidents; however, the increase in founded cases, while still high, was actually 126 per cent. Numbers are inflated in the 2002 paper, and figures are incorrectly labelled.[141]

In their 2005 paper, it is submitted that nine out of ten (89 per cent) of the grow ops brought to the attention of the police during the study period did not have firearms or other weapons or hazards.[142] Yet, in fact, only 6 per cent of founded cases included in the study were reported as having firearms on site, only slightly higher than the 5.5 per cent of the Canadian population overall who have valid firearms licences.[143] Rather than grow ops increasing in size and sophistication, as the authors claim, based on the data presented in their 2005 paper, one might speculate that the number of small grow ops are increasing at a higher rate than the number of large grow ops.[144]

The authors of these RCMP-funded papers recommend the establishment of more punitive policing strategies to eradicate marijuana cultivation, and they look to the State of Washington (prior to 2012) as a model for drug law and sentencing, advocating for harsher sentencing for marijuana cultivation and selling as a means to contain the domestic Canadian marijuana supply. Throughout both the 2002 and the 2005 reports, the statistics and numbers vary (with no explanation), and some of the numbers change between the 2002 and 2005 publications (again, with no explanation as to why).

In the 2002 and 2005 papers by Plecas et al., the raw data presented in the tables do not always match the authors' conclusions. For example, in the 2005 paper, the number of cases examined changes throughout. The 2005 Executive Summary refers to 15,436 cases of marijuana cultivation, but later on in the paper, reference is to 14,483 founded cases of marijuana cultivation.[145] The same summary states that the "number of individual incidents of marihuana grow operations increased by over 220% from 1997 to 2000."[146] This, is a misrepresentation, as they are, in fact, referring to "suspected" cases coming to the attention of the police, not actual founded cases. The number of actual founded cases increased only by 124 per cent from 1997 to 2003, still a large increase in the number of cases but by over 100 per cent less than the authors' original claim.[147]

In the body of the 2005 paper, the authors refer to 25,014 marijuana-cultivation cases coming to the attention of the police in British Columbia from 1997 to 2003 in a table with the heading, "Marijuana Cultivation Cases"; however, these are "alleged cases," not founded cases. Throughout the paper, the authors refer to "suspected and alleged" cases rather than founded cases, which has the effect, once again, of inflating the claims that the authors make.[148]

Unlike the scholarly research that highlights the diversity of marijuana grow ops, the findings of the RCMP-associated reports link grow ops with fire hazards, risk, and organized crime. This book reveals how RCMP-associated studies have been widely circulated by law enforcement agents, the media, and other claims makers, such as municipalities in British Columbia.[149] Thus, the claims made by the RCMP-sponsored authors may have inordinately shaped public perceptions and policy about marijuana grow ops in Canada, including support for the new Canadian federal crime bill, the Safe Streets and Communities Act, 2012, which introduced mandatory minimum sentencing for some drug offences including marijuana cultivation of as few as six marijuana plants.

A 2011 Canadian Justice Department report[150] was requested and released to the *Globe and Mail* under the Access to Information Act, and the findings of the study were presented in an article published on 24 October 2011.[151] We were able to obtain the report through a media contact; the federal government has not yet publicly released it. This raises questions about the lack of data available at that time to support the Conservative Party's efforts to enact the Safe Streets and Communities Act, 2012,[152] which as mentioned above, includes mandatory minimum sentencing for cannabis cultivation (among other increases in sentencing for drug offences). In contrast to the RCMP-associated research, the Justice Department findings challenge claims about organized crime participation in the cultivation of marijuana. By examining court cases involving indoor marijuana grow ops and drug labs in British Columbia, Alberta, and Ontario between 1997 and 2005, the Justice Department sought to better understand drug offences and drug offenders in Canada, with a focus on the production of marijuana.[153] The study draws from a random sample of 500 marijuana grow op cases from Crown prosecutor case files and RCMP criminal history files over an 8-year period. The findings indicate that half of the grow op sites had 151 plants or fewer, only 3 per cent of sites had over 1,000 plants, the largest had 3,629 plants, and just under 9 per cent of sites had fewer than 10 plants.[154] Of the total sample, 76 per cent of the accused were male, 52 per cent Caucasian, and 43 per cent Asian; 94 per cent were Canadian citizens.[155] The authors point out that the severity of penalties meted out to grow operators was directly related to the number of plants and types of charges laid. The probability of a prison sentence was related to weapons found at the site, a high number of plants, and prior criminal history.[156]

Of those cases where the accused was found guilty, fines were the most common sentence (39%) given for a smaller number of marijuana plants and for offenders who owned the grow op property and had employment. Sixteen per cent of the accused found guilty were sentenced to prison.[157] The literature on the production of marijuana and other criminalized drugs generally maintains that this activity is linked to organized crime and gang groups. However, this was not the case in the data: "from the sample of 530 cases, only 5% had any indication that the offender was affiliated with organized crime or street gangs. There were no charges for criminal organization in the collected data."[158] The authors conclude their report with the statement, "What impact organized crime has to play in this study's sampled cases is unknown."[159] They suggest that further research be conducted.

Other more general studies of Canadian drug law and policy have included brief analyses of cultivation mostly focusing on police activities and publications.[160] Kyle Grayson, for example, notes that the RCMP's construction of the problem of marijuana cultivation focuses on its potential to pose public safety threats because of supposed characteristics attributed to most if not all indoor grow ops. These include overloaded electricity bypasses, mould and other toxins, fire, carbon monoxide, and unsafe storage of chemicals. Grayson reports on the propensity of police forces in Canada to prepare and publish tips for spotting an indoor marijuana grow op in a residential neighbourhood. Law enforcement, he suggests, has constructed the gateway theory of drug production by arguing that the "proceeds from marihuana operations are frequently funneled into other criminal activities, such as the importation and trafficking of cocaine, ecstasy and heroin or are laundered to be reinvested in legitimate businesses."[161] He argues that in law enforcement discourses, these activities are often treated as the domain of foreign others including "Asian-based organized crime" syndicates. Grayson examines RCMP documents including reports prepared by its Criminal

Intelligence Service, but these same tropes can be found in Canadian newspapers, as we will illustrate.

Vancouver-based journalist Ian Mulgrew has contributed to the literature about marijuana grow ops. His 2005 book, *BUD INC: Inside Canada's Marijuana Industry*, provides a more personal journalistic account of the industry in British Columbia. He concludes that marijuana prohibition has failed and that the industry should be legally regulated.[162]

Conclusion

The scholarly research on cultivation suggests that cannabis production is far more diverse than what conventional media or police/RCMP present. Moreover, cannabis production is increasingly domesticated and quite normalized in some sectors of industrialized nations. This diversity of growers is apparent in a number of studies. As discussed above, their findings challenge widespread police claims about the extent of the control of marijuana production by organized crime and criminal gangs.[163] Drawing from the scholarly research discussed in this chapter, it appears that growers of cannabis in the "industrial world" are not just motivated by profit; many have a non-financial interest as well. This "ideological" aspect to cannabis cultivation problematizes conceptions of marijuana growers motivated only by profit and economic incentive,[164] and makes more visible the diversity of growers in and outside of Canada. Critical scholarly research is growing, and it describes a very different type of marijuana grower than the one presented by key claims makers, such as police, municipalities, and the media. Small-scale growers are diverse, non-violent, and interested in more than profit. Regardless of unfounded claims linking most cannabis growers to organized crime and violence, a number of scholars argue that cannabis consumption and culture is normalized in many Western countries. But, as we noted above, cannabis possession arrests make up the bulk of charges in Canada and the United States; and officially, law enforcement officers in these nations are opposed to "cannabis culture."

As we will see in the following chapters, drug scares, such as the panicked discourse that has emerged around marijuana grow ops, are not random events; nor do they emerge from nowhere. Our exploration of newspaper stories and photographs in this book allows us to establish what categories of persons are making claims about this drug and to analyse the content and character of these claims about the production of marijuana. These analyses are central to understanding how some ideas and beliefs about drug producers become prevalent and even inform policy and legislative changes. By linking marijuana production with public safety, crisis, disorder, crime, and violence, systems of meaning about "all" illegal drugs are reactivated and brought into focus. An analysis both of how media-based texts and photos transmit ideas about the scope of social problems and proposals for their regulation allows us to understand more fully how formal and informal modes of regulation evolve and become institutionalized in legal codes and policy frameworks.

1 A Brief Sociohistory of Drug Scares, Racialization, Nation Building, and Policy

This chapter examines the emergence of marijuana production as a social problem in media discourse in Canada, with an emphasis on British Columbia. We briefly review the history of Canadian drug policy, and several drug scares and media campaigns in Canada from the early nineteenth century to the present in order to contextualize the "marijuana grow-op scare." Although early drug policy centred on the criminalization of smoking opium, we focus on the tendency of contemporary newspapers to reiterate sensationalist and conventional ideas about drugs and the people who produce, sell, and use them.

A number of researchers have argued that the media have long been in the business of fuelling "drug scares." Reinarman and Levine noted that drug scares are "phenomena in their own right" and have been a popular media creation.[1] The phrase "drug scare" refers to "designated periods" of time where individuals, groups, and media identify and condemn a particular drug as a new social problem requiring increased attention and regulation. Drug scares are often fuelled by moral reformers, operating as vocal "claims makers" who attempt to produce authoritative knowledge about a social problem by diagnosing and defining the scope of the problem.[2] Illegal drug use and trafficking are most often associated with racialized people or other "scapegoats" such as biker gangs, "whose behaviour is presented as a threat to normative social and moral values."[3] Often, the drug threat is constructed as disproportionate to the "physical threat" posed by the actual levels of drug use.[4] In North America, drug scares have been shaped by long-standing, nation-building and race ideologies stemming from late nineteenth- and early twentieth-century social reform movements, including the anti-opiate and temperance movements. A number of Canadian scholars have argued that race, class, and gender concerns shaped early drug legislation and racial profiling.[5] Increased law enforcement and regulation, including broader police powers, harsher laws, and stiffer sentencing were most often the response to these real and imagined social problems.

The following section briefly describes the social and political environment in Canada prior to its first drug legislation and drug scare. Because the origins of Canada's first drug laws and drug scares are linked to colonization and racist discourses, we examine in some length in this section, temperance and anti-opiate movements, nation building, and the regulation of First Nations and Chinese people in the late 1800s and early 1900s.[6]

Canada's first drug prohibition was directed at First Nations peoples. The creation of racial distinctions was primary to Canadian nation building, and by 1876, the federal government had passed the Indian Act to regulate all aspects of the lives of First Nations people and to define and delineate legal "Indianness." One of the later provisions of the Indian Act, in 1886, was to prohibit First Nations people from buying or possessing alcohol. This legislation was not fully repealed until 1985. The law did not stop First Nations people from drinking alcohol; rather, it led to the arrest and imprisonment of thousands of people. First Nations writer Brian Maracle argues that law enforcement officials and Indian agents used the law to socially control First Nations people; and, in order to drink legally and to vote, First Nations people had to sign away their legal status.[7]

Colonization of what is now Canada played a significant role in racializing drug policy in Canada, especially on the west coast, including the territory that is now British Columbia. The west coast of Canada was not colonized until the mid-1800s, and early settlers, including politicians (federal and provincial), religious leaders, and labour advocates envisioned a strong white Canada and a "British" British Columbia, even though the region was long inhabited by First Nations people.[8] In British Columbia, racial distinctions and legal policy played a significant role in colonization, as it did in the rest of Canada. To make a white British colony and later a province of the Dominion, First Nations people were forced from their ancestral lands, and their social, political, and spiritual practices were outlawed by colonizers. The west coast became a British colony in 1849, and from the mid-1800s on, early politicians and city councillors in Vancouver, BC, sought to exclude non-white residents such as Chinese, Japanese, and South Asian people from permanently settling in the new province, and they were disenfranchised and denied the vote, both federally and locally.[9] The social practices of other groups characterized by white colonists as foreign were also constructed as deviant. White politicians in Vancouver hailed the recreational practice of smoking opium by some Chinese residents (rather than the copious amounts of opium-based elixirs and patent medicines that white settlers consumed) as an unchristian and immoral activity.

Chinese people, mostly men, came to the west coast during the gold rush in the mid-1800s. They were also recruited by the federal government to work on the construction of the national railway up until the mid-1880s. As racialized contract workers, they were given some of the most dangerous jobs building the national railway. They were paid between one-third and one-half as much as white labourers. After the completion of the railway, many Chinese men settled in Vancouver, and wage discrimination helped to fuel class conflicts that emerged between white and Chinese workers during the late 1800s and early 1900s.[10] So, too, did concepts of race such as the eugenics movement, white supremacy, and social Darwinism, which were strengthened during this era of British imperialism. Early white settlers constructed Chinese people as outsiders, an inferior "race," that was supposedly both immoral and threatening to the new province. The BC Legislature and Vancouver city councillors set about passing provincial laws and city bylaws to restrict Chinese people from representation in government, serving as jurors in both civil and criminal courts, working in a number of occupations, and living and owning homes and businesses outside of the designated "Chinatown."[11] Writing about the construction and segregation of Chinese people in Chinatown in the late 1800s, cultural geographer Kay Anderson points out in her book, *Vancouver's Chinatown: Racial Discourse in Canada, 1875–1980*, that the mayor and city council in Vancouver were "eager to lend whatever moral authority it could to the anti-Chinese vendetta," and they went out of their way to assure that Chinese people were deterred from settling in or near the city.[12] By the late 1880s, Chinese people in Vancouver were driven to the east part of town, and the Knights of Labour organized a boycott of all businesses that employed Chinese people.[13] Barriers to immigration were initiated at both the federal and provincial levels, including the infamous Head Tax.[14] In 1885, following the completion of the national railway, the first federal Head Tax of $50 was imposed on all Chinese people immigrating to Canada. By 1903, the Head Tax had increased to $500, a substantial sum at that time. No other group of immigrants was included in the Head Tax.

It is difficult to make clear the level of institutional racism and violence that emerged in the late 1800s and early 1900s towards Asian people in Canada.[15] Newspaper reports and citizen groups fuelled fears that opium smoking would spread further into white populations; these same sources promoted notions of "racial purity," and they stirred up racist fears about women's potential victimization at the hands of evil Chinese men. In this environment, Canada's first narcotic legislation emerged.

Local politicians, labour unions, police, and the media fomented much hatred towards Chinese people igniting two separate race riots in Vancouver in 1887 and, again, in 1907. Following the 1907 race riot, Mackenzie King, then deputy minister of labour, visited Vancouver to settle damage claims from the riot for Japanese and Chinese people. He was contacted by the Anti-Opium League and decided to investigate the possibility of suppressing the then legal opium industry. In this way, he hoped "to get some good out of this riot."[16] Following his report on compensation for the riot, Mackenzie King submitted another report, *The Need for Suppression of the Opium Traffic in Canada*, outlining the harms of smoking opium and recommending that as a moral law-abiding Christian nation, prohibition of the sale, production, and importation of this drug must occur to protect citizens from its "evils." Taking up Mackenzie King's recommendations, Canada enacted the Opium Act (the first federal drug legislation outside of alcohol prohibition for those labelled Status Indians according to the Indian Act), in 1908, with little parliamentary debate or pharmacological evidence to support the regulation of this drug.[17] The legislation was aimed at regulating opium in smoking form, as noted above, an activity linked to Chinese men. This legislation was not focused on the elixirs and patent medicines that contained opiates and other drugs such as cocaine and marijuana commonly used by white settlers. In his report, Mackenzie King drew from newspaper reports claiming that opium dens corrupted the morality of white women and men. Early legislation was enacted with the understanding that it would not be used against Anglo-Saxon Canadians.[18] Thus, Vancouver had the distinction of being the site of an anti-Asian riot from which Canada's first federal drug legislation emerged. The investigation of the anti-Asian riot and restitution for damages initiated a punitive law aimed at Chinese people, further adding to their status as criminalized outsiders to the nation.[19]

Following the enactment of the Opium Act, in 1908, Mackenzie King presented himself as the defining actor in determining drug policy in

Canada. In 1909, he attended the Shanghai Opium Conference, which served to elevate both his status and Canada's as pioneers in drug control.[20] The Shanghai Opium Conference, in 1909, was led by the United States, and its genesis stemmed from American concerns about the opium trade. Representatives from 13 countries attended this conference, including Canada. Mackenzie King is quoted in the *Globe*, after attending the Shanghai Conference, as declaring, "American delegations generously admitted that their legislation for the suppression of the traffic in the United States has been copied from Canada."[21]

The Shanghai Conference laid the groundwork for the first International Opium Conference where the first international drug treaty, the International Opium Convention, was signed at The Hague, in 1912.[22] Early international focus centred on curtailing the opium trade in Asian and South Asian nations. Although the United States was active in leading international drug control and pushing for prohibition of the opium trade, it did not enact federal drug control until 1914 with the passage of the Harrison Act.

In the early 1900s, newspaper reporting was a key component in racializing drug use in and outside of Canada. Vancouver newspapers depicted smoking opium, rather than liquid opium use, as a racialized threat to both the social and moral values of Anglo-Saxon citizens and the larger nation state.[23] These reports repeatedly constructed the opium den as a site of corruption of white women by immoral Chinese men. Fears about the Other, particularly "foreign" men corrupting innocent and supposedly moral Anglo-Saxons were further exacerbated by key social changes including immigration and urbanization. These fears were exacerbated by the first "Red Scare" following the Russian Revolution of 1917 and the First World War. Fear of groups like communists, socialists, anarchists, political agitators, and strike leaders culminated with the Winnipeg General Strike, in 1919, and led to the deportation from Canada of thousands of labour organizers.[24] Historian David Musto argues that the Red Scare and the First World War led to changes in perceptions about drugs, addiction, and foreign outsiders. Addiction was seen as a threat to the war effort, capitalism, and Western nationalism. Narcotics use was constructed as anti-social behaviour associated with foreigners, moral degradation, and the weakening of the nation.[25] In Canada, following the First World War and the Red Scare, politicians and the RCMP sought to root out and deport "enemy aliens" and those who threatened the morality of Anglo-Saxon society, including Chinese Canadians who smoked opium.[26]

Drug Scares and the Media

Against this backdrop, in the early 1920s, Canadians experienced their first "major" drug scare fuelled by anti-Chinese sentiments and media reports proposing solutions to these imagined problems. In 1920, Emily Murphy, a Canadian magistrate and moral reformer, published a series of sensationalized articles about drugs and trafficking in Canada's national *Maclean's* magazine. The "stated purpose of the series was to arouse public opinion to pressure the government for stricter drug laws."[27] Her articles, published in her 1922 book, *The Black Candle*, also introduced Canadian readers to ideas about dangerous Chinese traffickers who sought to seduce and corrupt supposedly innocent white Christian people. Chinese and Black drug traffickers were portrayed as enslaving white women into a life of addiction and immorality. Central to Murphy's argument was a strong desire to "protect" a Christian, Anglo-Saxon nation from the Other, and from the drugs associated with these racialized and demonized groups. Contributing to the production of racialized drug discourses in the 1920s, Murphy asserted that Chinese men would take over the world and contribute to an end to Anglo-Saxon civilization. She wrote that Vancouver's Chinatown was the site of drug traffickers and international distributors intent on this purpose. Murphy's writing and photographs reiterated strong anti-Asian sentiments and linked these beliefs to a need for drug prohibition that included harsh laws and increased law enforcement activities. Emily Murphy's magazine articles and book, and the print media in Vancouver, played a crucial role in shaping Canadian drug policy in the early 1900s.[28]

In British Columbia, provincial newspapers helped fuel the drug scare. A newspaper headline in the *Province* in 1922 stated, "Liberal Candidates Are Pledged to a White British Columbia."[29] Hatred and fear about the "Yellow Peril" continued unabated in Vancouver. Local politicians, moral reformers, the police, and the media contributed to the construction of Chinatown as a site of debasement, counterpoised to the rest of the city and British Columbia as a white moral and law-abiding space. In the 1920s, this led to harsher federal drug policy, racial profiling of Chinese people by the police, and the deportation of Chinese aliens. In 1924, 125 Chinese people were deported from Canada under the Opium and Narcotic Drug Act.[30] From 1908 to 1934, the majority of people convicted of drug offences in Canada were of Chinese Canadian heritage. For example, in 1922, 1,117 people whose country of birth was listed as China were convicted of a drug offence, compared with 733 "non-Chinese" persons. It was not until 1954 that "Chinese data" were no longer specified in criminal statistics.

Historian Catherine Carstairs examined the media-fuelled drug panic in Canada during the early 1920s. She found that newspapers in Vancouver (both the *Vancouver Sun* and the *Vancouver Daily World*) were important producers of racialized drug discourse. From 1920 to 1921, Vancouver's oldest newspaper, the *Vancouver Daily World* (merged with the *Vancouver Sun* in 1924)[31] "blamed Asians for the spread of the drug habit."[32] Anti-Asian discourse fuelled not only early drug regulation, but as mentioned above, restrictive and exclusionary immigration policy. Newspaper articles in the *Vancouver Daily World* argued that Anglo-Saxon Canadians needed to "defend themselves against" the supposed effects of drug use. These articles posed solutions for these problems in headlines such as "Deport the Drug Traffickers." Over the next several months, the *Vancouver Daily World* and the *Vancouver Sun* continued to produce stories accompanied by photos about "white victims and Chinese villains."[33] The *Vancouver Daily World* encouraged citizen groups and organizations to come together to create petitions and pass resolutions calling on the federal government to enact laws prohibiting drug use and trafficking. Echoing current Canadian media debates, these articles supported mandatory sentences for drug possession and trafficking and legislation to deport Asian people. Thousands of Vancouverites complied. The media, moral reformers, citizen campaigns (mass meetings), and the RCMP argued successfully for harsher federal legislation to regulate the use, production, and distribution of opium.

In the early 1920s, Canada committed to the use of criminal sanctions to control specific drugs such as opium and cocaine. In 1921, the Opium and Narcotic Drugs Branch was created, and in 1923, cannabis was added to the list of criminalized drugs with little debate or explanation in Parliament.[34] R.W. Cowan held the position of chief of the Narcotics Division from 1919 to 1927 and Colonel C.H.L. Sharman held that post from 1927 to 1946. After 1919, the RCMP had a more national presence; in fact, the organization was partially saved from being disbanded in the 1920s when it became the primary enforcement agency responsible for enforcing the new drug laws.[35] From its inception, the RCMP and other police forces were key knowledge producers about newly criminalized drugs such as marijuana. Their concerns overwhelmingly shaped law, drug policy, and media reporting. Social historian Steve Hewitt reports that the RCMP, a militarized federal police force, has become symbolically "synonymous with law and authority" in Canada.[36] To survive being disbanded, the RCMP set out to become the main player to enforce Canada's new drug offences, and successfully pushed for harsher drug laws and broader police powers.[37] Specialized RCMP drug squads were set up throughout Canada in the 1920s working with, and sometimes causing friction with, local police agencies.[38] As noted above, they also contributed to anti-Asian sentiment at that time and became ready sources for news outlets expressing hostility towards Asian people in Canada. Hewitt explores how the early RCMP was made up of mostly white British subjects, many of whom were ex-military men, and later white Canadian men, who expressed masculine values of "order, patriotism, militarism, and physicality."[39] The RCMP of the time sought to eliminate undesirables and foreign Others, including Chinese Canadian opium smokers and sellers and, later, those who possessed and sold cocaine, marijuana, and other newly criminalized drugs.

In the early 1920s, Mackenzie King and the Liberal Party were quite critical of the RCMP, accusing its members of being agents of a "police state."[40] Even as Mackenzie King's Liberal Party criticized the RCMP, and attempted to restrict its funding, "moral indignation" about the evils of opium, cocaine, and alcohol led to the creation of new government departments to regulate alcohol prohibition and newly criminalized drugs.[41] Giffen et al. observe that "a review of the history of the RCMP indicates that the Force had a great deal to lose if Parliament ever decided that a serious drug problem requiring their services did not exist in Canada."[42]

Marijuana Regulation in Canada and the United States

The *Indian Hemp Drugs Commission Report* (1894) is one of the most comprehensive studies of marijuana. The Commission systematically examined the physical, mental, and moral effects of marijuana. Its research findings consist of seven volumes (3,281 pages) produced by the British government in India. Seventy questions about marijuana and its effects were given to 1,193 witnesses (including civil officers, medical officers, private practitioners, cultivators, etc.). The Commission concluded that moderate use of hemp is the norm and that the drug "appears to cause no appreciable physical injury of any kind," nor does it produce "injurious effects on the mind" or "moral injury." Moreover, the Commission concluded, "There is little or no connection between the use of hemp drugs and crime."[43] Contemporary researchers have praised the *Indian Hemp Drugs Commission Report* for its depth, standards of thoroughness, and objectivity.[44]

However, objective scholarship about marijuana was short-lived; opposition in Canada (and other Western countries) to the drug emerged in the early 1900s, along with opposition to other drugs such as morphine, laudanum, heroin, and cocaine. As discussed above, these plant-based drugs were popular in patent medicines and elixirs and legally obtained and used by white Canadians to manage their health needs at this time.[45] But, by the 1920s, moral reformer Emily Murphy played on, and connected drug use to ideas about racial hierarchies so predominant in nineteenth- and twentieth-century colonial discourses. While persons of Asian descent were depicted through orientalist discourses as scheming and duplicitous,[46] Murphy drew on racist notions of primitivism to characterize Black men and their relationship to marijuana.[47] In *The Black Candle*, she quotes from a letter she received from the chief of police for the City of Los Angeles who asserts that people who use marijuana are driven "completely insane." He claims that "marijuana addicts" become "raving maniacs and are liable to kill or indulge in any form of violence to other persons, using the most savage methods of cruelty without, as said before, any sense of moral responsibility."[48]

Marijuana was criminalized in Canada in 1923 with no public debate. Yet, following its criminalization, opium and Asian users and sellers of it, not marijuana, continued to be the chief concern of law enforcement and news reports. Even though moral reformers such as Emily Murphy were clamouring about the dangers of marijuana, it was not yet a popular drug in Canada (or the United States). From 1923 to 1936, there are no recorded arrests for possession of marijuana in Canada. In 1937, four people were arrested. Marijuana arrests for possession remained stable until 1958, when 14 people were arrested for marijuana possession, followed by a slight increase to 21 arrests in 1960.[49]

Drug historian David Musto examines the demonization of foreigners, Chinese, Mexicans, Reds, etc., in his excellent history of the origins of drug control in the United States. He reports that the practice of smoking marijuana was introduced to some Black and white jazz musicians by Mexican labourers who immigrated to the United States in the 1920s. As the Great Depression set in, and jobs became scarce, Mexican immigrants who came north to work were increasingly made unwelcome and were stereotyped by moral reformers and print media as a group associated with crime, violence, and marijuana use, even though there was no evidence to substantiate these claims.[50] Marijuana became associated with Mexican immigrants, and moral reformers claimed that the drug was also a "sexual stimulant" that lowered "civilizing inhibitions."[51] By the 1930s, marijuana and the people who used it were depicted by moral reformers and the media in Canada and the United States as threatening to rural white middle-class society, especially youth.

Themes from the prohibitionist discourses of earlier anti-opiate reformers and alcohol temperance movements[52] became associated with marijuana. These themes linked drug use not only with the breakdown of the family and the Anglo-Saxon way of life, but with breaches of racial purity, and with potential victimization of "Others" by its users, who sold or gave drugs away to innocent and unsuspecting consumers, especially white youths. Once federal alcohol prohibition ended in the United States in 1933, marijuana became the number one enemy of the state and reformers.[53] By 1936, Harry J. Anslinger, the first commissioner of narcotics in the newly created US Federal Bureau of Narcotics in 1930, shifted his attention to federal marijuana control.

Law enforcement efforts to curtail marijuana use in the 1930s emerged at the same time as the Great Depression. The effects of the Depression were felt across the globe and affected many countries, including Canada and the United States.[54] This period constituted a curious mix of increased regulation of drug use alongside the implementation of the more progressive policies of US President Franklin Delano Roosevelt's New Deal, and the passing of the US Social Security Act of 1935.[55] Political instability and fears about the sustainability of capitalist Western societies not only shaped debates about social policy but also about drug policy and marijuana. Unlike the New Deal, which was, in part, the product of public pressure, political opportunity, and pre-existing policy pathways in the US context, US federal funding for drug control in this period was more a product of the idiosyncratic moral entrepreneurship of Harry Anslinger, the commissioner of narcotics.

Anslinger successfully used fears about social chaos precipitated by the dire social conditions of the Depression as his own form of political opportunity – and as a result, he enjoyed success in "using law enforcement to control public opinion regarding drug use and addiction."[56] He was influential in the production of a wide variety of anti-drug discourses during his long period in office as the US drug czar. For 32 years, Anslinger pushed to criminalize specific drugs and called for more international, national, and state laws to prohibit their use. He used radio, print media (newspaper and magazine articles and books), and film to "educate" Americans and others about the horrors of drugs like marijuana and concomitant dangerous drug dealers.[57] He encouraged citizen groups to take on the fight against marijuana and assisted them by providing written material and guest speakers from the Federal Bureau of Narcotics.[58] Anslinger also attempted to control the flow of scholarly research and artistic creations (including documentaries, fictive films, and books) about drug use, while at the same time producing, disseminating, and supporting anti-drug discourse.[59] His attempts to censor representations of illegal drugs that did not fit with his anti-drug ideology limited the availability of alternative information about marijuana, other criminalized drugs, addiction, and the law.[60] Anslinger also adopted imperialist approaches to the drug laws and policies of other countries. During his career, he pushed for Canada and other nations to adopt US-style anti-drug legislation and drug "education" efforts.

Anslinger publicly praised Colonel Sharman, chief of Canada's Narcotics Division for his unfailing law-and-order stance, abstinence ideology, and his opposition to maintenance treatment for people addicted to drugs.[61] In fact, Anslinger often cited Sharman and RCMP sources as initiators and supporters of harsh national policy. He drew examples from Canadian law enforcement to support the enactment of harsher US drug legalization.[62] Anslinger praised Canadian support for US efforts to coordinate and enforce international cooperation. Thus, the US commissioner and the Canadian drug chief were well acquainted, aware of each other's drug control efforts, and worked in tandem to increase enforcement efforts.[63] For a country like Canada, which did not have its own English-language fictive film industry yet, and whose citizens listened to US radio stations and read US-authored articles and books, US anti-drug discourse was significant in the education of Canadians about marijuana and other drugs.

It is believed that Anslinger and the US Federal Bureau of Narcotics supported the production of three anti-marijuana independent films produced in the 1930s in the United States. These films were also distributed outside the United States and were available to Canadian and British movie viewers on the independent film circuit. These films were produced prior to US federal marijuana regulation, in 1937, and at a time when moviegoers had little knowledge of the plant.[64] The three films, *Assassin of Youth* (1935), *Marihuana: The Weed with Roots in Hell* (1936), and *Reefer Madness* (1936), were originally created as educational films.[65] In these Depression-era cautionary films, white middle-class youth were depicted as vulnerable, not only to the negative effects of drug use, but to the seemingly parasitic and criminal ways of the people who sell drugs.[66] Whether intentional or not, these three films successfully captured many of Anslinger's views about marijuana, addiction, and the need for criminal justice regulation.[67] Anslinger's campaign to enact US federal regulation of marijuana culminated in the 1937 Marijuana Tax Act.

With the enactment of the Marijuana Tax Act in the United States, the Federal Bureau of Narcotics annual report for 1937 differed in tone from earlier reports on the cultivation of marijuana and hemp. These earlier reports were written in a "matter-of-fact" style without any dire warnings about ill effects of this plant.[68] The report for 1937 makes unsubstantiated claims about marijuana consumption reaching "serious proportions" in the United States, claiming that youth are especially "susceptible."[69] The Federal Bureau of Narcotics presented a number of "representational cases" describing suspects under the influence of marijuana. These suspects are depicted as savage and violent. A Denver, Colorado, judge is quoted in the report, saying, "I consider marihuana the worst of all narcotics – far worse than the use of morphine or cocaine. Under its influence men become beasts." A federal judge from Tennessee states, "There is no habit that can more encourage criminality in its worst form."[70]

Even though marijuana was a relatively unknown drug in Canada (as noted above, there had been no arrests for marijuana possession between 1922 and 1936, followed by four arrests each in the years 1937 and 1938[71]), the *Toronto Daily Star* carried a story in 1938 entitled "Marijuana smokers seized with sudden craze to kill: Officer warns insidious weed is even supplied to school children." A 1938 story in *Maclean's* magazine suggests, "Plants growing right here in Canada could produce enough of this drug which maddens, to send a large proportion of the Dominion's population to the insane asylum." The first full debate on marijuana in Parliament was occasioned by a bill introduced in 1938 to make the cultivation of marijuana an offence.[72] Parliamentary debate reflected the views of Canadian law enforcement agents, US-based negative media publicity about marijuana, US Commissioner of Narcotics H.J. Anslinger, and the Federal Bureau of Narcotics.

In 1939, at the request of the mayor of New York City, Fiorello La-Guardia, a committee of health professionals was formed by the New York Academy of Medicine to study marijuana smoking. Their work, *The LaGuardia Committee Report*, was published in 1944. Similar to the *Indian Hemp Drugs Commission Report* (1894), the *LaGuardia Committee Report* was praised by contemporary drug researchers for its "scope and thoroughness."[73] The research consisted of both a sociological and a clinical study. The researchers examined "tea pads" in New York City and other sites of marijuana use. Tea pads refer to sites where people came to smoke marijuana. The researchers found that the distribution and use of marijuana was centred in Harlem, and it was not widespread among schoolchildren, nor was juvenile delinquency associated with marijuana smoking. They found that marijuana was not a factor in the commission of crime, nor did marijuana use lead to heroin or cocaine addiction. Overall, they found that marijuana created feelings of adequacy among its users. The researchers also noted that publicity about the "catastrophic effects of marihuana smoking in New York City is unfounded."[74] The *LaGuardia Committee Report* differed in tone from Anslinger and the annual reports of the Federal Bureau of Narcotics from 1937 on. Musto suggests that the Federal Bureau of Narcotics sought to minimize the impact of the report's conclusions that marijuana use does not lead to moral, physical, or mental degeneration.[75]

There was little focus on drug regulation in Canada during the Second World War (Canada entered the Second World War a week after Britain and France in 1939, the United States entered the war in 1941); however, following the war, ideas about drugs as well as patterns of drug use shifted in Canada. In 1946, Colonel Sharman, former RCMP officer and chief of the Narcotics Division at this time, became the first international chair of the Commission on Narcotic Drugs and K.C. Hossick, also a former RCMP officer, replaced him as chief.

On the domestic scene, a small group of white users of heroin in Vancouver's eastside became the focus of police and media concern. By the late 1940s and early 1950s, the term *criminal addict* was adopted by law enforcement agents in Canada to describe heroin and cocaine users, and "addiction" was seen as secondary to what police typically described as "criminal" tendencies.[76] Similar to earlier drug scares in Canada, in the early 1950s, the *Vancouver Sun* and the *Province* contributed to societal fears by depicting an epidemic of youthful heroin use in the eastside of Vancouver, especially among vulnerable young girls.[77] Professionals in the City of Vancouver were divided about how to respond to heroin use; some called for medical care for "addicts" arrested for possession and harsher sentences for drug traffickers.[78] Yet, law enforcement called for more punitive drug laws, and they were successful in pressing for amendments made to the Canadian Opium and Narcotic Drug Act in 1954, including the addition of a new offence of "possession for the purpose of trafficking." At the same time, the Act further pushed the "burden of proof" of innocence onto the shoulders of the accused.

A Special Senate Committee was appointed in 1955 to report on the traffic in narcotic drugs in Canada. The Senate proceedings were mostly focused on narcotic trafficking and the "criminal addict." The proceedings of this committee highlighted the "amount of publicity" on the west coast about drug trafficking in the previous months and suggested it was a problem of both "alarming and increasing proportions affecting the youth of our country."[79,80] These proceedings solidified Canada's federal response to criminalized drugs, by advocating heavy penalties and increased enforcement. In the Senate proceedings, marijuana trafficking was not presented as a major problem in Canada.[81]

Law enforcement officials continued to push for new and harsher legislation, resulting in the Narcotic Control Act of 1961. These legislative changes gave Canada the distinction of enacting some of the harshest drug laws of any Western country.[82] The new Act furthered the socially constructed notion of the criminogenic nature of drug use, users, producers, and sellers.[83] In the same year, Canada signed the International Single Convention on Narcotic Drugs. The goal of the international treaty was to eliminate illegal production and non-medical use of cannabis, cocaine, opioids, and later, synthetic pharmaceutical drugs.[84]

Increased and sensationalist media reporting occurred again in the 1960s, at a time when white middle-class youth began to experiment with drugs such as LSD and marijuana. Although arrest rates tell us little about drug use rates, it is worth noting that, in Canada, there were only 21 marijuana arrests in 1960. However, as the 1960s progressed, marijuana use became more popular and was particularly associated with the counterculture movement, and arrest rates concomitantly skyrocketed.[85] Writing in the early 1970s, Brecher et al. argue that 30 years of anti-marijuana propaganda and increasingly harsh laws in the United States seemed to spur on marijuana use rather than deter it; a similar argument could be made about Canada.[86]

Debates about marijuana in the 1960s and early 1970s are best understood against the backdrop of the wider counterculture movement that encompassed a burgeoning civil rights movement, protests against the Vietnam War, increasing demands for gender equality, and challenges to conventional notions about family, religion, sexuality, the work ethic, capitalism, politics, and the arts. Political and citizen debates about marijuana and drugs such as LSD intersected with other social movement activities related to civil liberties, art, states of consciousness, and the appropriate role of the state and criminal justice. Whereas conventional society, lawmakers, and police considered the use of marijuana to be a threat to the dominant social order, counterculture movements embraced this drug. Social conservatives deemed counterculture youth (and not-so-youthful participants) to be rebellious and deviant, and these same conservatives considered drug laws to be a necessary tool to suppress these youth movements.[87]

During the 1960s, rising drug arrests, media attention, and conflict between youth and law enforcement personnel resulted in a wide range of groups with divergent views from politicians, the Canadian Medical Association, police and the RCMP, the pharmaceutical industry, to women's and youth groups.[88] These groups informed both public and not-so-public debates about marijuana. Heightened concern and scrutiny of this drug was, in part, driven by the fact that in most Western countries, marijuana users were categorically young, white, and middle class. Outside of their marijuana use, they tended to be law-abiding citizens.

One of Canada's responses to public debates about marijuana was the creation of the Canadian Commission of Inquiry into the Non-Medical Use of Drugs (also known as the Le Dain Commission) in 1969.[89] The Commission's role was to examine this phenomenon and make recommendations for domestic and international policy and legislative changes. The Le Dain Commission undertook a uniquely broad examination of magazine and newspaper reports about marijuana and LSD. It found that the number of newspaper articles about drug use increased significantly between 1966 and 1971. Because these representations of the use of marijuana and LSD associated the drugs with white middle-class youthful users, rather than working-class and racialized people, media reports gave more attention to perceived health and other medical dangers, rather than to their supposedly criminogenic effects on personality and behaviour.

The commissioners appointed to the Le Dain inquiry sought to understand how media reports shaped Canadians' perceptions about illegal drugs. This analysis included a questionnaire sent to 46 print media outlets in Canada. This survey found that early newspaper reports of illegal drugs, especially marijuana, relied on police and court sources; later reportage also included drug and alcohol institutions and the medical profession as news sources.[90] Henault, the researcher who conducted the survey, concluded that the media "amplified" the negative impact of marijuana and LSD. Goode noted that concerns expressed about drug use through media reporting in the United States, especially on LSD use in the 1960s, were "disproportionate to its physical threat"; a similar claim can be made for news reporting about marijuana in Canada.[91] As in previous eras, the photographs and drawings that accompanied newspaper stories played a key part in depicting the dangers of drug use; vivid and lascivious images depicting the worst effects of drug use often accompanied this reporting.

In its final report, the Le Dain Commission was critical of law enforcement and recommended less severe penalties for marijuana. It also recommended that prison time for possession of criminalized drugs such as heroin and cocaine should end.[92] The Le Dain findings on marijuana regulation resonated with many Canadians and politicians. However, critics noted that the recommendations did not go far enough to address marijuana reform. Marie-Andree Bertrand, a member of the Le Dain Commission, held a dissenting view from the committee and recommended the legalization of cannabis. Her views resonated with John Munro, the federal minister of National Health and Welfare, who proclaimed, in 1970, that the "federal government would legalize marijuana."[93] However, Canada's federal government did not implement most of the Commission's legal recommendations, including those related to marijuana.[94]

The Le Dain Commission met with well-resourced institutional resistance to its recommendations. Both the RCMP and the Department of Justice pressed the government and Canada's voters to reject the Le Dain Commission's findings. These two key groups saw the criminalization of marijuana as a "key component" of Canada's anti-drug strategy, and the regulation of marijuana use became a central concern for law enforcement.[95]

Some legislative changes did occur. In 1969, the penalty clause for simple possession of marijuana under the Narcotic Control Act was revised to allow for the possibility of summary conviction and a lesser penalty. This change gave judges more discretion about the types of penalties they could impose, although at the time, Department of Justice officials insisted that the Crown should proceed with a summary conviction for a first or second offence.[96] The Criminal Law Amendments Act of 1972 allowed judges to discharge a first offender, although no more than 10 per cent of individuals charged with cannabis possession received absolute discharges between 1973 and 1977.[97]

After the release of the Le Dain Commission's report, the Liberal government introduced Bill S-19 to move the regulation of cannabis from the Narcotic Control Act to the Food and Drugs Act (1974). This move was met with both support and resistance, in the latter case, most notably, from police organizations including the RCMP. As Martel's research into this period reveals, in the Senate hearings on this Bill, the "RCMP insisted on the changing nature of the illicit traffic. It stated that young people were involved in cannabis traffic during the sixties, but it was now organized crime groups that controlled it."[98] After these Senate hearings, the Bill was amended to provide for absolute or conditional discharge for possession of cannabis, but maximum sentences for trafficking were raised from the original proposal of 10 years to 14 years. This Bill was introduced in the House of Commons but was not approved due to a number of factors: opposition in Senate hearings and changing political and legislative priorities including the economy and inflation. Martel also attributes the RCMP with having a key role in preventing the transfer of marijuana to the Food and Drugs Act.[99]

In the early 1990s, the federal government moved to renew its legislative framework for the control of drugs in Canada. This process culminated in the passing of Bill C-8 in 1996, and the implementation of the Controlled Drugs and Substances Act. This Act had been preceded by an attempt by the Conservative federal government to introduce legislation to replace the 1961 Narcotic Control Act and an attempt by the Liberal government to do so in 1995. Debates about this legislation were shaped by the usual players, including police organizations, but they were also influenced by emerging harm reduction perspectives in Canada. Supporters of the new Bill claimed the new legislation was meant to focus on trafficking and organized crime, not on simple possession. The proposed act contained eight schedules, including one for cannabis.[100] As Fischer points out, spokespeople for Bill C-8 and its earlier version, Bill C-7, tried to convince its critics that it was going after "the big and bad guys."[101] Martel observes that similar claims were made when the federal government attempted to move cannabis into the Food and Drugs Act in 1974. As these researchers point out, however, evidence from both the 1970s and the 1990s indicates that law enforcement targeted simple possession of cannabis.[102] This discursive separation of the more innocent subject position of cannabis user from its evil-doing counterparts, the trafficker and producer, is one of the outcomes of debates about the regulation of cannabis in Canada since the 1960s.[103] It is the claim of this book that marijuana cultivators have emerged as a new iteration of long-standing notions about the evil trafficker.

The first National Drug Strategy was released in 1987. The Conservative-led government of the time allocated funds for the strategy. Renamed Canada's Drug Strategy in 1992, funding continued with a resurgence of prohibitionist policy. For example, drug literature and pipes were criminalized and drug law enforcement of people suspected of using and selling marijuana remained central.[104] However, debates about marijuana continued in Canada. Several bills were introduced in the 2000s to lesson penalties for marijuana possession, yet each bill died on the floor of the federal Parliament before being implemented. Public support for reform also culminated in the creation of two federal commissions of inquiry into cannabis regulation. Their extensive findings were released in 2002. The House of Commons recommended the decriminalization of cannabis. These potentially significant shifts in policy were followed in the same year by the report of the Senate Special Committee on Illegal Drugs, which recommended that cannabis be legalized. From 1998 until the release of their report, the non-partisan Senate Committee examined the scientific literature and heard testimony from a wide range of citizens, interest groups, researchers, and drug users. They concluded that drug addiction should be treated as a public health rather than criminal matter. They "found that the criminal prohibition of cannabis and other drugs is a patent failure."[105] The abridged version of their report, *Cannabis: Report of the Senate Special Committee on Illegal Drugs*, provides a comprehensive understanding of cannabis, Canadian policy and practice, and public policy options.[106]

Soon after the release of the Senate report, Liberal Prime Minister Jean Chrétien tabled marijuana reform Bill C-38 that proposed fines for possession of small amounts of cannabis. This proposed bill eventually died on the floor of Parliament. A new Liberal government led by Prime Minister Paul Martin did not reintroduce it. Although there has been little legal headway in relation to possession of marijuana, recent court decisions in the 1990s and 2000s about access to medical marijuana led to the implementation of the federal Marihauna Medical Access Regulation (MMAR) program (see chapter 4 for more detail and changes to the regulations).[107] Canada is the only country with a federal legal medical marijuana access program, although regulation changes by the federal government were announced in June 2013.

The election, however, of a minority Conservative government in early 2006 resulted in the introduction of a new National Anti-Drug Strategy in 2007 that favours law enforcement rather than public health perspectives on substance use. This strategy is openly hostile to harm reduction and allocates the majority of resources to enforcement and prosecution. The cornerstone of this new strategy has been a series of attempts to change Canada's Criminal Code to provide for mandatory minimum sentences for growing marijuana, including Bill C-26 (2007), Bill C-15 (2009), Bill S-10 (2010), and Bill C-10 (2011), which was enacted in 2012 and came into force in November that year. The National Anti-Drug Strategy was renewed for another 5-year period (2012–17) at a cost of $527.8 million. As part of this strategy, the RCMP's Drug Enforcement Program, focused on marijuana grow ops and clandestine drug labs, received $91.4 million from 2007 to 2012 and will receive $112.5 million in the second 5-year period.[108]

While debates about marijuana continue, older notions of "evil" and violent drug producers have been articulated to new sets of claims that feature marijuana grow ops as generalized threats to vaguely formulated notions of public safety. By the late 1990s, a host of key spokespeople including law enforcement officials, fire departments, citizen groups, and municipal, provincial, and federal politicians would figure largely in media reports. Indeed, the consistency of the claims made by these spokespeople has been successful in reiterating seemingly naturalized claims about the dangers of marijuana growers.[109] One of the arguments of this book is that as these claims grew in number, they provided a political opportunity for the relatively new Conservative government to implement the new National Anti-Drug Strategy, initiate legislative changes to support harsher sentencing practices, and sweep aside reasoned research about the necessity for reform of the regulation of marijuana and other drugs.

History demonstrates that anti-drug media and political discourse have often curtailed drug reform. Drug researchers Craig Reinarman and Harry Levine argue that the US "news media and politicians played the most important roles in establishing" what is now referred to as the "crack scare" in the mid-1980s.[110] In their analysis of the crack scare, they demonstrated that both media and politicians ignored and misrepresented evidence. The crack scare, and the refuelled drug war it propelled, provided a handy scapegoat and diverted attention away from growing urban poverty in the Reagan/Bush era. In this book, we argue that the contemporary marijuana grow op scare in Canada is a "phenomenon" in its own right, a drug scare *fuelled by the media, RCMP, politicians, and other vocal claims makers*. In these pages, we argue that news stories, photos, and headlines are cultural products that introduce and circulate "truth claims" and systems of meaning about the use, producers, and sellers of cannabis.

2 Problematizing Marijuana Grow Ops: Mayerthorpe and Beyond

As noted in the preceding chapters, since the mid-1990s, law enforcement agents, Canadian newspaper reporters, city and provincial task forces, and a number of politicians have identified marijuana grow ops as "dangerous and sophisticated," linked to violence and organized crime, and as a growing social problem requiring criminal and civil regulation. This chapter examines how the media, law enforcement agents, and politicians framed marijuana grow ops before, at the time, and following the murders of four RCMP officers in Mayerthorpe, Alberta, in March 2005. On a small farm in Mayerthorpe, James Roszko shot and killed four junior RCMP officers, Brock Myrol, Anthony Gordon, Leo Johnston, and Peter Schiemann. It is thought that Roszko took his own life immediately after murdering the four RCMP officers. Following the shootings, media coverage and law enforcement officials proclaimed that Roszko was a violent "cop-hater" and implied that he had been running a marijuana grow op linked to organized crime. Coverage of these shootings later turned to the grieving families of the four officers and their claims that Canada's weak drug laws contributed to the murders in Mayerthorpe. In this chapter, we argue that Mayerthorpe sparked a solidification of claims about marijuana grow ops and helped fuel a shift in discourse that called more urgently for harsher drug laws and associated punishments. This chapter highlights the process of "problematization": how problems such as marijuana grow ops are defined through the claims made by law enforcement agents, politicians, family members of the four officers, and the media.

In this first section, we examine media reportage about marijuana cultivators, police activities, the size of the problem, violence and grow rips, and claims about lenient sentencing prior to the events at

Mayerthorpe. We note that police/RCMP claims and media representations of marijuana grow ops prior to Mayerthorpe seek to "educate"
seemingly apathetic readers about this new threat to the nation. This
section is followed by a discussion of Mayerthorpe and the media coverage of that tragic event. We conclude with an analysis of media coverage following the events at Mayerthorpe, highlighting the shift in tone
in news reportage that highlighted demands for harsher drug laws. Instead of only commenting on the news articles, we provide substantial
quotes and headlines in this chapter so that readers can understand
how marijuana grow ops are represented in newspapers.

Newspaper Claims: Not Mom-and-Pop Operations

Our analysis of 15 years of media coverage found that newspaper reporting of the production of marijuana draws uncritically on vocal
claims makers and police/RCMP-based claims to illustrate the dangers
of these operations. In the years prior to the events at Mayerthorpe,
news reportage in our sample reflected the following themes:

- Claims that grows op are no longer the "mom-and-pop operations"
  they used to be, but rather, they are increasingly sophisticated,
  larger, and thus dangerous
- Police activities and police claims about the growing number of and
  size of marijuana grow ops
- Violence associated with cultivation either by cultivators or through
  "grow-rips"
- Claims about weak and lenient judges meting out ineffective
  sentences that supposedly encouraged the growth of marijuana
  particularly in British Columbia.

In the news articles and the reports we examined, we found that po-
lice/RCMP spokespeople magnified the dangers posed by grow ops
by attempting to dispel what they believe to be a supposedly "benign"
image of these operations held by members of the public.

Contemporary marijuana use in Canada has been associated with
youth and the counterculture since the 1960s. Over the decades, this
understanding of marijuana has grown: the non-violent "slacker"
marijuana user is now a cultural staple popularized in film, music, and
books. As we discussed in the introduction to the book, marijuana is a
popular recreational drug in Canada. We found no evidence that the

use of this drug leads to violent crime. Most marijuana users are white, middle-class, law-abiding citizens who consume a substance that is currently criminalized. Because of the extent of its use, it has become more difficult to demonize marijuana users; police and media attention has, in turn, shifted to growers of marijuana.

In our study period, media reports about the characteristics of marijuana growers changed considerably. At the beginning, reporters were more likely to describe growers of marijuana as enterprising individuals who cultivated cannabis to supply themselves and friends. In this early period, media reports would refer to some growers as "mom-and-pop operators," meaning individuals who had small grow ops that helped subsidize their annual income or who grew cannabis only for themselves and friends.

A 1998 *Globe and Mail* article describes the cannabis-growing efforts of farmers in Nelson and on Lasqueti Island, both in British Columbia. The City of Nelson located in the Kootenay region of southern British Columbia has long enjoyed a reputation as an alternative community because the surrounding region, including the west Kootenay region, was a destination for groups like the Doukhobors (a pacifist religious sect that immigrated from Russia to Canada in the late 1800s and early 1900s with the help of Leo Tolstoy) and for Americans fleeing the military draft during the Vietnam War, in the 1960s and early 1970s.[1] The region has become associated with pot growing in a folkloric sense. For example, Brian Taylor, the mayor of Grand Forks (re-elected in 2008) is a BC Marijuana Party member. Taylor is a vocal proponent of growing hemp for commercial purposes and is an advocate for medical marijuana and drug policy reform. Lasqueti Island, located off the eastern side of Vancouver Island, is known for its alternative approaches. In the 1998 article, both communities are discussed as places where the cultivation of marijuana had become a necessary economic supplement for a declining forestry sector. The first part of the article includes excerpts from interviews with growers and describes the activities of this underground economy:

Mr. Cantwell, co-owner of Holy Smoke Culture Shop [in Nelson], said pot harvested on mountainous Crown land around Nelson may not be as chemically potent as the genetically altered cannabis that thrives under light bulbs in thousands of BC basements and warehouses. But it does the job. And with BC's forest sector suffering from the Asian flu, pot is becoming the province's most cherished and reliable resource in communities such as Nelson, which is particularly famous for its alternative air.[2]

The second part of the article contains comments that would become a stable set of claims in later years: excerpts in this article from RCMP officers paint a very different picture of this underground economy. These spokespeople suggest that 70 per cent of grow ops in British Columbia are now controlled by organized crime, that marijuana is a gateway drug, and that its use has a negative effect on the health care system. Another spokesperson notes that gangs are involved in this underground business and suggests that the future holds more violence because of this development. Initially, this article presents an almost understanding tone towards growers; however, this mainly disappears in later reporting as writers come to rely increasingly on police spokespeople particularly when discussing issues such as organized crime.[3] Figure 2.1 provides a representational sample of news headlines asserting that marijuana is no longer benign.

In a number of articles, reporters freely report claims that the general public is apathetic about the dangers the marijuana trade poses to their lives. One news article quotes a senior federal prosecutor who "says that the public 'just doesn't buy' warnings about the marijuana trade and its consequences. Crown prosecutors believe that a '60's-era benign view

Figure 2.1. Headline Box: Pot Not "Benign."[4]

HEADLINES: POT NOT "BENIGN"

Kelowna drug trade "like fast cancer" (1998)

Dope-growing houses worry island fire chiefs: Laments one: We're going to lose a firefighter. Says a second: Lights are bombs (2000)

Grow-ops outpacing police efforts to smoke out plants (2002)

50,000 "grow" houses, police say: Law enforcement officers losing battle against illegal marijuana cultivators (2002)

Is there a grow-op next door? (2003)

Huge pot "factory" no ma-pa operation (2004)

Out of control: Criminal justice system "on the brink of imploding" (2005)

Higher THC levels are creating "pot 2.0" (2007)

Not the groovy '60s: Today's cannabis is harder and meaner (2007)

Seeing pot through benign soft lens ignores hard realities of grow ops (2009)

of marijuana as a relatively harmless substance is hindering efforts to fight a serious drug menace."[5] Another headline from 2000 reiterates police claims that grow ops are not victimless crimes: "Harsh pot sentence: Large grow operations are not the victimless crimes they're made out to be. Unless the courts impose harsher sentences, neighbours and children within the houses will be in danger."[6] Readers of these articles are, in turn, "educated" to understand that the cultivation of marijuana is an emerging danger that most of the general public does not fully appreciate.

Police Activities Establish the Size of the Problem

A typical way in which social problems are established by key claims makers is through the reiteration of numbers. Since the beginning of our study period, law enforcement officials have, in conjunction with newspaper reports, used the outcomes of their enforcement efforts to establish the size of the underground cannabis cultivation economy. Because marijuana cultivation is an underground economy, accurate estimates of its size are almost impossible to produce. But, to emphasize the dangers of these operations, newspaper articles rely uncritically on police claims about size and number of these operations. Many newspaper articles about marijuana cultivation simply highlight police raids and busts, and routinely note the number of plants seized and the police-based estimates of the market value of the seized crop. Over 700 articles (28%) in our sample routinely mentioned the number of marijuana plants found in a police raid. Most often, the news sources for these articles are police and RCMP spokespersons.

The character of these reports is reflected in some of the headlines of these articles: "Almost 7,000 pot plants found at old chicken farm city's biggest marijuana bust."[7] These estimates of crop size are often presented using dramatic language that reiterates that grow ops are a sizable problem. Headlines include: "Pot finds fixed at $2 million,"[8] "100 grow-op houses found in mortgage scam probe: How organized crime has infiltrated our communities."[9] RCMP in Comox, BC, say "they've seized enough pot from outdoor marijuana grow ops in recent days to make more than 11 million joints." Part of an annual aerial search by police, the RCMP reports that "the amount of pot could supply every person in a city of 75,000 with five joints every day for a month."[10] Figure 2.2 provides a further representational sample of these articles related to the number of plants and the size of the operations. These headlines and their accompanying articles consistently rely on modifiers such as "massive," "huge," and "large" or "largest" to emphasize that the

Figure 2.2. Headline Box: Size of Problem.[11]

HEADLINES: SIZE OF THE PROBLEM

Crime: 400 marijuana plants found in east side house (1999)

Massive pot operation raided: Police suspect city's biggest marijuana warehouse was set to expand (2001)

Almost 7,000 pot plants found at old chicken farm city's biggest marijuana bust (2004)

Princeton: Huge grow-op found (2005)

20,000 pot plants seized (2005)

RCMP seize 3,400 marijuana plants in raid on "sophisticated" growing operation (2006)

Island cops uncover thousands of pot plants: Police say this summer's program, the eighth, pulled in "the largest haul" (2007)

Cops take 4.8m joints out of circulation (2007)

Greenhouse pot bust biggest ever: Six suspects tending huge crop arrested by cops acting on tip (2008)

3,000 pot plants found in Richmond warehouse (2008)

B.C. seizes its biggest-yet marijuana grow-op (2008)

Police seize 9,000 pot plants from grow op (2009)

---

size of marijuana cultivation in British Columbia is part of the growing problem of cannabis cultivation. These articles repeatedly stress that the latest bust is the "largest" ever. These claims reiterate for the reader the sense that the problem is growing at an overwhelming rate and help to cloak the fact that police activities themselves are responsible for these finds and that accurate estimates of the underground economy are hard to establish.

Articles contain police estimates of the wholesale or retail value of BC's marijuana industry. A typical example from 1997 estimates the size of the marijuana industry and its overall value:

Police say that if there are 1,000 grow operations in the Lower Mainland – a very conservative estimate – then they are producing a minimum of $100 million worth of dope a year. Add another 1,000 grow operations for the rest of the province, and that doubles to $200 million a year.[12]

Newspapers report often repeated claims by British Columbia's Organized Crime Agency (OCA), which estimated the value of the underground cannabis economy to be worth $3 to $4 billion annually.[13] By 2002, the OCA's estimate of the value of the marijuana industry had risen to $6 billion with an estimated 15,000 to 20,000 grow ops in the province.[14] In November 2002, the police were quoted in a *Vancouver Sun* article claiming that there are 50,000 grow houses in Canadian homes and they face a losing battle against cultivation. This article was accompanied by a photo of a marijuana grow op that was discovered in a house in East Vancouver (see Figure 2.3).

Figure 2.3. "50,000 'Grow' Houses, Police Say." Reproduced with permission from the *Vancouver Sun*, 2002. Photo by Ian Lindsay.

In 2002 and 2003, increasing estimates of the value of the marijuana industry and number of grow ops were linked to reports that police were overwhelmed by the number of these operations:

> A study done for the RCMP found that between 1997 and 2000, BC grow operations grew by more than 200 per cent as organized crime shifted its efforts here from other parts of Canada and the US. During that time, BC police investigated 12,000 cases of marijuana cultivation, tore up 1.2 million plants – and could barely keep up. Swimming against the THC tide are the 30 members of the RCMP's Vancouver Island District Drug Section. Not a lot of people, considering all the coke-smuggling, heroin-dealing, marijuana-growing meth-makers they face.[15]

However, as we note in the introduction to this book, many of the numbers reported in the RCMP-associated paper referenced above were inflated, although the media did not challenge them. In fact, from 2002 on, we found that the media and the RCMP repeatedly and uncritically referenced the findings from the 2002 and 2005 papers by Plecas et al.[16]

In 2003, the influential US magazine *Forbes* published a story about marijuana production in Canada that grabbed newspaper headlines. *Forbes* estimated the size of the industry to be somewhere between US$4 billion and US$7 billion.[17] The oft-quoted 2004 report from the Fraser Institute in British Columbia, a conservative think tank, stated that police busts account for 10 per cent of the total number of marijuana grow ops.[18] The author of this report, economist Stephen Easton, estimates that there were upwards of 17,500 grow ops in British Columbia in 2000, with a retail value of approximately Can$7 billion.[19] Based on these numbers, however, Easton suggests that the wise public policy approach would be to legalize this industry given its potentially lucrative tax revenues. Responding to both the *Forbes* and the Easton estimates, BC's RCMP suggest that these numbers underestimate the size of the industry: "Yet, even that huge number," says Kelly Rainbow, a civilian analyst with the RCMP in Vancouver, is "conservative, laughably conservative."[20]

As we noted above, it is extremely difficult to estimate with certainty the size of the marijuana industry in British Columbia or the rest of Canada. But this fact does not stop claims makers from using estimates to describe the size of the problem. US drug policy researcher Beau Kilmer reveals how estimates of marijuana production for the United States and Mexico are "rife with mythical numbers." He notes that the same statistics are used repeatedly in media and other documents; this repetition encourages these statistics to become "trusted as common wisdom."[21] He points out that the statistics about marijuana production in the United States and Mexico reported by law enforcement agents were first published in reports by the US Drug Enforcement Administration (DEA), the US Office of National Drug Control Policy (ONDCP), the UN Office on Drugs and Crime (UNODC), and US State Department with no evidence to support such claims. Given the lack of hard evidence about the scope of marijuana cultivation in Canada, estimates of its overall size remain speculation. Yet this lack of evidence has failed to deter media reports from drawing on police-based assumptions as given facts. Still, in the absence of accurate estimates akin to ones available for legal enterprises such as forestry or agriculture, newspaper reporters draw on police-based claims without, for the most part, investigating the ways in which these claims support police demands for more resources.

Violence and Weapons

Newspaper articles prior to the events at Mayerthorpe problematize grow ops with claims about the violence, weapons, and "grow rips" associated with these operations and the risk of fumes, toxins, fire, and electrocution. Chapters 3 and 4 will discuss in more detail claims made about the relationship between organized crime, violence, and grow ops; chapter 5 examines claims about risks of fire, community safety, and city responses to these claims, including the enactment of civil bylaws. Here, we highlight only how grow ops are associated with threats to public and police safety through such issues as violence, weapons, and criminal types.

The extent to which the discovery of weapons in grow ops was reported in newspapers is one of the key ways that articles prior to Mayerthorpe establish the dangers of marijuana cultivation. The following excerpt from a 1998 article illustrates how police spokespeople link the presence of weapons to the cultivation of marijuana:

> The discovery [of weapons] prompted Cpl. John Furac of the Surrey Green Team to say: "This is some serious hardware that is likely tied into the outlaw gangs controlling the drug business. We are finding loaded guns and other weapons in almost every grow house we go into these days. But we seldom come across the number of machine-guns, including a

silencer-equipped machine-gun, like we did Tuesday." Furac said there is an increasing pattern of weapons being discovered in marijuana raids, an indication that high-powered gangs have taken over the lucrative marijuana trade, which brings top dollar in US markets. [Surrey RCMP Const. Grant] Learned said gangs are storing the weapons at home for fear they will be invaded by other gangs for their crop. He said that, because the grow operations are in residential areas, innocent civilians may be harmed should a gunfight erupt.[22]

This excerpt reiterates themes about gangs, violence, US exports, and general safety concerns and heightens these concerns with claims about the presence of weapons in grow ops. This occurs despite the fact that this article is about a raid in Surrey, BC, described in the following terms: "While the amount of marijuana found was small, the 'Green Team' of drug cops that went into the house was left 'buzzing over the exotic and sophisticated nature' of the weapons found,' said Learned."[23] It is impossible to tell from the article whether these weapons are typically found in grow ops, although police statements suggest it is part of a trend. Later reports do not support such clams.[24] In fact, the RCMP's 2005 study found that between 1997 and 2003, 89 per cent of the grow ops brought to the attention of the police in British Columbia did not have firearms or other weapons or hazards.[25] This is the case despite the fact that the Department of Justice estimates suggest that at that time 26 per cent of Canadian homes contained firearms.[26]

The following excerpt illustrates how generalized claims about the violence associated with grow ops continues to be articulated in newspaper reporting:

There is also a growing problem of violence associated with marijuana growing that puts the community at risk ... Growing operations are associated with such crimes as drive-by shootings, home invasions, assaults, extortions, murders, money laundering and cross border smuggling of guns and cocaine.[27]

This excerpt is from a 2003 article entitled "RCMP team dismantles 2 marijuana operations." It begins by describing two recent marijuana grow-op busts in Richmond, BC. It follows a format that many articles use by then, describing the more general dangers of grow ops without any reference to the specific busts described in the title of the article. The article then draws on a common narrative structure used in reporting about grow ops. It begins with a specific police bust and then goes on to reference a recent report by the RCMP Criminal Intelligence Division and draws on quotations from Vancouver RCMP Inspector Murray Dauk, who reiterates familiar themes noting the tendency for grow ops to be associated with violence, poor wiring, mould, and threats to children living in grow ops. This happens regardless of whether or not the grow op in question was the site of any of these problems. This narrative structure occurs repeatedly throughout reporting on the cultivation of marijuana. Other articles draw on a slightly different approach: they report on the size of a grow-op bust and whether or not weapons were found. These articles usually do not contain accompanying analysis of what this might mean; it is left to the reader to speculate on the connection between guns and grow ops.

Burglaries and Grow Rips

Starting in 2000, more frequent stories appear that describe a phenomenon known as "grow rips." These are usually explained as burglaries of known grow ops by persons hoping to resell marijuana for their own profit. Newspaper stories emphasize police claims about the possibility of violence associated with grow ops with headlines that dramatize the effects of "grow rips" such as "Pot thieves bring terror in the night."[28] Other excerpts from articles demonstrate these dangers: "Police issued a warning yesterday about a scary trend in the marijuana industry"; "'Grow-rippers' intent on stealing top-quality BC Bud are targeting grow ops – and mistakenly hitting the homes of innocent people who have moved into the site of a former grow op";[29] and "Violent 'grow rips' on the rise."[30] This excerpt draws on police-based claims to illustrate how dangerous it might be for innocent homeowners targeted by burglaries intent on stealing marijuana:

> This type of activity [in which] young [people] are contracted to steal marijuana crops is both inherently dangerous and also has serious criminal repercussions, the RCMP statement said. "These incidents highlight the fact that marijuana grow operations are a threat to public safety, especially since criminals frequently target the wrong home, where there is no grow operation."[31]

Articles with headings such as "Home invaders had the wrong address"[32] emphasize the threat to vulnerable citizens. Dozens of other articles emphasize the *possibility* that grow op rips pose a threat to innocent citizens. These claims, again, extend the possible safety risks of grow ops beyond their own boundaries to supposedly innocent citizens who could be drawn into their dangers by the actions of grow rippers.

It is important to note that we do not contest the danger of some grow rips, although to date it is impossible to accurately estimate the size of the problem. However, we draw attention to the fact that an unregulated illegal marijuana market may fuel the potential for grow rips, and we assert that a regulated marijuana market would reduce illegal trade, grow rips, and associated problems. We also note that the media and the police/RCMP have not been as ready to communicate when law enforcement agents and Green Teams investigate the wrong address and threaten innocent citizens.

Although drug laws and sentencing in Canada are quite harsh, especially for marijuana offences compared with the situation in the United Kingdom, a number of US states, and many European Union countries, newspaper articles in our study repeatedly make a causal link between the growth of marijuana grow ops and Canada's allegedly lenient court system. A 1997 *Province* article states, "Police are concerned that light penalties are fostering BC's reputation for the best pot in the world."[33] Another headline reads, "BC police say the disparity in sentencing has turned BC into a Mecca for pot farmers."[34] Figure 2.4 provides a sample of representational headlines related to lenient sentencing. Throughout the study period, the media reiterated the following headline: "Courts too lenient on pot growers: Minimum fines are needed to provide a real disincentive to illegal marijuana cultivation."[35]

The discussion above lays out many of the claims made by the media prior to 2005. As we can see, newspaper reports were offering Canadians the opportunity to become well acquainted with media and police claims about the dangers, size, and nature of the problems associated with marijuana grow ops. As will become evident in the following sections, many of these claims were further articulated in 2004, when the RCMP and the police hosted the first national conference on marijuana cultivation in November of that year. This conference received favourable coverage in newspapers with reporting emphasizing police claims about the dangers of grow ops. It was during this conference that then Public Safety Minister Anne McLellan called people who smoke marijuana "stupid." RCMP Commission Giuliano Zaccardelli also explained that grow ops are not "ma-and-pa operations, but

Figure 2.4. Headline Box: "Lenient" Sentencing.[36]

HEADLINES: "LENIENT" SENTENCING

Police blame judges for surge in grow ops (1998)

Traffickers "laugh" at the legal system: Following a major drug raid, a senior RCMP officer says BC penalties are too lenient (1999)

RCMP compiles booklet to help residents spot drug houses: The information describes what signs to look for and includes a victim-impact statement to promote stiffer penalties (1999)

A conviction in Alberta for growing pot could send you to jail for four years. In BC you'd probably get three to six months because ... judges show a soft spot for marijuana farmers (2000)

Our slack drug penalties lure major crime: US (2004)

Tougher laws and stricter enforcement needed to stop grow-ops (2005)

Judge pushes for tougher sentences involving grow-ops (2006)

Mandatory jail sentences will fill up our prisons (2007)

Judge wishes he could have jailed man over grow-op: Law should provide a deterrent, he says (2007)

Police release photos of city's worst thieves: Cops blame catch-and-release court cycle (2008)

BC calls on Ottawa to tighten drug laws (2009)

VPD opposes Senate move to soften penalty on grow-ops: Proposal would remove minimum sentence for less than 200 plants (2009)

---

dangerous organized crime businesses." He linked these operations to violence on Canadian streets. Other officials argued that marijuana use posed a significant health risk.[37] Again, policing claims about the harms of grow ops were reiterated in early 2005. The following excerpt from 2005 draws from a community impact statement prepared by the

RCMP in British Columbia and was reprinted in the *Vancouver Sun*. Its claims were included without debate, caveats, or comment by the press in Canada. The claims made in the community impact statement, detailed in the media excerpt below, illustrate the range of issues typically highlighted by police spokespeople and ones that we have now come to recognize as familiar from previous reporting on grow ops.

"COMMUNITY IMPACT STATEMENT" EXCERPTS

The RCMP's Coordinated Marijuana Enforcement Team has sent a draft "community impact statement" to all its detachments that can be presented during the sentencing of marijuana growers. The unit has asked detachments to update the statement with specific information on the impact of grow operations in each community. Following are some excerpts from the letter:

Organized Crime and Marijuana Grow Operations

"Intelligence and evidence gathered during police investigations indicate that organized crime groups control many of the marijuana grow operations located in the province of British Columbia. The marijuana trade requires the involvement of a large number of people playing a variety of roles."

Increase in Violent Crime

"In the past few years [name of town] has experienced a significant increase in violent crime. The city has recently experienced a number of marijuana grow 'rips.' A 'rip' takes place when individuals forcefully enter a residence where marijuana is being grown ... Due to the illegality of growing marijuana the 'rips' often go unreported to the police ... On occasion, suspects have attended the wrong address and threatened and/or assaulted innocent citizens."

Use of Weapons and Booby Traps

"Police are finding that more marijuana growers are arming themselves for protection from these 'rips' and as such pose an increased risk to the public and police. RCMP members are finding shotguns, assault rifles and various other weapons in residences where marijuana grow operations are present."

Potential House Fires

"The electrical bypasses and unsafe electrical wiring used in marijuana grow operations are a common cause of house fires. There is an ever present danger to fire fighters at any structural fire, however, there are increased risks when attending grow operations because of the unsafe electrical bypasses, booby traps, entanglement hazards caused by illegal electrical wiring, confrontations with attack dogs, and an array of toxic chemicals."

Structural Damage to the Interior

"Marijuana grow operations can cause extensive damage to the interior of residences. Over time, high humidity inside a marijuana grow operation will destroy interior drywall and produce mould. Many studies report that moulds found inside homes where marijuana grow ops are located are extremely toxic."

Harm to the Environment

"Marijuana growers typically discard used chemicals into the community drainage systems or backyards resulting in environmental damage."[38]

The article concludes with an excerpt from a police officer:

The spread of grow-ops comes at the same time as Canadians are becoming increasingly liberal in their attitude to marijuana use. But police officers such as Corporal Lorne Adamitz, a member of Edmonton's so-called Green Team of municipal and RCMP officers, strive to separate the two issues. "It's not a victimless crime," he said. "It's not just somebody wanting to smoke a joint."[39]

The question of liberalization of attitudes and laws posed by the police corporal above is clearly and strategically placed against the dangers

posed by residential marijuana grow ops. As coverage of the conference in 2004 illustrates, by 2005, newspapers had aligned their coverage of grow ops with the voices of police and claims makers who
sought to dispel the supposedly benign image of grow ops held by the
public.

Newspaper reporting on the shootings in Mayerthorpe picked up
and reiterated familiar themes about grow ops that had already been
prominent in past years. Issues like lenient sentencing, the violence
supposedly associated with marijuana cultivation, increasing concerns
about police safety because of the presence of weapons and booby
traps, concerns about the role of organized crime, and calls for harsher
and minimum sentences for production were retold in stories immediately following the shootings. These earlier references and claims
helped to contexualize the tragic events discussed below that unfolded
in Mayerthorpe, Alberta, in 2005.

Mayerthorpe

As noted at the beginning of this chapter, in March 2005, on a small
farm in Mayerthorpe, Alberta, James Roszko shot and killed four junior
RCMP officers and then, it is believed, he took his own life. The murders of the four RCMP officers are a terrible tragedy, especially for the
families of the men. It eventually sparked much public debate about
whether or not the murders could have been prevented. Immediately
following the shootings, media coverage and law enforcement officials
proclaimed that James Roszko was known to the RCMP. He was portrayed as a violent cop-hater who ran a marijuana-growing operation
linked to organized crime. Coverage of these shootings later turned to
the grieving families of the four officers and their claims that Canada's
weak drug laws contributed to the murders in Mayerthorpe. The murders in Mayerthorpe, and their subsequent media coverage, beg the
question of why some ideas about marijuana cultivation that stemmed
from police and government officials gained immediate and easy purchase in newspaper reporting. The case of Mayerthorpe also provides
a window to understand how media coverage shifted in tone during
2005 and how Mayerthorpe sparked a more rigorous alignment of
professionals (RCMP, police, real estate and insurance agencies, councils, mayors, BC Hydro) to enact harsher drug laws and sentencing for
marijuana-growing operators.

Events at Mayerthorpe: Contested Representations

Newspaper coverage in the immediate aftermath of the Mayerthorpe shootings attributed the murders to the presence of Roszko's grow op. They proclaimed that the murdered RCMP officers had converged on James Roszko's farm to investigate a marijuana grow op and stolen property. Yet, the 2011 *Report to the Minister of Justice and Attorney General Public Fatality Inquiry* makes clear that two civil enforcement bailiffs first approached the Roszko property on 2 March 2005 to repossess a motor vehicle because Roszko had failed to make his payments.[40] When the bailiffs arrived, the gate was locked, and shortly afterwards two large Rottweiler dogs appeared inside the property; the bailiffs saw a male moving around inside the property. They decided to call the RCMP for backup, a fairly common procedure, fearing that there might be a confrontation.[41] When two RCMP officers arrived, they and the bailiffs entered the property. It was believed that Roszko had fled the property shortly before the first two RCMP officers arrived. In a Quonset hut, the RCMP found evidence of a "chop shop" where parts of stolen vehicles were found along with evidence of a marijuana grow op. The RCMP and the bailiffs vacated the Quonset hut and requested a search warrant, the attendance of a Green Team and an Auto Theft Unit to proceed further with a criminal investigation.[42] The RCMP accessed Roszko's criminal record and saw that it showed six convictions, a caution/violence notation, and weapons prohibition.[43] The RCMP noted that Roszko was also designated as a "Special Interest" meaning he had an open file at the local detachment. The local RCMP knew that Roszko had a violent past.[44] There was a substantial risk that he possessed firearms.[45] The search of the property yielded evidence of a night vision scope and ammunition. Eventually, four officers were left to secure the property and to wait for the Auto Theft Unit scheduled to arrive the next morning. Following formal investigations of the event, we now know that the four junior RCMP officers were left on the farm without senior support and backup. We also know that the four RCMP officers were later ambushed and murdered on the morning of 6 March 2011 by Roszko alone (it was claimed early on that the ambush and murders were carried out by a number of people with Roszko) shortly after two other RCMP officers arrived on the scene from the Auto Theft Unit.[46] We know that, in 2000, the courts banned Roszko from owning firearms. Once the court imposes that ban, Alberta's chief firearms officer would have been notified. In spite of the ban, Roszko possessed weapons at the time of the murders.

Newspaper stories suggested that Roszko had a grow op with 20 mature plants and approximately 280 seedlings along with $30,000 worth of growing equipment. As the excerpt from the *Globe and Mail* illustrates, this early media coverage claimed that Roszko's grow op was part of a larger operation with other properties and criminals involved. The article also noted that grow ops were popping up everywhere, including small rural towns:

> Four Mounties were shot dead during a raid on a marijuana grow operation in central Alberta yesterday, the force's biggest loss of life in a violent act in 120 years. The killings sent shock waves of grief through this remote, rural community and sparked calls for stricter laws to control the explosive growth of grow-ops ... Alberta Solicitor-General Harvey Cenaiko, who is a former Calgary police officer, also spoke out against grow-ops. "It goes to the seriousness of the fact that organized crime, illegal cultivation of marijuana ... is all around us, including in a small town like Mayerthorpe," he told reporters.[47]

A week after the murders, RCMP Commissioner Guiliano Zaccardelli linked the killing of the four RCMP officers in Alberta to marijuana cultivation by denouncing marijuana grow ops as "a plague on our society." Further, he took the opportunity to promote his view that drugs are dangerous, there are no safe drugs (we assume he is not referring to alcohol and legal and prescribed drugs), and legalizing drugs will not solve anything:

> RCMP Commissioner Giuliano Zaccardelli expressed hope the incident will encourage Canadians to reconsider their views on marijuana. "Hopefully this type of a tragedy will make us review and rethink and reflect and bring a perspective to some of these issues as Canadians," he said. "Drugs are illegal and they're extremely dangerous and people have to understand that. And when you have people who are promoting the issue of safe drugs or [that] there are harmless drugs, I think that is something that we better understand is not the right way to go. We don't solve anything in society by legalizing things or by pretending they're not harmful to society."[48]

Then Public Safety Minister Anne McLellan was one of the first politicians to blame the RCMP murders on marijuana grow ops. She stated the government would introduce stiffer penalties to punish grow operators:

Anne McLellan, the Deputy Prime Minister and Public Safety Minister, also offered her sympathies to the families of the slain officers. She promised that Ottawa would consider toughening laws against grow-ops, calling them a rapidly expanding organized-crime threat. Without providing details, she said the government would consider changes to a bill before the Commons to decriminalize marijuana, which includes stiffer penalties for grow operations."[49]

The article described the four RCMP officers as "paying the highest price to fight this fight" against marijuana grow ops, and both McLellan and Zaccardelli called for harsher laws.

Along with the calls for harsher drug laws, several articles linked Mayerthorpe to drug production because of its rural location. Although claims about rural space and grow operations were based mostly on speculation, they contributed to a sense of encroaching danger threatening small communities:

"It's happening more and more in the rural areas," he said. "I'm speculating that farmhouses and sheds are harder to find [for police]. It's cheaper, and it's hidden away from prying eyes." The area and highways surrounding Mayerthorpe have been singled out as a drug-trafficking concern by police and politicians. Grow-ops are "in rural places and can quickly transport to British Columbia and then south," said one police officer, who asked not to be named. Dan Bryant is a 26-year-old oil-patch worker in nearby Whitecourt who says this part of Northern Alberta is perfect for marijuana grow-ops.[50]

This excerpt helps to expand the domain of the problem to include rural areas specifically because they are unlikely to receive the kind public attention thought to be common in the city. The claims in this excerpt are, again, vague but potent. Referring to highways as having been singled out for concern by the police tells the reader almost nothing but implies a great deal. In other words, this excerpt manages to draw in not only rural but also unnamed roadways as potential sites of drug-related criminality without producing anything specific to verify this claim. Another article suggested that the shootings heightened US fears about Canada as a drug-producing country:

The incident has still managed to generate fresh irritation and fear in America over the growing flood of potent Canadian pot into the US. As

if the two countries needed another irritant, the murders have only un-
derlined concern among officials and politicians here that Canada's relatively lax treatment of grow-op criminals is fuelling the influx of drugs ...
"We've tended to view Canada as our front door. And we've certainly
come to the point where we don't feel that we can leave the front door
unlocked any more," said Chris Sands, an expert on Canada at the Center for Strategic and International Studies in Washington. "Stories like
the one about the officers being murdered and increasing violence associated with this trade are going to only make the Americans think what
we usually think about these things – that we're right and maybe you'll
finally realize it."[51]

In the wake of Mayerthorpe, such hyperbolic claims about police being murdered and increased violence stemming from the marijuana
drug trade were not unusual. The article above goes on to suggest
that Canadians are not taking grow ops seriously enough and then
concludes that marijuana and crystal meth from Canada are "ravag-
ing" the State of Washington: "Senator Patty Murray of Washington
state is among the politicians who have called for more policing of
the northern border" and "Washington state is being ravaged by the
influx of BC bud and meth," she said last fall."[52] There is, of course, no
concrete proof given to substantiate these claims. Yet this article pro-
ductively links marijuana cultivation to other drugs and to the possibility that Canada is not a good neighbour to the United States. Figure
2.5 provides examples of representational headlines about the events
at Mayerthorpe.

Media coverage of the Mayerthorpe shootings was especially concerned that the supposedly benign image of the harmless marijuana
smoker and grower should be challenged. The news cartoon (Figure 2.6),
published in the *Vancouver Sun* a few days after the murders, exemplifies
the representation of "slacker" marijuana users as contributing to violent
murder.

This cartoon reiterates fears that underneath the supposedly
slacker image of the pot smoker lies culpability for the violence associated with this underground trade. These types of images effectively
locate the problem of underground economies in the individual pur-
chaser and hide any analysis of the role that drug policy itself might
play in creating violence in an unregulated underground economy.
Nor does this image or the newspaper articles refer to the numerous
small to mid-size cannabis growers who are not associated with other
crimes.

Figure 2.5. Headline Box: Mayerthorpe.[53]

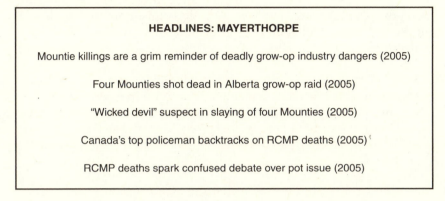

HEADLINES: MAYERTHORPE

Mountie killings are a grim reminder of deadly grow-op industry dangers (2005)

Four Mounties shot dead in Alberta grow-op raid (2005)

"Wicked devil" suspect in slaying of four Mounties (2005)

Canada's top policeman backtracks on RCMP deaths (2005)

RCMP deaths spark confused debate over pot issue (2005)

Figure 2.6. Cartoon, "Smoking Pot Kills Cops." Reproduced with permission of Roy Peterson and Simon Fraser University Library Special Collections.

Reportage and news headings, such as this one, "Nothing benign about grow-ops," also exemplifies the shift in discourse about marijuana use and growing. The key message is this: now the media and the RCMP assert that they have proof that marijuana grow ops are dangerous:

> Sadly it has taken the deaths of four RCMP officers at a grow-op near Mayerthorpe, northwest of Edmonton, Thursday to provide us with incontrovertible proof of that [danger]. No one can assume any longer that cultivating marijuana is just some relatively harmless pursuit of simple country folk, a cottage industry run by moms and pops or confused pot-heads.[54]

This article continues by noting that the assailant James Roszko had previously exhibited personality problems. However, contrary to early claims by the RCMP and the media about links to other criminals, Roszko had no connection to organized crime groups and worked alone on his grow operation or possibly with a neighbour, Shawn Hennessey. Later, Hennessey was arrested and convicted of manslaughter of the RCMP officers who were killed at Mayerthorpe.[55] However, media coverage continued to focus on how grow ops pose dangers to law enforcement agents and the public because of their links to organized crime.

In a different article, the Victoria, BC, police chief echoes these prevailing ideas about grow ops in his references to Mayerthorpe:

> These are not Mom and Pop who are growing a few plants. These are wide-scale organized crime events and they are dangerous and they're dangerous to the public. They are dangerous to some electrician showing up to repair a panel if it has been booby trapped and they're dangerous to some kid knocking on the door if there is a paranoid guy guarding it with a gun.[56]

Other hyperbolic claims by police were reported without comment in the media. In the following excerpt, BC's Attorney General Geoff Plant is quoted, saying:

> the tragedy should dispel any doubts people might have about the dangerous nature of marijuana growing operations. "I think there is an attitude that is part of our culture in British Columbia that thinks that a grow-op is just your neighbor making a couple of bags of marijuana for

some of his friends," Plant said in an interview at the legislature, shortly after learning of the deaths. "Whether that was ever true – 20 or 30 years ago – it's sure not true today. We're talking about the commercial manufacture of marijuana for the purpose of participating in an international organized crime activity. That's very serious business."[57]

In the media excerpt above, BC's attorney general and the reporter reiterate fears that Canadians are simply not taking grow ops seriously enough; to underscore this point, these spokespeople suggest that the character of grow ops has shifted to a much more dangerous problem over time. The attorney general's comments were not reflective of the actual events at Roszko's farm in Mayerthorpe in 2005, since his grow operation was relatively small and not linked to other criminal organizations.

In the coverage immediately after the Mayerthorpe shootings, columnists, politicians, law enforcement agents, and others called for harsher penalties for cultivating marijuana – echoing concerns that had been well established in earlier media coverage. The following excerpt from an opinion piece, written just after the shootings, illustrates how newspaper reporting refers to claims made about Mayerthorpe. The author characterizes growers as inevitably criminal:

> Growers being apprehended in BC today have, on average according to police, a 13-year criminal history and seven previous convictions, of which 41 per cent are for crimes of violence. They're not only turning up on the edges of small farming communities. Three-quarters of grow-ops are in residential areas, subjecting neighbouring families to the fallout from their turf wars, to home invasions and health hazards.[58]

The writer of this piece, who remains anonymous, calls for harsher penalties for growing marijuana and lists numerous dangers associated with the production of this plant. The writer does not provide a source for the information contained in the excerpt above, but uses it to illustrate that a particularly dangerous criminal type is routinely involved in growing marijuana, an unsubtle reference to James Roszko.

Initial and subsequent media coverage of the events at Mayerthorpe gave varied information about the number of plants founds at the farm. Some estimated it as low as 20 mature plants. Based on information collected by the CTV investigative news program *The Fifth Estate*, it's likely that about 280 plants in various stages of maturity were found at the farm. Like other news stories on grow ops, the number of plants found at any given site is used as an indicator of the level of danger posed by these operations. These articles presuppose that the larger the number of plants, the larger the grow op and the danger to society and possible links to organized crime. The 2011 *Public Fatality Inquiry Report* does not expand on the number of plants founds, so we can only go on media reports rather than evidence about many claims related to the plant count at Mayerthorpe.

In the days following the tragedy, media reporting began to reflect some of the questions raised about attribution of these deaths to the issue of marijuana grow ops. Letters to the editor and editorial stories suggested that blaming the cultivaton of marijuana for the events at Mayerthorpe overlooked the history of Roszko's crimes and his history as a menace over a long period of time in the town of Mayerthorpe. A letter to the editor in the *Globe and Mail* challenged MP Randy White's claim that marijuana production was responsible for the events at Roszko's farm.[59] Another article described marijuana activist Marc Emery[60] and lawyer Kirk Tousaw's[61] objections to the reporting and noted that it was unfair to demonize marijuana growers for the events in Alberta.[62] Other editorials urged lawmakers not to act hastily to alter Canada's drug regulation regime given that the events in Mayerthorpe were the fault of a lone gunman with a history of violence.[63] Even the RCMP's Commissioner Guiliano Zaccardelli later suggested that his "condemnation of grow-ops just hours after the shootings may be inappropriate, because police and politicians did not have the full details of the particular case and background of cop-killer James Roszko."[64] Once the marijuana links had been challenged, newspaper coverage also quickly shifted to examining the past history and individual character of James Roszko by quoting community members:

> Violently self-righteous, a convicted pedophile who denied all wrongdoing and spurned all treatment, the hermit who shot dead four Mounties was by every account a walking time bomb whose rage resembled a hissing fuse.[65]

Articles with titles such as "They knew he was loopy for an entire decade," for example, provided salacious details of sexual assault by Roszko on "Mike," an adult resident in the area.[66] These same articles gave lengthy details of Roszko's past crimes and his convictions including a ban on possessing firearms.

But the shift in tone of the coverage also created a political opportunity for writers to ask questions about the value of harsher sentencing practices such as mandatory minimums. Newspaper articles with titles such as "It's too early for a political solution"[67] announce opinion essays that criticize the notion that minimum sentences would deter individuals such as Roszko, at the same time as they suggest that politicians made too much of the links between organized crime and grow ops. Other articles suggest that police procedures, equipment, and the failure of Canada' gun registry were culprits in the shootings. Notably, however, newspapers avoided discussion of the criminalization of marijuana or drug prohibition as fuelling violence associated with the drug trade, instead, relegating these analyses to letters to the editor.[68]

Following the official investigations, today we also know that the killings at Mayerthorpe were an isolated incident and that Roszko was well known to the police for past violent offences. Rosko just happened to have marijuana plants on his property but they were not the cause of the violence that ensued. Despite these facts, later in the year, newspaper articles suggest that the shootings in Mayerthorpe contributed to the failure of a Liberal-sponsored bill to decriminalize possession of small amounts of marijuana while increasing penalties for growers. As the following news excerpt illustrates, police claims about Mayerthorpe and its association with marijuana cultivation and violence had a significant impact on public policy: "With an election on the horizon, and following a show of 5,000 police and peace officers over the weekend for a Parliament Hill memorial of all officers slain over the past year, [Justice Minister] Cotler said the government is not going to press MPs to push the legislation ahead."[69] At the same time, some family members of the slain officers are quoted as calling for "a minimum sentence of two years in prison for anyone convicted of running a grow-op, and decried the lenient sentences that have been handed down for drug growers and dealers: 'I'm sure the Roszko's of this world are laughing at us.'"[70]

The meanings promulgated about Roszko's actions and marijuana-growing operations are only partly the result of media and other institutionally based spokespeople such as the RCMP and the federal and provincial governments. As we noted above, our examination of media representations of Mayerthorpe reveals that a variety of people challenged the claims made by these spokespeople. Although the RCMP have privileged access to media representations of drug production,

they did face challenges in letters to the editor and from some columnists who contested the easy links made between the events in Mayerthorpe and grow ops in general. Yet given the lack of a fulsome public
debate and scrutiny of these events, and continued overt and covert
references to the dangers of violence posed by grow operators, the initial representations of Mayerthorpe as a grow op linked to dangerous
crimes and even more risky persons lingers. In the next section, we
question how the murders of four RCMP officers were used to support a law-and-order agenda, even though the events at Mayerthorpe
ultimately had little to do with the cultivation of marijuana. We also
question the close relationship between law enforcement agents and
the media and reveal how Mayerthorpe and the calls for increased regulation of marijuana grow ops are linked to wider social and political
shifts in Canada.

Mayerthorpe and Beyond: Law-and-Order Discourse

Even years after the events stemming from the tragedy at Mayerthorpe,
newspaper reporting on marijuana grow ops continued to reference
these events to underscore the dangers of marijuana cultivation. These
themes reflected the worst-case scenarios and focused on the most heinous of problems associated with the production of marijuana. The solutions heralded by spokespeople continued to reiterate the need for
more "law and order" in Canada because of the Mayerthorpe tragedy.
A 2008 article in the *Globe and Mail* exemplifies this theme. The article
covers a BC Supreme Court ruling related to a defendant's Charter
rights and "knock and announce rules." In her ruling, Madam Justice
Catherine Bruce of the BC Supreme Court harshly criticized police actions during a marijuana raid. She stated that the officers endangered
their own lives and the life of the accused when they smashed in the
side door of a Surrey home with their guns drawn. The RCMP were investigating a marijuana grow op in a basement of the home. The judge
noted that "the abrupt and violent entry executed by police went well
beyond what was necessary." In response to the judge's ruling, BC's
Solicitor-General John Les stated, "I was profoundly disappointed.
We've been making good progress in terms of getting after grow operations." The news article states that he wonders "what police have
to do? ... Are they supposed to wait longer to give people the opportunity to lock and load?"[71] Surrey RCMP spokesperson Sergeant Morrow

claimed that "the culture of grow operations means officers must assume high-powered weapons are involved and that the homes they're about to search may have been booby trapped." Madame Bruce's ruling noted that "this kind of violent and forceful entry with guns drawn appears to be standard practice for the Surrey RCMP even where no evidence exists of weapons."[72] Yet, as we have seen in this chapter, the media and police spokespeople continue to claim that weapons and potential violence at marijuana grow ops are the norm, regardless of lack of evidence to support these claims. As noted earlier, a 2005 RCMP-supported study found that 89 per cent of grow ops identified in British Columbia were not potentially violent,[73] and only 5 per cent of grow ops in a 2011 Department of Justice study could be said to have links to violent organized crime groups.[74]

Well into 2007, news stories drew on the same themes that had helped to shape public understanding of the Mayerthorpe events. Newspaper stories still offered economist Stephen Easton's estimates discussed at the beginning of this chapter, but also increasingly linked them to RCMP claims about the types of problems that the cultivation of marijuana poses for BC citizens:

> A study by the Fraser Institute estimates the real value of BC's marijuana industry at $7 billion in 2006, the same year the value of all the agriculture, forestry, fishing and hunting in BC totaled $5.3 billion. The institute says "there were 17,500 grow-ops province-wide that year." "Don't think that all that money [$7 billion] is coming back to British Columbia," Rintoul says. "Some of that money is going to other countries to support other organized-crime activities" involving cocaine, handguns and human smuggling.[75]

This excerpt is part of larger article that contains RCMP claims not only about the connections between grow ops and violence but the potentially serious health problems that marijuana can cause. Following Mayerthorpe, claims about the size of the industry and links to organized crime are rarely contested by the media even though they have potentially serious consequences in relation to the direction of drug policy and the demonization of marijuana cultivators.

The movement for harsher sentencing and punishment for people who cultivate marijuana has grown since the events at Mayerthorpe. Newspaper writers often make their critiques about a lenient court system in a comparative manner, usually contrasting Canadian sentences with those given in the United States:

"Lenient sentences given to marijuana growers by BC's courts are encouraging criminals to set up shop here and ship their product south of the border," an official with the US border patrol said Monday. "It's grown up [in BC] because it's much more lenient up there," said Gene Davis, deputy chief of the US border patrol in Blaine, Wash. "It makes a much better growing environment up there than down here ... They've gone north to grow it because it's pretty low risk."[76]

Another editorial excerpt from the Vancouver *Province* simultaneously reiterates police-based claims that Canada's sentencing practices are lenient at the same time as it praises US-based sentencing as effective at containing grow operations:

Consider the case of marijuana grow-ops. Anyone in Washington state convicted of running a grow-op can expect a minimum five years in jail. If they're growing on their own property, they've just lost their house. If they have young children, they can expect social services to remove them. What happens in BC? The grower loses his light bulbs, and might pay a fine equivalent to a couple ounces of product. And he's back in business the next day. Consequently, grow-ops are not a problem in Washington state while in BC, they number in the thousands. So let's lay the "tough penalties don't deter" myth to rest.[77]

This article goes on to suggest that while funding for treatment is important, "that doesn't necessitate we roll our eyes in disgust at the mention of increasing sanctions and resign ourselves to the fast-diminishing quality of life that BC's law-abiding citizens are experiencing."[78] In this passage, the author draws on long-standing drug discourses that contrast "good" citizens against bad drug users. Here, however, this discourse has been extended symbolically to divide drug producers, in this case, marijuana-growing operators from "good" citizens. This allows the author to claim that harsher sentencing practices can have a positive impact on the quality of life of "good" citizens regardless of how these sentences impact the lives and civil liberties of others. This article and others rarely problematize whether or not harsh sentencing and punishment are effective deterrents. In our study period, reporters rarely investigated the fiscal and personal costs of long prison sentences, nor how tax dollars diverted to prison building and the maintenance of prisons could leave other publicly funded institutions such as health care and education underfunded. Yet the residents of Washington State were considering these very issues, and in a November 2012 referendum, they voted to abolish the prohibition of cannabis. Adults in the State of Washington can now possess one ounce of marijuana, licences will be issued to grow cannabis, and stores will be set up to sell marijuana to consumers.[79]

Prison sentencing for a drug offence became an ongoing concern for Marc Emery, a prominent Canadian marijuana policy reform activist living in British Columbia. A few months after the events in Mayerthorpe, the Vancouver police arrested Marc Emery. It is believed that the US Drug Enforcement Administration (DEA) requested his arrest. Following a number of legal challenges, in 2010, Canada's Minister of Justice Rob Nicholson extradited Marc Emery to the United States to stand trial for selling marijuana seeds through the Internet. Emery's extradition was approved even though he had claimed and paid Canadian taxes on his business for years. In Canada, his alleged crime would have been subject to a fine; however, in the United States, he was given a 5-year prison sentence. In a Kafka-like twist, in April 2012, the former US District Attorney for the western district of Washington State, John McKay, who prosecuted Marc Emery, called for the legalization and taxation of marijuana in Canada and the United States, and as noted above, Washington State did vote to legalize small amounts of cannabis in November 2012. However, McKay's change of heart does not extend to Marc Emery. McKay is quoted saying that he did not regret prosecuting Emery because he broke US law. McKay now believes that the war on marijuana has failed, and the laws that keep marijuana illegal "no longer serve any purpose, but allow gangs and cartels to generate billions in profits." As we write, Marc Emery is still serving his sentence in Washington State, and there is no indication so far that cannabis offenders convicted prior to 2012 will be released from prison or granted leniency.

Although Emery was caught in the net, the issue of lenient sentencing is linked to the dangers posed by grow ops, rather than the selling of marijuana seeds. For example, one reporter writes:

> Grow-ops use more than 93 kwh of electricity per day, three times normal consumption. And they are 24 times more likely to catch fire than ordinary houses. Homes are guarded by dogs, "deliberate booby traps," guns and axes. Rintoul said the weapons are not directed at the public but designed to thwart ripoffs. Convicted operators are likely to serve sentences of "a few months."[80]

This article is typical of many of its kind that skips easily from describing the harms of cultivation to the claim that the justice system is too lenient. The reader is left to make the connections, although anyone who has followed this issue in the preceding years would be well aware of the supposed connections between these ideas.

By 2009, the Conservative government in Ottawa had made several attempts to pass changes to the Criminal Code that would have instituted mandatory minimum sentences for some drug crimes. An article from this same year again reiterates a seemingly causal relationship between harsh penalties and reduction in drug crimes despite evidence to the contrary. Below, a police spokesperson suggests that the efforts by Canada's Senate to soften the penalties proposed in a bill to introduce mandatory minimum sentences for growing marijuana would be detrimental to public safety:

> "If they remove the minimum sentencing for grow ops under 200 plants then they will, without a doubt, create a huge industry where we will see a proliferation of grows with 199 plants because there will be less penalty," he said.[81]

The speaker, Inspector Brad Desmarais, from the Vancouver Police Department (VPD), suggests that softening the penalties will only make the problem of grow ops worse and will lead to many more smaller operations equally as likely to pose safety risks. Newspapers continue to uncritically publish these claims, despite the existence of a wide variety of evidence that suggests enforcement approaches have limited effects in deterring drug demand and supply or increasing overall public safety.[82] In general, tough sentences do not deter people from committing crimes.[83]

During our study period, suggestions to decriminalize and/or legalize marijuana use are generally limited to the pages of the letters to the editor, and news stories are more likely to feature police-based perspectives. These same stories often draw on police statements to claim that neither decriminalization nor legalization will eliminate the link between organized crime and growing operations; nor will alternate regulatory mechanisms reduce the number of grow ops in British Columbia.[84]

Prior to Mayerthorpe, police routinely made claims about the links between marijuana grow ops and guns, fire hazards, and organized crime. These claims did not seem to capture the public imagination in the same way that the events at Mayerthorpe did; in fact, the media and police/RCMP complained that Canadians were ignorant of and apathetic to this pressing danger. Events at Mayerthorpe and subsequent media reporting operated as a lightning rod that crystallized anxieties about violence, marijuana grow ops, and lenient courts. Mayerthorpe provided the specific case that seemed to prove what the police/RCMP and the media had claimed all along. However, as we have demonstrated, many of the claims about events at Mayerthorpe were either exaggerated or faulty. This did not, however, dissuade newspapers from focusing on these issues, as the next chapter will illustrate.

3 Marijuana Grow Ops and Organized Crime

As we discussed in the preceding chapter, since 1995, marijuana grow ops in Canada have increasingly been linked to organized crime. In this chapter, we expand on our analysis of news articles about marijuana grow ops linked to organized crime, a dominant theme that emerged in our analysis of media representations. We examine here how the media characterize the links between the profitability of the marijuana industry and organized crime. Then we reveal how media reports portray organized crime as a phenomenon that is infiltrating supposedly safe neighbourhoods to set up marijuana grow ops. We discuss media-based concerns about exports across the Canada/US border, and, finally, turn our lens to how the media represent marijuana grow ops, organized crime, and violence.

In our sample, 280 news stories (11%) discussed the links between organized crime and marijuana grow ops. The excerpts from news stories included in this chapter are representative of the numerous articles about organized crime and marijuana grow ops. Although we discuss how this is racialized, we provide a fuller discussion of this theme in the next chapter. We also highlight here how the varied themes intersect with one another to produce an increasingly potent mix of claims about grow ops. Figure 3.1 graphs the number of articles about organized crime and marijuana grow ops found in our sample.

Organized Crime

Canada, like some Western countries including the United States, is committed to eradicating illegal drug use, trafficking, and cultivation both domestically and around the world. Canada is a signatory to the

Figure 3.1. Articles about Marijuana Grow Ops and Organized Crime, by Year.

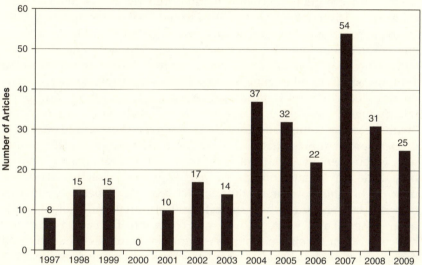

Number of Articles about Organized Crime by Year

1961 UN Single Convention on Narcotic Drugs, one of three international drug control treaties that determine how the drug trade will be controlled. Researcher Michael Woodiwess notes that the United States was very influential in shaping this UN initiative; as a result, the global drug prohibition regime reflects both US interests and its particularly punitive, prohibitionist, war on drugs.[1] Although Canada is often viewed as having a more liberal drug policy, the reality is actually rather different. Canada's drug laws are quite harsh compared with many European countries' (e.g., in 2001, Portugal decriminalized possession of all criminalized drugs, including marijuana). Regardless of the relative punitiveness of drug control regimes, drug offences have risen steadily in Canada since the early 1990s.[2] In 2011, cannabis offences in Canada accounted for 69 per cent of all drug offences, and 52 per cent of all drug offences were for cannabis possession.[3] Similarly, in 2012, 52 per cent of all drug offences were for cannabis possession.[4] The high arrest rates for cannabis possession since the early 1990s have been rendered invisible by a hyperbolic discourse about the production of marijuana and organized crime (both local and global organizations) promoted by law enforcement agencies in both Canada and the United States.

Since the advent of drug prohibition, fears about racialized crime syndicates have prevailed. In the 1990s, new versions of these racialized fears were generated about Latin gangs by media reports especially in the United States; beginning around 2000, Asian and especially Vietnamese criminal organizations became a predominant focus of law enforcement agencies in Canada. Both the media and these law enforcement agencies have repeatedly reiterated their claims about the "outlaw" status of biker gangs and their links to the production of marijuana. Media reports typically represent the Hells Angels and other biker gangs as racially unmarked "Others." Richard Dyer's work on "whiteness as an ethnic category" in the media is pertinent to our study on newspaper representation.[5] Dyer contends that most often whiteness is represented as natural and, thus, an invisible category; this is one of the ways that white power and supremacy "secures its dominance."[6] But, media representation of white outlaws clearly delineates between law-abiding white subjects and criminal and violent white biker gangs. Thus, white biker gangs come into focus as a problematic category but their racial status is unmarked, unlike other racialized groups such as Asian and Vietnamese crime gangs who are "marked by colour."[7] Woodiwess notes that ethnic- and alien-conspiracy theories and stereotyping were an important part of the propaganda accompanying drug prohibition in the United States, and the same can be said of Canadian drug policy and discourse on organized crime in the past as well as in contemporary times.[8]

Canadian Media and Organized Crime

Figure 3.2 provides a representative sample of titles of news articles about organized crime. Given that three out of four of the newspapers analysed in this study were BC based, the majority of these articles described the issue of marijuana grow ops in British Columbia as an escalating social problem, partly because of the increasing involvement of organized crime over time. As we noted in the previous chapter, these articles claim repeatedly that marijuana grow ops are not "mom-and-pop" organizations or small-scale operations run by law-abiding people; rather, they are supposed to be large-size operations, involving increasingly dangerous booby traps and weapons, and increasingly sophisticated growing techniques, all linked to organized crime, especially Asian organized crime. An early 1998 opinion essay in the *Province*, written by a Vancouver police officer, associates grow ops with

Figure 3.2. Headline Box: Organized Crime and Gangs.[9]

HEADLINES: ORGANIZED CRIME AND GANGS

Police sweep massive grow-op: "Sophisticated organized crime" behind pot, police say (1998)

New RCMP unit specializes in busting Langley pot operations: Growing BC marijuana has become such a lucrative business that organized crime has moved in (1998)

39 charged, drugs and cash seized in major cross-border crackdown: After a month-long surveillance operation along the border from Langley to Chilliwack, a team of Canadian and US officers strikes against the trade of BC-grown marijuana for cocaine and cash (1999)

BC living easy for foreign thugs: Word is out around the world that province is soft on crime (1999)

Gangs "franchise" grow-ops (2000)

Organized crime controls it (2001)

U.S. syndicates use BC as hub for pot smuggling (2001)

RCMP fears gang warfare over marijuana operations (2003)

Police overwhelmed by surge in organized crime's grow-ops (2003)

Police fear gang war over pot: Price drop expected to ignite violence between crime groups (2004)

Marijuana bankrolling other crimes (2005)

Satanism, hard-core pornography, fighting dogs, cocaine use, and biker gangs.[10] The Organized Crime Agency of British Columbia (OCABC), a key early spokesgroup in newspaper articles about grow ops, is quoted in a 2000 *Province* article: "Grow ops are not about the occasional use of marijuana ... they are about large amounts of money, violence and intimidation."[11] These articles describe marijuana as a cancer spreading into our neighbourhoods, or a poison in our communities, reaching epidemic proportions.[12] Articles often focus on grow ops supposedly located in "nice neighbourhoods." These articles help to shape the notion that grow ops pose dangers to innocent persons and represent a perilous encroachment of organized crime into otherwise normal middle-class spaces.[13]

As we noted previously, municipal police forces and the RCMP were the majority of claims makers found in newspaper stories. Rarely do claims about organized crime and marijuana occur alone; rather, news articles tend to make links between claims about grow operations and violence, exportation of marijuana to the United States, and the high value of the crop. Individual organized crime members are represented as greedy, violent, and racialized Others. Over time, this achieves the effect of naturalizing not just the individual claims, but also the links between these claims. The supposed value of the marijuana industry in British Columbia, in particular, is the subject of repeated and now familiar claims linked to organized crime. This approach to reporting occurs at the beginning of the study period and continues throughout the years. The linking of these claims is illustrated by the following excerpt from a 1997 article in the *Province*:

> They say much of the profit from BC's biggest cash crop – worth an esti-
> mated $1 billion a year – is going straight into the pockets of organized
> crime. And they say members of BC's notorious Hells Angels motorcycle
> club are among the main players in the lucrative dope-growing business.
> "There is no question about it, marijuana has become big business, and BC
> has the dubious distinction of growing some of the most powerful mari-
> juana in the world," said RCMP drug awareness co-ordinator Sgt. Chuck
> Doucette.[14]

This article establishes and assumes a causal link between the claims that the majority of the profits from growing marijuana go to organized crime and the size of the underground economy estimated at that time at $1 billion a year. In other words, gangs, rather than the demand for marijuana, are the cause of so much underground marijuana cultivation.

An important component of claims about organized crime is the con-
tention that these groups control the majority of marijuana cultivation. In 1998, police spokespeople claim that organized crime groups control the bulk of marijuana grown in British Columbia:

> Although police confidently assert that "70 per cent of commercial grow
> operations are controlled by the Hells Angels," no biker has yet been con-
> victed of such an offence. Nevertheless, Const. Vince Arsenault of the Sur-
> rey RCMP drug section insists: "The evidence we have is that the Hells
> Angels control these operations and that the people doing the growing are
> just the babysitters."[15]

Typically, newspaper articles do not always provide exact sources for these claims. A 2002 article in the *Province* describes a national police operation called "Operation Greensweep III." The article highlights police spokespeople who claim that 80 per cent of grow ops are controlled by organized crime and that 80 per cent of pot is grown for export to the United States.[16] This article makes explicit, once again, the unsubstantiated link between the profits from marijuana cultivation and organized crime. An excerpt from a 2002 article in the Victoria *Times Colonist* entitled "Police seek more power to shut down grow houses" illustrates how estimates of the size of the industry have grown in the intervening years:

> The grow operations now bring in billions of dollars in profit annually. Police say that 95 per cent of the operations are run by criminal gangs, who smuggle their marijuana to the US for sale ... British Columbia remains the country's marijuana-growing capital, where the annual business is estimated as high as $6 billion. The business is not confined to run-down rental properties. Growers are increasingly buying homes, and in some cases entire blocks are devoted to the lucrative business.[17]

This excerpt is illustrative of how a set of claims is linked together to expand the domain of the problem that grow ops pose. This article is exemplary in that these comments are preceded by claims about the reach of organized crime, the invasion of otherwise safe neighbourhoods by grow ops, the increasing use of upscale homes for these operations, the use of stolen electricity and dangerous electrical power bypasses, and the potential for dangerous toxins and fire. The article then links the need for increased police resources for what police describe as a battle they are losing against a "clear and present danger" posed by these growing operations and organized crime. The article concludes by noting both the risks to children living in grow ops and the unsuitability of penalties given by judges to convicted grow operators.

The following excerpts also illustrate how newspapers easily link claims about the size of the industry to other issues including organized crime:

> Marijuana cultivation in BC is a massive industry and massive problem for citizens and police. The province accounts for 39 per cent of all cultivation cases in Canada, more than any other province. BC's 79 grow-ops per 100,000 people is well over the national average of 27. The street value of BC bud tops $7 billion. BC produced 80,000 kilograms in 2003 and in the

process stole $3.2 million in electrical power. Detection of grow-ops out-paces police forces' ability to deal with them. BC RCMP get about 4,500 reports of grow-ops a year, but can only bust 1,500 of the largest.[18]

This newspaper article makes causal links between the involvement of organized crime and the profitability of the industry.[19] The article also illustrates how these claims are linked to other concerns about stolen electrical power and lack of sufficient police resources. Another 2008 article illustrates how police claims about the size of BC's industry are linked to organized crime in the later part of the study period:

Metro Vancouver is one of three Canadian hubs for organized crime, crime that is becoming more sophisticated and high-tech, according to a report by Canada's spy agency. Criminal Intelligence Service Canada's 2008 report identified 900 gangs across Canada and found the drug trade remains the largest criminal activity. In BC alone, marijuana and grow operations generate $6 billion in revenue every year, said RCMP BC spokesman Sgt. Tim Shields.[20]

Sgt. Shields' admonition that marijuana is a $6 billion industry is identi-cal to the one made in a previously noted article from 2002. The multiple and intersecting themes in these articles reflect the key findings of other chapters of this book; the linking of claims about organized crime to other concerns about marijuana cultivation potentially exacerbates the dangers of these operations. At the same time, these articles do not attempt to sub-stantiate the extent of police-based claims about the control of the industry.

Broadening the Scope of the Problem of Organized Crime

A 2003 news report highlights a claim that is increasingly made by both the police and the media: the police are overwhelmed by the supposed number of grow ops. In an article about Richmond, BC, police spokes-people estimate that the number of grow ops in their city is 600. These spokespeople argue that they can only attend to two a week, and the reporter estimates, in turn, that it would take six years to clean up all the grow ops in Richmond providing more were not initiated. These figures are combined with other claims about the role that organized crime plays in these operations in the following excerpt:

The establishment of the marijuana industry is the most stunning victory organized crime has had over police authorities in the province. Growing operations have become so numerous that the industry has acquired the resiliency and attributes of a herd. The police can run around like a pack of wolves picking off a victim here or there, but the greater part carries on unmolested.[21]

Another story from 2003 again emphasizes the crisislike state of organized crime in British Columbia and its relationships to the cultivation of marijuana. This article is part of a special series on crime in Vancouver:

From being little more than a landing stage for heroin and humans smuggled into North America, BC has sprouted a major criminal industry of its own – the cultivation of marijuana, estimated to be worth $4 billion a year in sales. Employing a sophisticated marketing, distribution and horticultural workforce numbering in the thousands, marijuana production has completely overwhelmed police efforts to control it. It has brought organized crime into every neighbourhood in the Lower Mainland – from the mansion district along Marine Drive to the humble homes of east Vancouver. Thirty years ago, it would have been difficult for the average citizen to be aware of organized crime, but break-and-enters and car robberies in the Lower Mainland – mostly by persons seeking money to buy drugs – have destroyed the public's sense of security. People now live in a world of discarded needles and condoms, street prostitution in every major community, police routinely breaking down the doors of neighbourhood grow-ops, merchants who won't keep cash around at night or won't change $100 bills.[22]

This reporter attributes to organized crime the destruction of neighbourhoods, skimming over the role that economic and other social and legal policies have contributed to the impoverishment of some of Vancouver's neighbourhoods. Once the diagnosis of the problem of grow ops is established, the article then links the elimination of grow ops to the need for renewed powers for police and the formation of the Organized Crime Agency of British Columbia.

Exports to the United States and Organized Crime

Over time, newspaper discussions of organized crime become increasingly focused on the issue of exports to the United States. News reports and law enforcement agents on both sides of the border claim that Canadian marijuana, especially "BC bud," is smuggled into the United

States for sale and distribution. In fact, newspaper reports describe grow ops as agents in not only the expansion of organized crime but also of the intensification of US concerns about its border with Canada. A 1999 article provides an example of this claim:

> Constable Rintoul, who is the media relations officer for BC's drug enforcement program, said organized crime groups now view Canada as the route of choice into the United States for heroin, cocaine and marijuana. He conceded that British Columbia has become a haven for drug traffickers doing business in BC's $3-billion-a-year marijuana industry. "Organized crime groups laugh at us in Canada. We are an easy mark."[23]

Other claims in this article include several conflicting arguments as to why Canada is rife with drug production. The reporter initially expresses US-based concerns about Canada becoming a drug-producing country, and then highlights BC-based politicians who, in turn, blame decreasing federal funding for the lack of drug control initiatives. In the same article, an RCMP spokesperson suggests that lenient sentencing contributes to the growth of organized crime and also makes the claim that organized crime finds an easy and lucrative haven in Canada. Then Foreign Affairs Minister Lloyd Axworthy is quoted as opposing US suggestions that Canada be blacklisted as a drug-producing country. Axworthy suggests that Canada prefers to work on a more cooperative international stage in support of the "war on drugs." Axworthy's comments are vague in terms of what he means by cooperation, but are clearly an attempt to counter US claims that Canada is a drug-exporting country.

In some cases, Canadian officials are the source for claims about Canadian marijuana being exported to the United States. Nevertheless, US concerns about Canadian-grown marijuana are featured routinely by the media outlets we studied. One such example is an article from the *Vancouver Sun* in March 2006.[24] This article draws the bulk of its assertions from a report released by the US State Department. It quotes a 2006 US report and then also draws on RCMP sources for its claims:

> "Though outdoor cultivation continues, the use of large and more sophisticated indoor grow operations is increasing because it allows year-round production," the document says. "The RCMP reports the involvement of ethnic Chinese and Vietnamese organized crime organizations in

technologically advanced organic grow methods that produce marijuana with elevated THC levels."[25]

The article reports that the US State Department calls for increased regulatory and enforcement efforts in Canada to stem the tide of drug production in this country. The reporter is uncritical of US efforts to influence Canadian drug policy, including permitting US law enforcement agents and the US DEA to operate on Canadian soil.[26] In 2003, the DEA set up a permanent office in Vancouver, BC. One of the DEA's priorities is to eradicate the production and trafficking of marijuana.[27] None of the news media in our study reported about the DEA in British Columbia or on what long-term implications the DEA might have for Canada's drug policy.

This article reveals how claims about organized crime are circular. RCMP reports become the basis for US reports about Canada. In doing so, the dangers of organized crime groups are linked to the growing of marijuana with purported "technologically advanced" methods that produce increased THC levels. The US source quoted in the article above complains about lenient sentencing in Canada as a causal factor in the marijuana trade and exportation to the United States. The reporter offers no proof from the US source to support these claims. Both US and Canadian sources assert that Canada has weak laws and sentencing, and both sources assume that harsh sentencing deters the drug trade. These claims are continuously naturalized in media reports, highlighted as if they are established fact when, in fact, they are not. In the United States, where broadened police powers, harsher drug laws, and harsh sentencing practices were set in place in the 1980s, the illegal drug trade and drug-related violence has not decreased.[28] During our study period, evidence that suggests drug prohibition and harsh laws and sentencing fail to deter the drug trade is rarely reported by the media – and when it is, it is often limited to editorials; see chapter 7 for a larger discussion of alternative media reporting.

The above article refers to organic methods of cultivating marijuana as a particularly deviant form of cultivation associated with high THC levels. Between 1997 and 2002, newspaper articles uncritically draw on UN and police sources to report that THC levels had increased to as high as 35 per cent.[29] Articles repeatedly compare the THC content of marijuana with that used in the 1960s. These claims often originated from police spokespeople who contended that current marijuana use was more dangerous than in the past. One such article entitled "Enforcers challenge cannabis liberation movement: Activists who want lawmakers to take lighter view on the use of marijuana face police who maintain the drug is dangerous," suggests:

> contemporary marijuana, which is produced from the cannabis plant, is much stronger than it was in the 1960s. They [police] say marijuana's THC levels are much higher today than they were 20 years ago ... "Right now, the THC level in marijuana is between 16 and 20 per cent. Twenty years ago it was between 3 and 5 per cent," said RCMP Constable Scott Rintoul, who is part of the force's drug-enforcement unit in Vancouver.[30]

A 2002 article claims, "There are concerns that pot is not the same 'soft' drug it used to be. Genetic manipulation has produced strains 10 to 20 times more powerful than the weed smoked at long-ago pop festivals such as Woodstock."[31] Although claims about the dangerous potency of marijuana grown in British Columbia declined over the years, a 2007 opinion essay by Margaret Wente in the *Globe and Mail* reiterates the claims that marijuana has become increasingly dangerous with the article title "Not the groovy '60s: Today's cannabis is harder and meaner."[32] Wente goes on to attribute a variety of social problems to the strength of marijuana:

> Today's harder, meaner cannabis is a scourge in many of Canada's poorer neighbourhoods. It is a spreading affliction on native reserves and, in the cities, is intimately linked with the deadly duo of guns and gangs. It has an especially devastating effect among certain ethnic minorities.[33]

Wente blames changes in cultivation techniques including greenhouse technology and the cross-breeding of seed stock from Asia and the Middle East for the increase in the potency of marijuana. We will address in detail below the issue of marijuana potency and media reports that link organized crime and higher THC levels. Racialization of marijuana grow ops is discussed in chapter 4.

Estimates of the potency of marijuana in the United States usually originate from the US National Institute on Drug Abuse–funded Marijuana Potency Monitoring Project at the University of Mississippi. Peer-reviewed research from this project indicates that the overall strength of marijuana has increased since the 1970s. This project, however, separately measures different types of marijuana including ditchweed (defined as > 1% THC), marijuana (includes leaves, stems, and seeds), and sinsemilla (flowering tops of unfertilized female cannabis plants). With high and low percentage THC outliers excluded, these researchers find that the strength of ditchweed has remained relatively similar; the potency of marijuana has increased from a mean of 3.4 per cent THC in 1993 to 5.7 per cent in 2008; the average of THC content of sinsemilla has increased from 5.5 per cent to 11.4 per cent in the same period. There is a great deal of variability in THC content in the samples used for these estimates. The variability of THC in domestic samples of marijuana can fluctuate, for example, from less than 0.01 per cent to as high as 24.7 per cent, and the THC content of sinsemilla can vary from 0.1 per cent to 33.1 per cent. These researchers suggest that comparability of THC measurements is somewhat compromised by the lack of randomness of samples, correct identification of samples, plant maturity at harvest, different definitions of cannabis, and different analytical techniques.[34]

Similar longitudinal detailed surveillance data are not routinely collected in Canada. The most recent report from the RCMP, in 2009, suggests that the potency of cannabis seized in Canada has increased but this report provides no data to support this claim.[35] A report from the US DEA suggests the following: "The average THC content of marijuana analyzed in Canada continued its rise in 2006. THC content of samples analyzed in 2004 was 9.78 percent, followed by 9.96 percent in 2005, and 10.25 percent in 2006."[36] Caution must be exercised about these data, however, as there is no way to verify the findings of the RCMP. Comparison between the United States and Canada is further complicated by differing approaches to measurement. The DEA draws its US data from the Marijuana Potency Monitoring Project (noted above) and its Canadian data from the RCMP. The DEA report points out that in Canada "marijuana exhibits are submitted for THC analysis for court purposes and are comprised almost exclusively of the flowering heads or buds of the female cannabis plant, which in the United States would be classified as sinsemilla. Canada tests all marijuana but does not classify it by type."[37] These differences make comparisons between the United States and Canada difficult and also suggest that the average reported THC content of Canadian cannabis may be generally higher because of testing methods. Our analysis of newspaper articles indicates that information on THC content primarily originates with RCMP spokespeople and reports. Claims that the THC content of Canadian cannabis has reached 20 per cent to 30 per cent likely originate with a few samples, but do not accurately represent the average THC content.

What effects these increases in potency have on health are difficult to estimate because there is a lack of data on how users titrate their dose according to the strength of cannabis.[38] Two newspaper articles dispute the dominant discourse about the dangers of high-potency marijuana. One article quotes the 2002 Senate report on cannabis law reform to suggest that prohibition itself is responsible for the increases in potency given the unregulated character of this underground economy.[39] The second article, also from 2002, quotes Neil Boyd, a criminologist and drug policy researcher at BC's Simon Fraser University:

> One of the biggest health risks of marijuana use, he [Boyd] said, is the inhaling of smoke from joints – which can cause lung problems similar to those experienced by cigarette smokers. "The more THC in a joint," Boyd said, "the less the user needs to smoke to get the same effect – making them more healthy not less."[40]

As Boyd argues, higher THC levels may be interpreted as a health benefit rather than a negative event because users could ingest or smoke less of the substance in order to achieve the same effect.[41] Critics further note that the cannabis plant is made up of 460 known compounds, THC being only one of them; thus, the sole focus on THC is misguided.[42]

As early as 2001, newspaper articles report that high-potency Canadian-grown marijuana is the key product smuggled to the United States by organized crime groups.[43] But high-potency marijuana and organized crime connections are not the only concerns US politicians and claims makers have about Canada. In 2002, a federal parliamentary committee recommended that Canada decriminalize the possession of small amounts of cannabis. This event prompted a flurry of articles in the *Globe and Mail*, many of which reported on US objections to decriminalization. These articles included numerous examples of how claims like the high potency of "BC Bud" are used by US commentators to challenge Canadian attempts to decriminalize possession of marijuana. Several of these articles quoted John Walters, director of the National Drug Control Policy in the United States at that time:

> Mr. Walters said any moves to liberalize marijuana laws in Canada could result in longer waits and tougher scrutiny at the border, already heightened in the wake of the US terrorist attacks last year.[44]

The newspaper report above goes on to quote Walters' earlier claims that Canada produces a highly potent type of marijuana that contributes to increasing rates of youth addiction in the United States. In another article, Walters is quoted as saying that "marijuana poses a greater danger to the United Sates than heroin, cocaine or amphetamines."[45] He then claims that the potency of Canadian marijuana is four times stronger than it used to be and calls for more cooperation between Canadian and US law enforcement agents. In another 2002 article, Walters asserts that there is no medical use for cannabis and accuses Canadian policy makers of being naive for being persuaded of the medical benefits of cannabis.[46] For the most part, these comments are reported uncritically. Unlike Canada, US drug laws are enacted at both the federal and state levels. Since the 1990s, there has been an ongoing conflict between federal and state law in the United States in relation to marijuana. The US federal government and the DEA deny that cannabis has medical benefits and defy state law that has legalized medical marijuana by raiding compassion clubs and dispensaries and arresting activists, organizers, and patients. However, in August 2013 the US Justice Department announced that it would allow states to implement their legal medical marijuana programs and ballot initiatives in Colorado and Washington.

Earlier in 2002, the *Globe and Mail* carried a story that challenges the view that decriminalization would "stir the wrath of the US." This article draws on critical drug policy spokespeople including lawyer Eugene Oscapella and MP Libby Davies who supported decriminalization[47] But in 2004, when the federal Liberal government attempted to reintroduce legislation to decriminalize possession of small amounts of cannabis, newspapers like the *Vancouver Sun* carried articles that warn of a negative US response: "Only weeks before the Martin government plans to revive a marijuana decriminalization bill, the US has taken another pot-shot at Canada by saying its slack drug penalties amount to an invitation to organized crime."[48] The article concludes with an excerpt from a US Whitehouse spokesperson, who reiterates the need to stem the tide of marijuana imported from Canada because of its high potency and its links to organized crime. The claims about the dangerousness of Canadian-grown marijuana are thus magnified by asserting its connections to organized crime seen to be responsible for increases in its THC content.

A typical example from a 2008 *Province* article, entitled "Gangs cast shadow over Bible-belt Abbotsford: Organized crime is growing in might as the Fraser Valley city expands – but churches and the community are fighting back," explores the link between the proximity of the Canadian-American border to communities in the BC lower mainland and the growth of organized crime in places like Abbotsford, BC.[49] The article repeats concerns about young men entering gangs and offers several explanations for this occurrence, stating that gangs provide a like-minded community and a sense of belonging, as well as a source of easy income. Liberally sprinkled throughout the article are excerpts from key BC spokespeople including Plecas, an RCMP university research chair. In this article, Plecas comments on the growth of gang life, not just marijuana. Police spokespeople also make the link between gang life and drugs by asserting that marijuana grown in BC's lower mainland is sold to US customers causing the ranks of organized crime to swell. The article suggests that the increase in gang violence in BC is drug related but that police have brought resources to bear that will decrease the amount of organized crime in the area.

British Columbia is, of course, not the only region of concern in the newspaper articles we studied. Another article from the same paper, in July 2008, introduces its concerns about the burgeoning industry in Ontario with the following lead-in: "Another day, another grow-op busted – and tomorrow there'll be another, as Ontario's homegrown marijuana industry hums and thrives, shipping its potent product across the US border by the tonne, some things don't much change for the Toronto police drug squad."[50] This article repeats the claim that organized crime plays a key role in the increase of grow ops and attributes this increase to lack of risk because of lenient sentencing and high profits that accrue from exporting marijuana to the United States. This article, too, uses quotations from Plecas, who argues that marijuana is the "largest single revenue source for gangsters" in British Columbia. A police officer is then quoted in the same article as he asserts that the same is true in Ontario. Yet, as we discussed earlier in this book, there is no empirical evidence to support such claims, and in fact, a comprehensive 2011 Canadian Justice Department study refutes these claims.[51]

Exporting Marijuana and Cultivation Skills

As the articles described above suggest, concerns about Canada as a drug-exporting nation, increase over time. Coverage of the 2006 RCMP report, *Drug Situation in Canada*, reiterated RCMP claims that exports of marijuana to the United States were a key part of organized crime activities in Canada. This article supplements its claims with quotations from Darryl Plecas that BC expertise is now being exported:

"Smuggling of Canadian-grown marijuana to the United States continues to be a concern for both countries," the report states. Plecas said BC's level of sophistication in the marijuana market has spread to other parts of the world, most notably Britain, Australia and New Zealand. "That level of sophistication developed here in BC is being found in other jurisdictions," he said. "They'll tell you about their BC connections ... It's such an outrageously profitable business. It always boggled me why there weren't more [grow ops] everywhere. Once it was established it can be produced in a three-level home with a basement, why wouldn't you have 20 of them?"[52]

Here, Plecas reiterates claims that Canada not only exports marijuana but also its seemingly unique growing techniques. In contrast to the scholarly literature that reveals very diverse marijuana growers and styles of growing in the United Kingdom, Belgium, Australia, and New Zealand,[53] Plecas asserts that British Columbia is leading the way in exporting knowledge and organized crime connections when, in fact, the scholarly evidence does not substantiate such claims. Plecas states how lucrative the business is by emphasizing how easy it is to grow profitable marijuana. In contrast, the leading North American marijuana magazines, *Cannabis Culture* and *High Times*, dedicate considerable space in each issue to the difficulties of growing marijuana, both indoors and outdoors. For a humorous and informed account of marijuana growing, see *Romancing Mary Jane: A Year in the Life of a Failed Marijuana Grower*.[54] These accounts are in sharp contrast to Plecas' statements. Like other sources of information, newspaper articles rarely contest these claims, nor do they ask for any evidence to support the allegations made by key spokespeople – especially by RCMP and municipal police officers.

Another 2007 article, entitled "BC exports grow-op skills," also claims that organized crime groups export marijuana and their skills at growing plants:

A different kind of brain drain is under way in BC as pot growers share their billions of dollars' worth of skills with a worldwide audience. "We think they're exporting their expertise," says RCMP Superintendent Paul Nadeau, director of the Mounties' national drug branch and the former head of Vancouver's drug section. "We've heard of it on an international scale."[55]

This article draws on quotations from Toronto municipal police officers to suggest that the exportation of cultivation skills to the United States was preceded first by the movement eastward of these skills, and they say that this accounts for an increase in grow ops in places like Ontario.

The idea of BC growers "exporting their expertise" deflects attention away from the fact that the United States has a large illegal domestic marijuana-growing industry and drug trade. In 2010, the US Office of National Drug Control Policy reported that marijuana cultivation is most prevalent in seven states – California, Hawaii, Kentucky, Oregon, Tennessee, Washington, and Virginia – and that California is the lead state for indoor cultivation (based on number of plants eradicated), followed by Florida and Washington.[56] Twenty US states and the District of Columbia have sanctioned legal medical cannabis and growing for these purposes. Founders of BC's Compassion Club drew from the expertise of US medical cannabis dispensaries that were first established in California.[57] In November 2012, two US states, Washington and Colorado, voted to repeal cannabis prohibition. Now adults may possess up to one ounce of cannabis for personal use in these states, and legal marijuana dispensaries will be set up for the sale of cannabis. In Colorado, adults may grow up to six cannabis plants in their home for personal use.[58]

Cocaine and Marijuana

Stories often claim that "BC bud" is so valued and potent that organized crime groups are willing to exchange marijuana for cocaine in the United States. This claim appears in various forms throughout the study period. An article from 2004 is representative of media reportage about the relationship between cocaine smuggling and BC-based marijuana production:

> Nadeau said the marijuana export trade has become the No.1 money-maker for organized crime groups, which use profits from the trade to finance other ventures, such as the importation of cocaine and guns. "It's becoming more and more apparent that every organized crime group is looking to grow-ops to generate money that supports other criminal activity," said Nadeau. "It's become their money machine." Det. Jim Fisher, a Vancouver police department expert on Asian gangs, said even Chinese gangs such as the Big Circle Boys, which traditionally focused on importing heroin into BC, are getting involved in pot. "The profit is as good as heroin," said Fisher. "I don't think people understand how big it is. It's changed the dynamic of organized crime here."[59]

Drawing on police sources, this article argues for the causal relationship between growing marijuana and the ability of organized crime to fund other ventures including the importation of cocaine.

Another 2004 article, in the *Times Colonist*, reports the problem of organized crime in British Columbia in the following way:

"In BC organized crime is involved in drugs, money-laundering, the gun trade and the sex trade. Hells Angels are the 'biggest and the worst' organized crime group, but Asian gangs, Indo-Canadian gangs and a small Russian gang component are also active in the province," he said. "People with grow-ops are part of the organized-crime network because the distribution and marketing system is run by organized-crime groups and anyone who freelances is in trouble," he said. "About 80 per cent of marijuana grown in BC goes to the United States where it is traded kilo for kilo for cocaine," the solicitor general said.[60]

This article is rich in unsubstantiated and interlinked claims. It simultaneously evokes racialized tropes, other crimes, and claims about the extent of control of marijuana cultivation by organized crime to underscore its central claim: BC-grown marijuana is so potent and prized in the United States that it can be traded for cocaine and guns, without the exchange of money.

A later 2007 article describes the findings of the RCMP's Criminal Intelligence Division and its recent report, again making the claim that marijuana is exchanged for cocaine in the United States.[61] Another 2007 article from the *Vancouver Sun* suggests that the mainstay of the Hells Angels is their cross-border smuggling of marijuana in exchange for cocaine brought back to British Columbia.[62] These articles broaden the domain of the problem of marijuana production, giving it a causal role in not only supporting organized crime, but also in making cocaine more readily available to residents of the province.

Newspaper reporting does not provide any context for why cocaine might be a popular drug, nor does it really distinguish small-time growers from those associated with organized crime. In contrast to claims in news articles about cocaine coming from the United States and traded for BC marijuana, the rate of cocaine offences fell steadily from 2007 to 2010 in Canada, with a 5 per cent decrease from 2009 to 2010.[63] There is little evidence that cocaine is flooding the country, regardless of unsubstantiated media and police/RCMP claims. Thus, claims of such large amounts of marijuana in Canada being traded for cocaine from the United States are suspect. Claims about guns being traded for marijuana may also be suspect. In 2012, *Maclean's* reporter John Geddes revealed that the number of guns seized by the Canada Border Services Agency was grossly inflated by Justice Minister Rob Nicholson on

CBC radio. Geddes questions the federal government's commitment to stopping handguns from being smuggled into Canada. He points to the scrapping of the federal gun registry by the Conservative government and the comparatively small budget allotted to curtailing the illegal trade of guns compared with the much larger National Anti-Drug Strategy budget.[64]

Violence and Marijuana Grow Ops

As we make clear above, early on in the study period, newspaper articles make simplistic and causal links suggesting that the production of marijuana underscores a great deal of violence and organized crime especially in British Columbia. Figure 3.3 provides a representative sample of news headlines linking marijuana production, organized crime, and violence. One such article from 2007 illustrates media claims about grow ops and attempts to implicate marijuana users in fuelling gang violence:

> A lethal intersection of American guns, sea routes to Asia and rapidly proliferating marijuana grow-ops has given rise to a volatile gang scene in British Columbia, police say. In other parts of Canada, established gangs provide some measure of stability to their illegal industries – although they can be every bit as brutal – but in British Columbia, the composition of gangs is constantly shifting. The result is a more dangerous situation in which new gangs are aiming to carve out territory or establish their reputation, putting them on a collision course with existing criminal outfits ... What they all have in common is a profit motive built on BC's massive marijuana exports, which allow gangs to smuggle hard drugs and high-powered guns into Canada, he said ... And grow-ops are proliferating, giving gangs every incentive to resort to violence, even murder, to grab a bigger piece of the profits ... Pot may have a benevolent reputation, he said, but any users who aren't growing their own supplies are fuelling the war playing out on the streets of the Lower Mainland. "Ultimately, you're contributing to the violence."[65]

This excerpt is part of a longer article that suggests that the gang scene in British Columbia is unique because of its connections to marijuana. It also evokes themes described earlier in this book by drawing simplistic causal relationships between marijuana use and gang warfare on the streets in the lower mainland of Vancouver.

Figure 3.3. Headline Box: Violence and Grow Ops.[66]

HEADLINES: VIOLENCE AND GROW OPS

Mayor vows to reclaim neighbourhoods: Lois Jackson says North Delta's war on marijuana growers is just a first step in improving the quality of life in older residential areas (2000)

Pot house invaded by three men (2001)

RCMP says illegal drugs fund foreign terrorists (2002)

Neighbours cheer as police raid marijuana-growing operation (2003)

BC bud buys guns for Afghans (2004)

Police alarmed by number of grow-rips (2004)

Violent "grow rips" on the rise (2004)

Murder linked to grow-op: Man, 51, called 911 after shooting but died in hospital (2005)

Man slain at grow-op: Police find 200 marijuana plants in Coquitlam home of victim (2005)

Terrified family wrong target of grow-op rip (2006)

A finger that's in jail can't pull a trigger (2006)

Elderly couple victims of daylight home invasion (2006)

Three adults face charges after cops discover grow-op and loaded handgun (2007)

Missing woman's body found at grow-op (2008)

Two men face charges after grow-op murder: Pot dealer was found beaten to death (2008)

BC bud's sinister role in the violent drug trade (2009)

In 2007, a spate of shootings in Vancouver prompted the police chief and others to comment on the relationship between gangs, violence, and the production of marijuana. The following excerpt adeptly illustrates how claims about marijuana production and violence are linked to US exports:

The problem, police said, is too many gang members are packing guns for protection and are prepared to use them to settle personal scores and "business" disputes – police estimate 90 per cent of gangs are linked to the illegal drug trade, especially BC-grown marijuana, which is being shipped across the US border in exchange for cash, cocaine and firearms. "Those responsible for opening fire in public places like schoolyards or restaurants should face stiffer prison terms," Solicitor-General John Les said Friday.[67]

Here, we see how the safety of children is linked to the issue of violence by organized crime and marijuana cultivation. In turn, Solicitor-General John Les uses these claims to bolster his argument to support the imposition of harsher prison terms.

A number of articles appearing after 2007 focus on portraits of individuals arrested and/or tried for crimes related to violence. These articles serve to individualize and racialize drug traffickers who are thought to be members of gangs. As we have noted earlier, Reinarman and Levine suggest that, since the twentieth century, "a core feature of drug war discourse in the media is the 'routinization of caricature' which depicts worst case scenarios as the norm and sensationalizes and distorts drug issues."[68] Drug policy debates, including those about marijuana grow ops, are full of these spectacular and representative figures (injured elderly people, abused children, violent racialized gangsters).[69] Yet these representations render invisible key differences between and within these groups: differences of income, class privilege, size and characteristics of grow ops, and motivations for growing marijuana. Instead, these representations support law-and-order agendas focused on punishment as a means to eradicate marijuana cultivation.

One representative 2008 article describes the crimes of Jong Ca John Lee associated with the UN (United Nations) gang in the lower mainland of British Columbia. The article describes the gang's alleged involvement in numerous violent incidents in the Vancouver area, including descriptions of violent acts committed by gang members.[70] A number of shootings and other incidents in 2009, again, led to increased reportage and the trade in marijuana is specifically held to be the cause of gang violence that erupted in Vancouver during this period. A 2009 article discusses the Canadian federal government's introduction of Bill C-15, which would increase prison sentences and establish mandatory terms for growing marijuana. The article quotes the then Minister of Justice Rob Nicholson, who claims that the Senate's delay of this Bill "risks lives":

Federal Justice Minister Rob Nicholson slammed the Senate Wednesday for not pushing through new legislation implementing mandatory jail terms for drug producers, smugglers and traffickers ... "They also lead to more crime and gang violence on our streets and more risk to law enforcement officers as organized criminals fight to establish and protect their turf." He [Rob Nicholson] said the bill would deter those willing to set up clandestine labs and growing operations ... Nicholson said there is ample evidence that marijuana is the currency of organized crime and that much of the market for Canadian pot is foreign.[71]

This article links violence, grow ops, and gangs to public safety and innocent lives, helping to establish harsher penalties as the solution to these problems. The news reportage fails to mention how the Conservative government's previous crime bill died on the floor when Parliament was dissolved. Nor does it make clear that the Senate was not delaying the Bill nor risking lives. Instead, the Senate was raising important questions about the financial and social costs of mandatory sentences. The Bill eventually died when Prime Minister Stephen Harper prorogued Parliament, for the second time, in December 2009. It was not until after our study period ended that more vigorous news reporting appeared about both the cost of the reintroduced crime bill (introduced again in 2011 as the Safe Streets and Communities Act and passed into law in March 2012) and the limitations imposed by the Conservative government on the Senate and its debates of this Bill. Overwhelmingly, the articles in our sample highlight spokespeople such as the RCMP, or Minister of Justice Rob Nicholson who support harsher sentences for marijuana cultivation. Harsher laws and sentencing, expanded police powers and budgets, and prison building were offered as the solution to the problem.

Crime in Canada

In contrast to media reports about the marijuana industry fuelling more crime and violence, in 2010, the overall crime rate fell in Canada, both in volume and severity of crime. In 2010, the crime rate reached its lowest level since the early 1970s. In 2012, the overall crime rate reached its lowest rate since 1972, a downward trend that has continued for over 40 years.[72] In 2010, British Columbia reported the largest decline in both the volume and severity of crime reported to the police, although there are regional variations; Kelowna saw an increase in violent crime in 2010 and Abbotsford-Mission experienced a decease.[73] However, the homicide rate in British Columba was at its lowest since the early 1960s, continuing a general decline in the province over the past 25 years, although again, there are regional variations.[74] In 2012, British Columbia had a 16 per cent decrease in homicide from the year before.[75] Although the police believe that gang-related homicides have been rising since 1991, over the past decade, homicide rates in Canada were stable and there was a sharp decline in 2009, 2010, and 2012.[76] The incidence of homicides resulting from gang activity are not always assessed based on court evidence or closed cases; rather, incidents are classified as gang related when police "believe" the homicide to occur as a consequence of organized crime activities.[77] Nationwide, 17 per cent of all homicides were believed to be gang related in 2010.[78]

In Vancouver, BC, the homicide rate fell 42 per cent in 2010 from the year before.[79] The police believe that a third of the homicides in Vancouver in 2010 (12 out of 36) were gang related.[80] Statistics Canada reports that in 2010 the most common drugs identified in drug-related homicide were cocaine (51%) and cannabis (31%).[81] However, we found no scholarly research, aside from Statistics Canada, that examines the gang affiliations of individuals involved in homicides (from reporting to sentencing) in Canada. These homicides are most often unsolved, and there is little empirical evidence revealing what proportion of these homicides were, in fact, related to gang activity.[82] This is an area of scholarship that needs in-depth attention given that speculation about homicide and violent crime rates associated with the drug trade are routinely provided as proof by vocal claims makers and the media who purport that harsher criminal and civil interventions are required to curb the marijuana trade in Canada.

As the overall crime rate in Canada (including BC) declines, only drug offences have increased, a trend that began in the early 1990s. Yet, as noted earlier, marijuana possession arrests made up 52 per cent of all drug charges in 2010. Regardless of politicians' and law enforcement agency statements to the contrary, marijuana users continue to be the focus of police attention rather than high-level marijuana producers and traffickers.[83]

We are not disputing the fact that marijuana-growing operations exist in Canada, or that organized crime plays a part in this illegal enterprise, nor do we condone drug trade–related violence. Rather, we argue that the size of the illegal marijuana business is unknown, as is the rate of gang-related homicide, even to law enforcement agents. Claims reported by law enforcement agents and the media that the value of the underground marijuana industry is allegedly anywhere from $1 billion to $8 billion a year in British Columbia alone speak to uncertainty about the industry's real profits. In addition, police and media reports fail to represent the diversity of marijuana growers, highlighting mostly those thought to be associated with organized crime, especially motor-cycle gangs and racialized Asian criminal groups. In the introduction of this book, we drew from the scholarly research on marijuana grow ops to discuss the diversity of marijuana growers represented in these studies. For example, we noted that according to a 2005 paper funded by the RCMP in British Columbia, no firearms or other weapons and hazards were found at 89 per cent of the grow ops brought to the attention of police during the period under investigation, 1997 to 2003.[84] Rather than grow ops increasing in size and sophistication, as the authors claim, based on the data presented in their study, one could easily conclude that the number of small grow ops is increasing more than the number of large grow ops.[85] We also discuss, in the introduction and in this chapter, a 2011 Canadian Department of Justice[86] study examining court cases involving indoor marijuana grow ops and drug labs in British Columbia, Alberta, and Ontario between 1997 and 2005.[87] The authors of the Department of Justice study state that the literature on marijuana production claims that this activity is linked to organized crime. However, their findings do not support this claim. From their study sample of 530 cases, "only 5% had any indication that the offender was affiliated with organized crime or street gangs."[88]

Conclusion

Legal experts argue that the definition of an organized crime group in the Criminal Code of Canada is so broad that many people producing, buying, or selling drugs collectively to reduce costs or to better obtain criminalized drugs for personal use will be at risk of arrest, especially poor and marginalized people.[89] In Darcie Bennett and Scott Bernstein's 2013 study, *Throwing Away the Keys: The Human and Social Cost of Mandatory Minimum Sentencing*, many of the low-income illegal drug users in Vancouver and Victoria, BC, interviewed for their study, had "been involved in small-scale production" of marijuana in the past. They argue mandatory minimum penalties and tough on crime measures for marijuana production will impact poor, racialized, and marginalized people rather than higher-level producers (similar to mandatory minimum drug penalties in the US).[90]

Woodiwess asserts that the construction of organized crime as an alien and racialized entity has been vital to law enforcement in the United States and elsewhere; organized crime is also constructed as calculating and relentless in its search for "weak spots" and vulnerability

in the "armour" of the morality of the nation state; thus, vigorous policing and harsh laws are necessary to make the nation safe.[91] Yet, when
examined more closely, it is evident that organized crime is a fluid and
shifting enterprise with participants from every level of society and every ethnic background involved (including governments, banks, drug
law enforcement agents and agencies) and the demand for drugs and
the criminalized status of these drugs fuels organized crime and the illegal market.[92] Just as important, research findings, as well as journalistic and personal accounts, demonstrate that many people who buy, sell,
and grow marijuana are not personally involved with or connected to
criminal gangs or organized crime, but rather, marijuana use and buying is a normative activity given its popularity in Canada. Cultivation
of marijuana is also a means to obtain the plant for personal use or to
supplement income. Given the limited research studies to draw from,
trying to determine what proportion of grow ops are the product of organized crime and what proportion are mom-and-pop organizations is
nearly impossible. Such studies as are available do not support a major
link with organized crime. Nevertheless, expanding police powers, law
enforcement budgets, and harsh laws and civil bylaws in Canada are
most often premised on the fear of male organized crime and the racialized Other, including white outlaw groups such as the Hells Angels,
who are depicted as violent and as posing a threat to national and community security and supposedly threatening innocent and vulnerable
citizens (especially youth) because of the encroachment of drug crime
into suburban spaces.

US drug eradication programs in other countries such as Mexico,
where toxic defoliants such as paraquat were used on marijuana fields
in the 1970s, helped to fuel marijuana production at home. Consumers turned to safer domestically grown marijuana.[93] Still, the US 2010
National Drug Control Strategy, which outlines US drug policy, praises
drug law enforcement agencies for their operations against marijuana
cultivation in and outside of the country.[94] So does the 2012 *US International Narcotics Control Strategy Report*. The report praises Canada
for introducing the Safe Streets and Communities Act, which includes
mandatory minimum sentencing for a range of drug offences, including
marijuana production.[95] Protecting the border from the drug threat is
one of their top priorities in the US war on drugs. Mexico, Canada, and
Latin America have long been viewed as threats to the United States
because of perceived incompetence in regulating illegal drugs at home
(see past and current publications of the US Office of National Drug

Control Policy and the US Bureau of International Narcotics and Law Enforcement Affairs). The construction of Canada (and other countries) as an unreliable drug source country with a one-sided porous border deflects attention away from the fact that the United States has a large illegal domestic marijuana-growing industry and drug trade, a seemingly insatiable appetite for illegal and legal drugs (including over-the-counter and prescription drugs), and the largest prison industry in the world – where many prisoners are serving time for drug offences.[96] The North American Congress on Latin America (NACLA) claims that, in the early 2000s, about one-third of marijuana consumed in the United States is grown at home; it also notes that marijuana production supports economically depressed communities.[97] Canadian newspapers in our study also say little about the incursion of US law enforcement agents on Canadian territory. They do not critique US agents working in Canada such as the DEA stationed in Canada or US police stopping cars in the interior of British Columbia.[98]

What remains striking over the 15-year span of our media project is the hyperbole and unsubstantiated claims about marijuana grow ops and organized crime expressed by a small group of spokespeople, mostly RCMP, police, and some government officials, and reported, for the most part, uncritically, by the print media. Taken at face value, the newspapers we analysed depict Vancouver, and British Columbia in general, as a war zone of racialized, violent, greedy, drug gangs vying for profits, endangering law-abiding citizens, and moving rapidly into suburban spaces. Drug-related crime is depicted in a number of articles as a natural outcome of greedy racialized gangs intent on destroying the fabric of the nation. Little critique of this dominant discourse is evident in media coverage. Yet, internationally and at home, a wealth of research points to prohibitionist drug policy and law-and-order initiatives as fuelling drug-related violence, organized crime, and the illegal market. Law-and-order prohibitionist policy has done little to stop illegal drug use, selling, and marijuana cultivation in Canada (or the United States). There is no empirical evidence demonstrating that harsh drug laws and penalties deter marijuana production or any other type of drug offence. Indeed, a growing body of scientific research reveals that drug prohibition and increases in drug law enforcement result in higher rates of drug market violence and fail to reduce the prevalence of drug use.[99] The rush to punish marijuana cultivators, as expressed by the media, claims makers, and vocal RCMP/police spokespeople in our sample, ignores this empirical fact.

4 Racialization of Marijuana Grow Ops

In chapter 1, we explored the racialization of drug scares and the construction of the criminal "Other" in Canada. We agree with sociologist Clayton Mosher that "the racialization of crime has a long history in Canada."[1] As we illustrate, news reports racialize marijuana cultivation as the purview of the Other, an age-old trope that constructs some racial and ethnic groups as outsiders and culprits. We have discussed how the media and drug war advocates employ the "routinization of caricature" – which promotes worst-case scenarios – as the norm[2] and links marijuana grow ops to racialized groups. As noted in the previous chapter, numerous articles depict biker groups such as the Hells Angels as white outcasts, and another 68 stories (3%) primarily focus on "Asian organized crime" groups.

A number of critical and feminist theorists have brought our attention to the processes through which racialized groups and people are criminalized through techniques of erasure, trivialization, categorization, and culturalization.[3] These scholars explore how racialization is a process that goes far beyond simple racist remarks and is embedded in ideologies, texts, government documents and policy, institutions, science and social science research, legal decisions, art, media, and popular culture. These ideas are often made concrete by policy and legislation.[4] As scholar Sunera Thobani argues, the "exalted" Canadian citizen is white; all others are, thus, more easily constructed as lawless, outsiders, and a threat to the nation.[5] National mythologies render the violence of colonization and white dominance invisible, including the relationship between law and race.[6] Historically, drug scares link specific drugs to racialized groups in Canada, including "white" outsiders. Indeed, this racializing practice seems evident in

Figure 4.1. Headline Box: Organized Crime.[7]

HEADLINES: ORGANIZED CRIME

US officials troubled by expansion of Asian Canadian drug gangs (2006)

British pot grow-ops skyrocket, linked to Vietnamese (2007)

"We've chopped the head off the snake": Raids here and abroad net $168 million in drugs, 100 arrests, 5.5 tonnes of drugs, $300,000 worth of vehicles, $6 million in real estate, 17 prohibited weapons, $2.1 million in cash (2007)

For gangsters, life is often cheaper than the rings on their fingers (2007)

---

recent RCMP reports that claim that Asian organized crime "groups continued to dominate indoor" marijuana production and threaten national security.[8] In our study, we found that newspaper articles increasingly began to link marijuana grow ops with racialized gangs and organized crime. Newspaper claims are supported by RCMP reports and spokespeople, yet empirical evidence to support their claims is sorely lacking. Figure 4.1 provides a representational sample of news headlines that illustrate how racialized concepts shape crime news.

As early as 2003, newspaper articles began appearing that link marijuana grow ops, violence, and organized crime to race. A typical example is an article from 2003 that suggests that Asian organized crime groups are taking over marijuana cultivation in the lower mainland of British Columbia:

> Vietnamese-based organized crime groups produce "a significant portion" of BC-grown marijuana through thousands of indoor growing operations. They have expanded their grow-ops from BC across Canada, especially into Ontario. As of 2002, Vietnamese crime groups and the Hells Angels were thought to control about 85 per cent of the marijuana production and distribution in BC, including 15,000 to 20,000 growing operations in the Lower Mainland.[9]

Another 2003 article also refers to a special section of the Organized Crime Agency of British Columbia (OCABC) set up to address the issue "Asian-organized crime." This excerpt quotes Inspector Brad Parker, head of the Asian Organized Crime section of the OCABC. Here, he racializes the nature of this phenomenon drawing on stereotypes of familial connections between Asian persons who supposedly help to facilitate connections to organized crime:

> Determining the size of the Asian problem is more difficult, but every major immigrant group has brought with it a criminal subculture. "They don't wear patches on their backs, are very fluid and don't consider cultural boundaries an impediment and will move around the country doing business," Parker said ... "There is a natural bond between many of these guys because they all came over together and now they've split into different groups. They have relatives in Seattle, San Francisco, Montreal, Halifax and Toronto and it's developed into a real network," he said.[10]

Another 2003 article, entitled "RCMP fears gang warfare over marijuana operations"[11] describes marijuana cultivation as the key factor in the increase in organized crime, particularly in British Columbia and suggests that most large-size operations are run by Asian organized crime:

> Lax laws have made Canada and especially BC a "haven" for indoor marijuana-growing operations, raising fears of a violent turf war in the Lower Mainland between the Hells Angels and Vietnamese gangs, according to an RCMP report. The analysis from the RCMP's Criminal Intelligence Directorate reveals that Vietnamese gangs, known for their "extreme violence," have been steadily encroaching on the lucrative pot-growing industry historically controlled by outlaw bike gangs in Ontario and especially BC. "The gradual arrival of Asian criminals in the marijuana-growing business in British Columbia originally raised serious concerns within the law-enforcement community about a potential all-out turf war with the Hells Angels," according to the report from the RCMP's Criminal Intelligence Directorate.[12]

The article later suggests that this expected violence *has not emerged* but the reporter draws on the RCMP report to suggest that police do not know how long the "respective tolerance" between these groups will last. The article insinuates that lenient sentencing practices in Canada fuel the rise of marijuana cultivation. It also suggests that most large-size operations are run by Asian organized crime:

> Vietnamese gang activity in Vancouver's cannabis cultivation industry has increased almost 20-fold between 1997 and 2000, according to police

data. Southeast Asian growers have gradually expanded their operations to the suburbs of the Greater Vancouver Area, as well as to other cities across BC.[13]

This excerpt illustrates how newspaper articles racialize the growers of marijuana and link these activities to violence and the threat of further social chaos. The article concludes with comments from then member of Parliament Chuck Cadman:

> Canadian Alliance MP Chuck Cadman said the government doesn't appear aware of the gravity of the indoor grow-ops phenomenon, despite [Solicitor-General Wayne] Easter's recent visit to BC to discuss the matter. "These are occurring in upscale homes that cost in excess of half a million dollars each. These homes are being paid for with bags of money," said Cadman (Surrey North). "And they're in neighbourhoods where there's children playing. Organized crime is involved. Some of these places are booby trapped. There are drive-by shootings. There's been attempted murders."[14]

Cadman emphasizes a complaint that the Liberal federal government, in 2003, did not understand the serious nature of the marijuana-cultivation problem. This story also suggests that children are at risk because of these groups, particularly, in upscale neighbourhoods.

In the following excerpts from a 2004 media report, police express concerns about possible violence between Vietnamese, biker, and possibly Chinese gangs. This violence is linked to a drop in price precipitated by the growth of the marijuana industry in Ontario, and increased security at the Canada-US border since 11 September 2001. This report claims that the marijuana trade is no longer the domain of mom-and-pop operations or motorcycle gangs; rather, Vietnamese gangs threaten to dominate the trade, fuelling turf fights between rivals such as Chinese gangs:

> In the 1980s and early 1990s, police say, the province's marijuana trade was dominated by outlaw motorcycle gangs like the Hells Angels and a smaller number of independent, "mom and pop" operations. But since the mid-1990s, according to police intelligence reports, Vietnamese gangs have come to dominate the province's pot trade ... According to an RCMP intelligence report produced two years ago, police had some concerns that the Vietnamese gangs' rapid takeover of the pot trade could lead to conflicts with biker gangs ... "It's becoming more and more apparent that

every organized crime group is looking to grow-ops to generate money that supports other criminal activity," said Nadeau ... Det. Jim Fisher, a Vancouver police department expert on Asian gangs, said ... "I don't think people understand how big it is. It's changed the dynamic of organized crime here."[15]

Here, police spokespeople suggest that gang violence will be precipitated by the "takeover" of the industry by Vietnamese crime groups. The article is speculative. It also creates a hierarchy of organized crime groups and suggests that Asian organized crime is somehow more dangerous and insidious than other crime organizations.

News stories claim that Indo-Canadian gangs are rivals in the drug trade. An article from 2004 describes the individual "redemption" of "Indo-Canadian mafia" member Bal Buttar, who was shot in 2001, leaving him blind and a quadriplegic. In this article, he admits to killing another gang member, and he claims that he has turned against gang life because of the violence he saw in his community. Buttar describes other violent acts he committed as a gang member and makes the following assessment of its origins:

> But the more he kept hearing of the continuing violence plaguing his community, the more Buttar began to regret his contributions to the problem. He now thinks God allowed him to survive two bullets to the head to help youth stay away from violent gangs that have been glamourized for years. "It's because of the easy money. We have marijuana here and people say it is a beautiful drug," he said. "But when people deal big quantities of that, there is murder. All of this violence is caused by marijuana. A lot happens with marijuana."[16]

The reporter easily accepts Buttar's assessment of the origins of gang violence in BC's lower mainland and, in addition, does not dispute the naturalized link between Buttar's evocation of racialized tropes and gang violence.

Articles uncritically carry excerpts from federal RCMP reports that provide little in the way of evidence to substantiate their racializing claims. One such article from 2005 based on an RCMP report offers the following assessment of marijuana cultivation in British Columbia:

> Outlaw motorcycle gangs continue to be the largest organized crime group in BC, followed by Asian-based outfits and Indo-Canadian gangs, says a

2005 RCMP report obtained by The Vancouver Sun ... Asian-based groups are ranked the second-most violent, for their involvement in importing heroin and synthetic drugs, growing pot, the sex trade, extortion within the Asian community and financial crimes.[17]

Here, we see Asian people depicted by the RCMP and the media as not only violent, but also likely to be involved in a plethora of illegal activities. Not surprisingly, the reporter fails to mention police profiling of ethnic groups in Canada, nor does he mention the criminal activities of Caucasian Canadians. Nowhere in media coverage does whiteness appear as a causal agent of crime in the same way that it does in the above-noted excerpts. As Dyer, Thobani, Razack, and others have revealed, whiteness is noted by its absence in media representations.[18]

Another 2005 article about this same 2004 report prepared by the RCMP's Criminal Analysis Section and obtained by the *Vancouver Sun* through a freedom of information request, reiterates now familiar claims about the racialization of grow ops. This article details how different groups have come to dominate certain sectors of the trade. Vietnamese gangs, for example, are thought by the RCMP to largely grow the marijuana plant because of their "higher work ethic":

"Vietnamese marijuana growers improved on previously established methods of producing a marijuana crop, using innovation and new technology," the report states. "They applied a higher work ethic, which has resulted in increasing the profitability of growing marijuana." Indo-Canadian gang members are primarily involved in smuggling marijuana into the United States, often in cargo trucks. And members of the Hells Angels, the report says, help run the show – overseeing networks of growers and coordinating smuggling runs to the US. "Hells Angels assert a very strong and stable presence in the grow-operation industry," it states.[19]

This article uncritically adopts the racist language of stereotypes that allows spokespeople to make claims about the work habits of racialized groups. The "higher work ethic" of Vietnamese citizens, which would normally be constructed as a positive if stereotyped attribute, is framed as leading to their success in the drug trade. The RCMP continue to assert that the Hells Angels, a mostly white group, help organize the marijuana trade. These white outsiders are continually constructed as violent lawbreakers who dominate the higher echelons of the marijuana trade.

Although BC newspapers do not carry many articles about marijuana cultivation in other parts of the world, an article published in the *Vancouver Sun* in 2007 is striking because of the claims it makes about the racialization of marijuana cultivation in the United Kingdom:

> Criminal gangs are trafficking hundreds of children into Britain and forcing them to work in cannabis factories, with at least one child per week being found by police ... there has been a five-fold increase in the practice in the past year alone. Children as young as 13, many from Vietnam, were being brought to Britain to work as "slaves" for organized criminals to push production of the drug to record levels, it says. The kids are forced to tend cannabis plants grown in suburban houses and often forced to sleep in cupboards, with little chance of escape for fear of being caught ... Police believe the problem has emerged after organized crime gangs, many of them Vietnamese, moved to dominate the British cannabis market after the narcotic was downgraded from a Class B to Class C drug in 2004.[20]

This article is particularly salacious in its claims, but it provides little in the way of documentation to support its assertions. The article is potent in a BC context because it appears alongside other BC-based reporting on marijuana cultivation that claims that Vietnamese groups are attempting to control the trade. It is also effective because it links the racialization of human trafficking in children with changes to drug legislation in the United Kingdom that lessened penalties, giving these changes almost a causal relationship with increases in child slavery.

Another article from the *Globe and Mail* in 2006 describes a $6 million drug bust in a Toronto high-rise. The article uses this incident to illustrate the role that Vietnamese criminal groups play in smuggling marijuana:

> A US Department of Justice report on the cross-border narcotics industry released this month nonetheless concluded that "high-potency marijuana production, smuggling and distribution by Canada-based DTOs [drug-trafficking organizations], primarily of Vietnamese ethnicity, is increasing."[21]

This article goes on to describe the various groups involved in organized crime and marijuana grow ops in Canada, taking care to depict the ethnic and racial backgrounds of these groups.

In a 2007 article from the *Globe and Mail*, the reporter reiterates a series of claims about cannabis cultivation and organized crime:

The Mounties say the involvement of organized crime has significantly expanded the Canadian drug trade, with outlaw motorcycle gangs and Asian groups the reigning kingpins of the marijuana industry.[22]

These claims originate in the RCMP's 2006 annual report entitled *Drug Situation in Canada*. The RCMP's annual report on illicit drugs in Canada serves as a backdrop in this article for claims about the role that organized crime plays in exporting marijuana to the United States. The report highlights marijuana smuggling as an issue for both Canada and the United States. It also gives the Hells Angels and "Asian organized crime" equal billing as leaders in the marijuana trade. The news article fails, however, to critique the information in the 2006 RCMP report even though the report itself provides little support for its claims.

In 2007, a familiar RCMP spokesperson quoted numerous times in our study reports that "[Paul] Nadeau said at the time that many of Ontario's illicit growers were British Columbians of Vietnamese descent who had relocated to that province to grow marijuana in order to tap into a vast and growing market of drug consumers on the US East Coast."[23] The article also quotes a British researcher who is investigating the migration patterns of Vietnamese persons to see if there are links between British grow ops and British Columbia. These comments are, indeed, significant given that, by this time, all news reporting of Vietnamese involvement in grow ops is assumed to be done by organized crime groups. An article from the late fall of 2007 describes the rising problem of gangs in Vancouver and calls for an integrated police force. At the end of the article, it offers an oft-repeated set of descriptions of gangs in British Columbia that draws on profiles of the racial backgrounds of these groups except for the Hells Angels, who are assumed to be white. The text accompanying these profiles makes links between race, ethnicity, violence, and drugs, and the need for harsher drug laws.

One typical article provides detailed information on gang involvement in grow ops using police sources and sweeping statements such as "the hells angels likely control many Greater Victoria marijuana grow ops, as do the Vietnamese gangs and other Asian groups such as Indo-Canadian gangs."[24] The same article links Asian organized crime with grow ops and makes pernicious claims about the "nature" of these persons:

> Vietnamese gangsters are known for being ruthless and unpredictably violent during confrontations. Other Asian crime groups are more low-key, not wanting to attract police attention, but will resort to violence and murder to protect their criminal interests.

This article quotes police who depict "young Indo-Canadian criminals as 'mama's boys' who often live at home or close to parents."[25] The articles not only racializes the drug trade, but also promotes "white western nuclear families" and individualism as the legal and social norm in Canada while associating racializing traits with particular ethnic groups. For example, Vietnamese citizens are portrayed as more "ruthless," "unpredictable," and "violent" than white Canadians, and Indo-Canadian men are depicted as "mama's boys." Over the years, a plethora of articles about gang violence includes similar descriptions, reinforcing racialized markers for each ethnic (and non-white) group. These racialized claims are now familiar tropes and most often remain uncontested in news articles and RCMP reports.

Conclusion

As we discussed in chapter 1, Canada's earliest narcotic laws were racialized, class based, and gendered. Early on, newspapers, politicians, and moral reformers claimed that Chinese Canadians who smoked opium corrupted the moral values of white women and men. Opium smoking was depicted as deviant and different from the liquid opium–based patent medicines consumed by white Canadians. The opium den was depicted as a site of deviance and corruption that destroyed white Christian morality and neighbourhoods. In the 1920s, the media and the RCMP continued to fuel anti-Asian sentiment and relied on stereotypical images of the Other to justify their claims and to support their campaigns for broader police powers, new and harsher drug laws, and longer prison sentences. Newspapers continue to rely on racialized representations to tell the "story" of marijuana cultivation.

Ironically, these claims are disputed by RCMP-funded research. In their 2005 report, Plecas et al. found that, in 1997, only 6 per cent of "suspected" grow op growers in their study are members of non-white ethnic groups in British Columbia.[26] This same study notes that the numbers of non-white participants in the marijuana trade have increased to 46 per cent in 2003. Despite this last claim, the 2011 Justice Department report and the unpublished reports by Plecas et al. reveal that the majority of offenders and suspects found at grow ops are Caucasian males.[27] The Justice Department reports that 43 per cent of the offenders examined in their study between 1998 and 2005 were "Asian"; there is no further breakdown or definition of the term "Asian." Ninety-four per cent of all offenders in their study were Canadian citizens.[28] Plecas et al. claim that the number of Vietnamese suspects is rising, yet provide no empirical data to support this claim in their 2005 paper.[29] Plecas et al. also state that 74 per cent of the suspects in their study were born in Canada, yet there are no data provided on whether other suspects were Canadian citizens (having applied later in life).[30] These claims about race and grow ops fail to take into account potential police profiling of suspects, a further reason to interpret these findings with caution. It appears that suspected growers and offenders in these two studies were not foreign "Others"; rather, they were overwhelmingly Canadian. Nevertheless, in Canada, as Grayson suggests, the threat that drugs pose to the nation is continually constructed as originating in foreign bodies including organized crime. Foreign and criminalized bodies include racialized bodies: Vietnamese, South Asian, First Nations, Black, Latino, and white outlaws such as Hells Angels. As the newspaper articles illustrate, the participation of non-white groups in the cultivation of marijuana is treated as a gateway to other types of crime and drug use including cocaine, ecstasy, importation of weapons, and money laundering.[31]

The racialization of marijuana grow ops has material consequences. Researchers argue that racial profiling by police is magnified by stereotypical, individualized, and negative media representations.[32] Racialized growers of marijuana are depicted in the media as deserving of special police attention and punishment. Since the advent of drug prohibition, racialized people have been vulnerable to stereotypical and negative media reporting, police profiling, and arrest. In Canada, early on, Chinese Canadians were overrepresented in relation to drug arrests. Mosher found that Black and minority drug offenders in Ontario were subject to disproportionate police profiling and differential treatment in Ontario criminal courts between 1892 and 1961. As early as 1995, the Commission on Systemic Racism in the Ontario Criminal Justice System reported that since 1992 Black women and men were more negatively impacted by drug laws and policy in the province than their white counterparts.[33] The 1996 Royal Commission report, *Bridging the Cultural Divide: A Report on Aboriginal Peoples and Criminal Justice*, highlights the impact of colonization, police profiling, and institution-alized racism in Canada's criminal justice system.[34] As a consequence of these systemic practices, minority offenders and First Nations peo-ple continue to be overrepresented in Canadian prisons. Furthermore, critics of the Safe Streets and Communities Act assert that Aboriginal, racialized, and marginalized people in Canada will be profoundly im-pacted by the new legislation.[35]

The 2012 Office of the Correctional Investigator's final report, *Spirit Matters: Aboriginal People and the Corrections and Conditional Release Act*, discusses how the Corrections and Conditional Release Act, in sections 81 and 84, makes reference to the needs and circumstances of Aborigi-nal Canadians in federal prisons. These sections were meant to help mitigate the overrepresentation of Aboriginal people in federal prison and "long-standing differential outcomes for Aboriginal offenders."[36] Although these sections came into force over 20 years ago, between 2001 and 2011, the number of Aboriginal Canadians in prison has been rising steadily.[37] In 2012, 21 per cent of federal prisoners were Aborigi-nal, and Aboriginal women accounted for over 30 per cent of feder-ally incarcerated women.[38] In the Prairie provinces, Aboriginal people comprised more than 55 per cent of the total prison population at Sas-katchewan Penitentiary and 60 per cent at Stony Mountain. Provincial rates were even worse; 81 per cent of people in provincial custody in Saskatchewan were Aboriginal in 2005 even though they made up only 15 per cent of the total population. In addition, 76 per cent of youth admitted to provincial custody in Saskatchewan were Aboriginal.[39] The report makes clear that these statistics cannot, and must not, be attributed to a greater propensity for criminality by Aboriginal people but are the long-term consequences of colonialism and current racist practices in the justice system. The report also illustrates that both drug treatment and healing supports are inadequate in Canada's prisons.

The 2012 final report found that in British Columbia, Ontario, Atlan-tic Canada, and the North, that there were no section 81 Healing Lodge spaces for Aboriginal women. Healing Lodges offer a "healing path based on traditional cultural and spiritual practices."[40] In addition, be-cause Healing Lodges limit intake to only minimum security offenders, and the majority of Aboriginal offenders are sentenced to medium and maximum security prisons (although Aboriginal women have limited access to Healing Lodges in minimum and medium security prisons), 90 per cent of Aboriginal offenders were excluded from being consid-ered for a transfer to a Healing Lodge.[41] The report notes that there was "limited understanding and awareness within CSC [Correctional Service of Canada] of Aboriginal peoples" and their diverse cultures, spirituality, and approaches to healing.[42] The practices of the CSC are not in keeping with the landmark Supreme Court of Canada decision of *R. v. Gladue*, which affirms section 718(e) of the Criminal Code that states that all options other than imprisonment should be taken into consideration in sentencing, especially in relation to Aboriginal offenders. This section of the Criminal Code is meant to recognize and remedy the "overrepresentation of First Nations offenders in prison" which is "systemic and race-related, and that the mainstream justice system was contributing to the problem."[43]

An earlier 2000 review of drug offenders by the Correctional Service of Canada demonstrated that there has been a steady rise in drug offenders being sentenced to prison. More recent reports from the Correctional Service show that new admissions to federal prison for drug-related offences continue to increase. In 2009, one-quarter (25%) of all women and men in federal prisons were there for a drug charge.[44] For 3 years prior to the release of a Correctional Service of Canada's 2009 report, drug offences increased for new admissions for both First Nations (14% to 15%) and non–First Nations offenders (27% to 32%).[45,46]

Further, women's federal incarceration rates have risen steadily since the 1970s in both Canada (it has tripled) and the United States (where it has risen 800%).[47] In provincial prisons such as in BC (for those serving time for 2 years or less), First Nations persons are overrepresented.[48] The BC Corrections Branch reports that between 2006 and 2007, 42 per cent of provincial prisoners in custody for drug charges were there for possession.[49] A 2013 report by the BC Provincial Health Officer also states that Aboriginal people will be more vulnerable to incarceration stemming from the enactment of the Safe Streets and Communities Act in 2012 and its provision of mandatory minimum sentencing and increased penalties for some drug offences.[50]

Increasingly, provincial incarceration stems from breeches of court conditions such as failure to meet the conditions of probation or administration of justice offences by a court or by the police.[51] These breaches are not criminal acts; rather, they involve disobeying a court order, such as being in a "no go zone," failure to appear in court, or failure to attend a probation appointment. In British Columbia, between 2003 and 2010, there was a steady increase "in the number of charges laid by police," rather than by probation officers, for administration of justice offences.[52] Police have discretion in regards to whether they will lay charges. These breaches comprised up to 45 per cent of the BC Provincial Court's caseload in 2011.[53] Thus, a minor drug offence could lead to prison time following an administration of justice offence.

A 2012 Office of the Parliamentary Budget Office report estimates that had the new limitations on conditional sentencing (which are now a provision under the new Safe Streets and Communities Act) been in effect from 2008 to 2009, approximately 4,500 offenders would no longer be eligible to serve their sentence in the community; instead, they would have been sentenced to prison.[54] In addition, the cost would have increased 16-fold, from $2,575 to $41,006 per offender.[55] Thus, the impact of the new mandatory minimum penalties enacted in 2012 will be economically and socially costly for Canadians.

The United States has recorded a similar if not more dramatic phenomenon; one out of three young Black men are likely to be incarcerated in his lifetime. The United States also has the highest incarceration rate in the world, fuelled by police profiling, drug arrests, and mandatory minimum sentences.[56] Black and Hispanic people are overrepresented in US prisons and jails for mostly non-violent drug offences, making up two-thirds of the prison population. In 2010, over 850,000 people in the United States were arrested for marijuana offences; 88 per cent of these were for possession of small amounts of marijuana. Other race-based discrimination and disparities are also evident in marijuana possession charges. A 2013 report by the American Civil Liberties Union (ACLU), *The War on Marijuana in Black and White*, reveals that even though marijuana use rates are similar for Black and white people in the United States, Black people were 3.73 times more likely to be arrested for marijuana possession than white people in all 50 US states and the District of Columbia between 2001 and 2010.[57] There have been over 8 million arrested in the United States for marijuana possession between 2001 and 2010.[58] The ACLU estimates that the annual enforcement of marijuana possession costs about US$3.614 billion.[59] The ACLU calls for an end to the "War on Marijuana" and recommends the legal regulation of marijuana.

In terms of the State of California, since the 1990s, California arrested 850,000 individuals for possession of marijuana; half a million of these arrests took place in the past 10 years. Black and Latino people, especially young men, were disproportionately arrested for marijuana possession over this time period.[60] In 25 major cities in California, police have arrested Black individuals for "marijuana possession at four, five, six, seven, and up to twelve times the rate of whites."[61] Many of these arrests did not result in long prison sentences; however, these arrests result in jail time and permanent criminal records that can disqualify individuals from employment, housing, student loans, etc. For some of these people, arrests and charges are complicated by failure to appear in court, failure to pay fines, or breech of probation, all of which lead to further prison time and tax resources.

Since 1990, "arrests for nearly every serious crime have declined in California. Yet arrests for possession of marijuana, usually for very small amounts, have tripled."[62] Similar increased arrest rates for marijuana possession are evident in other US states and cities, including New York City, even though there is no evidence that people in these places are smoking or consuming more marijuana than in the past. In 2010, in New York City, over 50,000 people were arrested for possession of marijuana. The cost of these arrests for taxpayers is approximately US$75 million each year, and approximately half a billion to US$1 billion between 1997 and 2010.[63] Surveys of drug use reveal that young white people have higher marijuana use rates than young Black and Latino people in New York City. Yet the police in New York City arrest Black people seven times more often and Latino people four times more often than white people for marijuana possession.[64]

Just as marijuana possession arrests and prison sentencing are race based, so too, are media representations of the people who use, produce, and sell illegal drugs. In Canada, since the 1990s, the racialization of marijuana grow ops by the media, law enforcement agents, and government representatives, and the linking of these masculinized groups to violence, increasing levels of organized crime, and criminal gangs renders invisible the diversity of cannabis growers. More importantly, it fuels legal and social discrimination, which is linked to social exclusion, police profiling, overrepresentation in arrests, prison sentences, and inequalities of power.

5 Civil Responses to Marijuana Grow Ops

In this chapter, we examine two related phenomena: media representations about how municipal governments view grow ops and the implementation of provincial and municipal laws, bylaws, and programs aimed at reducing the cultivation of marijuana within city and town borders. Specifically, we analyse the ways that municipal programs to eliminate residential marijuana cultivation extend the reach of regulatory initiatives beyond the domain of the criminal justice system. This chapter illustrates how abundant newspaper coverage of the public safety risks of marijuana cultivation sensitized readers to the need for more regulation at the municipal level. We also examine court decisions and the news coverage of a Supreme Court of British Columbia legal case that challenges amendments to the BC Safety Standards Amendment Act (2006) and the Court of Appeal for British Columbia decision of this case in May 2010.[1] Amendments to this Act allowed some BC municipalities to develop programs that use electrical inspections of private residences – without a search warrant – to detect grow ops. Despite legal challenges to this Act, BC municipal officials, particularly in Surrey, claim that their efforts have been successful at displacing growing operations, and they have moved to "export" their initiatives to other municipalities. This chapter also examines a class action lawsuit, initiated in 2011, to challenge the Controlled Substance Property Bylaw in Mission, BC. This bylaw allows "safety inspection" teams to enter private homes suspected of having a marijuana grow op. We conclude with a discussion of Canada's legal medical marijuana program and recent challenges to it by municipal officials, the RCMP, and Health Canada.

The Regulation of Marijuana and Its Cultivation and the Policing of Residential Neighbourhoods

As discussed in chapter 1, in Canada, drug offences fall under federal jurisdiction and are regulated under the Controlled Drugs and Substances Act (CDSA) of 1997. The Act includes eight schedules; each schedule regulates a set of drugs. Schedule 1, for example, prohibits opiates including heroin, while Schedule 2 prohibits cannabis. Types of offences and their possible penalties accorded to each schedule are outlined in section 4 of the Act. Even though the federal law that regulates marijuana is quite harsh, municipalities in British Columbia, including Surrey and Mission, have implemented multipartner civil initiatives that draw on a hybrid of regulatory mechanisms that do not rely on these federal statutes. These activities have focused mainly on using municipal bylaws to control the cultivation of marijuana and the production of methamphetamines. These initiatives have been the result of collaborative efforts between a number of partners including municipalities, fire departments, BC Hydro, BC Safety Authority, and the RCMP. With the help of familiar claims makers, municipalities such as Surrey have developed these programs aimed at eliminating residential marijuana grow ops. As discussed in earlier chapters, all three of these claims makers are authors of papers on marijuana grow ops referenced repeatedly by the media.

Newspapers, Public Safety, and Marijuana Grow Ops

Although this chapter examines municipal initiatives to curb marijuana cultivation, an examination of newspaper reporting is key to understanding how an important theme in our analysis was established early on in this medium. We contend that media coverage helped link marijuana cultivation to concerns that go beyond their criminality to include "grave" public safety concerns. In the analysis that follows, we offer some examples of how these links were made in newspaper coverage. In our sample, there was ample evidence to support our findings. There are 179 articles (7%) about municipal programs and 58 (2%) about municipal bylaws; most of these articles praise local initiatives to regulate marijuana grow ops. There are also 228 articles (9%) about electrical power supplier BC Hydro and its partnerships with the RCMP and municipalities. Each of these articles mentions the use of these partnerships to eliminate residential cultivation of marijuana. As with other news stories discussed in this book, newspaper coverage of municipal initiatives intersects with other key themes related to marijuana cultivation such as damage to residences, mould, health effects, crime, violence, and children.

Starting in 1997, newspaper reporting helped to establish marijuana grow ops as a danger to public safety. An early example from the study period echoes future claims about the dangers of residential marijuana production. This 1997 article, entitled "Pot 'deathtraps' growing," states:

> Potentially deadly pot-growing operations are springing up on Vancouver Island, costing taxpayers millions of dollars. Fires that destroyed rental houses and theft of electricity from BC Hydro are the byproducts of the burgeoning home-based hydroponic marijuana growing trade.[2]

This article is typical of many similar stories that link house fires to grow ops. Claims about fire are also repeatedly linked to the claim that grow ops are poorly wired and/or steal electricity from electrical power providers, both of which present a fire hazard.

Newspapers routinely report that marijuana grow ops release chemical toxins and fumes, and these houses are depicted as potential fire hazards because of their overloaded heating and wiring systems.[3] By 2002, newspaper stories begin to link the safety risks of grow ops to the overall safety of neighbourhoods:

> Fire has become an all too common business risk for basement marijuana producers who pirate electricity to avoid being detected by police forces and hydro utilities that watch for the unusual consumption patterns created by hydroponic operations. That, in turn, has become a problem for neighbours who have no clue that the home next to them is sheltering a small part of a pervasive illegal operation. In the past year in the Toronto area alone, more than two dozen of these suburban, indoor farms have caught fire. Pot farms conceal deadly risks: hydro stolen to run the hydroponic labs has led to fires and fears of electrocution.[4]

The two studies commissioned by the RCMP conducted by Plecas et al.[5] are key sources for linking grow ops to public safety in newspaper articles. As early as 2002, newspaper reporting draws uncritically on the first of these two papers by Plecas et al. to reiterate the public safety dangers posed by grow ops, as this excerpt illustrates:

> The evidence indicates that, over the period studied, marijuana grow operations became larger and increasingly sophisticated, often involving greater technological enhancements. This, in turn, has led to greater risks to the communities in which these illicit operations took place due to the increased risk of fire, the report states.[6]

The news excerpt above is similar to other police claims that suggest that grow ops are becoming increasingly "sophisticated" and thus pose greater public safety dangers to other presumably innocent citizens.

As these excerpts illustrate, newspaper articles do not simply reiterate claims about public safety dangers, but link these dangers to other issues such as the potential financial costs of grow ops to citizens or the dangers of residential marijuana production to otherwise innocent or safe neighbourhoods and first responders. One article illustrates claims about the costs of grow ops:

> the hydro industry says that consumers are paying the price because growers illegally tap into the power supply for the massive quantities of electricity they need to operate high-voltage lamps and maintain hothouse temperatures, draining the system of hundreds of millions of dollars annually.[7]

Although newspaper articles repeatedly stress the role that grow operators play in stealing electrical power and creating unsafe electrical bypasses and wiring, a 2011 Canadian Department of Justice report shows little evidence of such dollar amounts.[8]

This news coverage has helped support the emergence of BC's electrical supplier, BC Hydro, as a key claims maker about grow ops. The website for BC Hydro includes a page of information on grow ops that describes their dangers, including stolen electrical power and damage to the electrical grid. The site encourages readers to call the police if they suspect their neighbours are growing marijuana indoors, and it directs readers to the RCMP's webpage on grow ops that, again, describes the "public safety dangers of grow ops" and includes a tip sheet on how to spot a grow op.[9] Newspaper stories echo these key claims makers by repeatedly carrying information on how readers can spot a grow op. Some of these tips are vague and effectively encourage neighbours to spy on each other and to become police informants. These stories appear as early as 1997, and one such story from that same year describes an RCMP booklet issued to residents of Pitt Meadows, BC, aimed at helping them detect the presence of grow ops:

> The booklet contains a checklist to help identify a drug operation: People and vehicles constantly coming and going; dark coverings over the windows; unusual or modified wiring on the outside of the home; hoses running from doors or windows; growing equipment and supplies seen but no garden or flowers evident; and visitors parking down the street and walking to the home.[10]

Once residents had filled out the booklet, it was supposed to be returned to the RCMP for evaluation.

In an article entitled "Is there a grow op next door?" the newspaper reporter identifies the public safety risks of grow ops, emphasizing that most residents do not know they have a grow op in their neighbourhood, and ends the article with a list of tips on how to spot a grow op.[11] Over the years, many such articles appear in newspaper coverage. Articles that suggest that neighbours may not know they have a grow op next door inadvertently dispute the claim that grow ops are inevitably disruptive to residential neighbourhoods. But, the claims about the dangers posed by grow ops, especially their public safety risks, endorse the views of key claims makers that all such operations pose significant dangers. This coverage, in turn, links the elimination of these dangers to the need for neighbours to spy on one another in an effort to limit these risks.

Innocent Others and Evil Growers

Newspaper coverage tries to pit "innocent" views of grow ops against their supposed dangerous reality. One 1999 article suggests:

> Many people view marijuana growing as a victimless crime ... fire has destroyed several local homes. These homes are usually owned by a landlord who is unaware of the tenant's illegal activity.[12]

In an excerpt from a 2000 *Vancouver Sun* article, the writer reiterates claims about public safety dangers of grow ops and links these claims to the safety of children:

> Amateur rewiring to BC Hydro meters is often the cause of fires which endanger neighbours, and explosions from hydro heaters used to dry

plants are a common danger. For just those reasons the province has apprehended more than 40 children living in houses where marijuana growing operations were busted in the last six weeks.[13]

The reader is left to assume that the apprehended children were found
in improperly wired homes, although no evidence for this claim is
provided. Another article from 2000 suggests that the characteristics
of grow ops are not only dangerous to neighbours and children but to
firefighters:

> It's only a matter of time before a firefighter is injured or killed in a blaze
> caused by a marijuana-growing operation, a Victoria-area fire chief has
> warned. "I'm afraid if the court system does not address illegal grow-op-
> erations adequately, we're going to lose a firefighter," Bob Beckett of the
> Langford fire department said Saturday. He made his comments after a
> fire leveled a rented house. Equipment in the home suggested it sheltered
> a growing operation. Thirty firefighters attacked the inferno, which con-
> sumed the building.[14]

This article represents a trend in reporting that increases into the mid-
2000s as BC firefighters become key spokespeople about the dangers of
residential marijuana production. A very similar version of this article
appears in the *Times Colonist* on 21 February 2000. By 2003, fears about
the safety of firefighters are reported in an increasingly alarming tone:

> A firefighter who ran out of air Tuesday while fighting a fire in a build-
> ing containing a suspected marijuana-growing operation says he wants
> stiffer penalties for people who put firemen at risk while flouting the law.
> Captain John McQuade, a 26-year veteran of the Burnaby fire service, said
> he thinks owners of growing operations where fires break out should be
> charged with murder if firefighters die putting out the blazes.[15]

The article offers no rebuttal or alternative perspective on the claims
that grow op fires are akin to murder.

In our study sample, we found 156 news articles (6%) focusing primarily on fires and explosions related to marijuana grow ops. Often,
Surrey's Fire Chief Len Garis or Darryl Plecas are quoted highlighting
the risk of fire hazards in grow ops. Garis argues that residential grow
ops present rampant fire hazards; this claim substantiates his assertion
that fire departments should play a role in regulating residential cannabis cultivation. Drawing on the RCMP-commissioned research written

by Plecas et al.,[16] Garis suggests that grow ops are 24 times more likely to catch fire due to unsafe electrical practices such as electrical power bypasses and poor wiring associated with grow lights and other equipment.[17] These issues, Garis warns, have the potential to spill over into the lives of innocent others. Yet there is little evidence to substantiate Plecas' and Garis' claims about indoor marijuana grow ops and the increased risk of fire in British Columbia. The tables provided by Plecas et al. in their 2005 publication on BC fires do not provide sufficient evidence to back up this claim.[18] Data in the *Annual Statistical Fire Report: 2001–2003,* prepared by the Office of the Fire Commissioner, which include various statistics for all fires responded to in British Columbia for the years 2001, 2002, and 2003, suggest that the numbers are lower than those presented for the same years in the Plecas et al. 2005 report. For example, Plecas et al. state that the proportions of indoor grow operations resulting in fire were 3.5 per cent in 2001, 3.7 per cent in 2002, and 4.7 per cent in 2003; however, using the data found in the *Annual Statistical Fire Report*, the actual proportion of fires in British Columbia related to grow ops would be 1.21 per cent, 1.01 per cent, and 1.30 per cent, respectively. These contradictory statistics suggest that claims about the links between grow ops and fires may be exaggerated in the reports that routinely appear in newspaper stories.

Media reports also suggest that grow ops are booby-trapped, and as a result, the police officers who try to discover and eliminate these operations face terrible dangers from these operations. An article from 2001 states:

> Hazards increasingly faced by police and pot-patch intruders include: Shotguns poised to go off if a wire is disturbed; razor blades embedded in plant stalks; fishing hooks that dangle at face level from fine line; boards bristling with nails; and bear traps that will crush a human ankle. Then there's alarms, also trip-wired, and surveillance cameras that will trigger an usually armed response.[19]

Yet a study commissioned by the RCMP of the period in British Columbia between 1997 and 2003 found that only 2.1 per cent of marijuana grow ops contained hazards such as booby traps, explosives, or dangerous chemicals.[20]

The following excerpt is typical in that it suggests that otherwise safe neighbourhoods are at risk and that grow ops are more likely to be run by renters (rather than home owners) in residential areas. Like the newspaper coverage about organized crime, these articles

confirm the link between marijuana production and supposedly undesirable outsiders:

> Vancouver media liaison officer Constable Sarah Bloor said one of the
> main objectives of Green Sweep was to encourage the public to be aware
> of growing operation activity and the physical dangers that the opera-
> tions can pose for people living near them. Captain Rob Jones-Cook of
> the Vancouver fire department said firefighters are "extremely concerned"
> about the operations because of the risk of fire and explosion – which pose
> a risk to other homes in the vicinity – from unauthorized and unskilled
> modifications of electrical and heating systems. Homes used as growing
> operations are typically rental homes where the landlord or a manage-
> ment company has not exercised vigilance in screening or keeping up to
> date with the activities of the tenants.[21]

This excerpt contains several different sets of claims, but it quickly links
these issues together by listing the dangers of grow ops in rapid-fire
order. The result is a pastiche of claims about the problems related to
grow ops linked to rental properties.

In late 2002, police and representatives of the electricity and real
estate industries met in Ottawa to push for increased attention to the
production of marijuana in Canada. News articles that reported on
these meetings emphasized delegates' objections to a House of Commons proposal to decriminalize possession and cultivation of small
amounts of marijuana. The coverage of these meetings reiterated many
of the same themes about the public safety dangers of grows ops, and
it particularly emphasized risks of marijuana cultivation to otherwise
"good" neighbourhoods as well as the Canadian insurance industry:

> Pot-growing, they [delegates to the meeting] announced, steals power and
> is threatening to push hydro rates even higher than they're going anyway.
> Grow-ops also lower the tone of even upscale neighbourhoods, under-
> mining house and property prices and driving up insurance premiums.[22]

On that same day, the same newspaper carried another article that
emphasized the dangers that grow ops pose to "good" neighbours particularly because of the supposed increase of renters seeking homes
strictly for marijuana production:

> According to [RCMP Cpl. Brian] Kerr, head of the West Shore street crime
> unit, marijuana grow operations almost always used to be housed in

rundown, nondescript rental properties. Police identified them by their windows, which were covered up 24 hours a day. Now, the grow-ops are moving into better neighborhoods, becoming more upscale. And the scams to rent in better neighbourhoods are becoming more sophisticated.[23]

Claims about the public safety risks of grow ops are magnified by making these dangers seem contagious. More innocent neighbour-hoods, especially in upscale areas, are depicted as potential sites of public safety risks brought by dangerous criminals who do not belong. Renters are thus represented as possible criminals. Another excerpt · from an article in the *Vancouver Sun* in 2003 re-emphasizes the dangers that grow ops pose to communities:

> Most grow-ops are in residential areas where neighbours have no idea about what is happening next door. That's a big problem, say police, because grow houses are a serious danger to communities. They can also be a serious pain in the pocket book to real estate investors. Electricity supplies are tampered with and the house is usually a total mess by the time the police step in and shut down the operation. Worse, police estimate that one in 10 of indoor grow-ops will eventually go up in flames: fire is a constant danger.[24]

The article is representative of an emerging trend in newspaper report-ing: exaggerating claims of fire and electricity theft and a presumption of an overwhelming number of grow ops appearing in residential BC communities such as Chilliwack and Abbotsford.[25] Abbotsford city council amended their zoning bylaw in 2005 to include the "growing, production, manufacture, sale, distribution and trade of drugs listed in Schedule 1 of the *Controlled Drugs and Substances Act*, including canna-bis, or any by-product of cannabis."[26] As noted earlier, cannabis is listed in the Controlled Drugs and Substances Act as a Schedule 2 substance.

Newspaper coverage also extended the public safety dangers of grow ops to include threats to the viability and profitability of the real estate industry (see Figure 5.1). These articles link the public safety dangers of grow ops to the condition of homes on the market, particularly for unsuspecting buyers. Other articles extend these same concerns to the home insurance industry. The following excerpt illustrates this trend:

> Real estate agents aren't the only ones alarmed by the increasing number of quiet, suburban homes being used to grow lucrative crops of high-qual-ity marijuana. No longer solely the concern of law enforcement, the rapid

Figure 5.1. Headline Box: Real Estate.[27]

HEADLINES: REAL ESTATE ISSUES

Realtors want drug declaration added to BC seller's disclosure (2004)

Clues that your dream home might have been a grow-op (2007)

Homes used to grow pot pose serious mould risk: But no sure way to know if property once used as a drug house (2008)

It's already going to pot, home buyers discover (2008)

---

spread of such grow-ops is changing the way agencies from insurers to municipalities do business.[28]

This article charts the trajectory of a suburban grow op and suggests that it inevitably ends up in a bust by police, and an empty house now destroyed by indoor agricultural production because of the mould and other toxins produced by moisture accumulating on the walls of these houses. The article describes steps taken by insurers and real estate associations to curb these trends including insurance riders that require disclosure of a home's history. It also extends the domain of the problem of grow ops to municipalities by noting the extra work hours required to inspect sites of former grow ops.

Starting as early as 2000, news stories focused on the need for municipalities to regulate drug production inside city limits. The following except exemplifies the tone of these stories:

Frustrated and frightened, police in the lower mainland are pushing municipal councils to enact bylaws to stop the alarming spread of marijuana grow operations in their communities.[29]

Later on, stories carry positive assessments of municipal efforts:

Municipalities such as Chilliwack, BC, respond to its reputation as "Columbia North" today with what officials say is the toughest anti-marijuana growing bylaw in BC.

This article further reinforces the dangers of grow ops and praises a municipal bylaw that forces landlords to keep tabs on their rental properties.[30]

By 2006, claims about the public safety dangers of grow ops are routine as are articles detailing initiatives undertaken to curb the spread of these operations. The following excerpt exemplifies the consolidation of claims about the dangers of grow ops. This excerpt is from an article about a "Block and Grow Watch" program in a neighbourhood in Chilliwack:

> "Grow-ops are a cancer among us," Don Van Beest of the Chilliwack fire department tells a crowd of 75 Block Watch leaders gathered in Chilliwack's municipal hall to learn about Block and Grow Watch. "It's not if this building catches fire, it's when," the fire prevention officer says as he flashes slides of deadly wiring and pails of toxic chemicals. In 2005, Chilliwack launched its local pot watch, believed to be the first of its kind. Grow Watch works with police to educate residents to report suspicious activity. Residents sign up and once a block gets an 80 per cent participation rate, they are trained and Grow Watch signs go up, warning: "Neighbours are watching, recording and reporting."[31]

The article noted above offers no critical appraisal of these initiatives and, instead, provides more information that serves to reinforce the dangers of grow ops to unsuspecting persons. As these excerpts illustrate, the problem of public safety is extended by either more broadly defining the scope of the problem or by suggesting that it affects more people than it did in previous years. In these ways, police claims and media reports helped to create an environment for the introduction of municipal programs to restrict residential marijuana grow ops. Linking "public safety" concerns to the cultivation of marijuana provided a political opportunity for some municipalities to begin to develop their own regulatory initiatives. Valverde claims that urban municipal law in Canada is rarely guided by "constitutional principles" or individual rights. Although she does not discuss the regulation of marijuana grow ops in her analysis of Toronto's municipal governance, Valverde makes clear that city governance "has its own dynamics" that are "little-understood."[32] However, to be clear, "zoning is a mechanism by which municipalities, through authority conferred on them by provincial statute, are empowered to regulate land use through bylaws."[33] In the following sections, we examine municipal bylaws and discuss three interrelated programs: the introduction of electrical inspections in Surrey, BC, in 2005; the introduction of the BC Safety Standards Amendment Act, in 2006; and the subsequent proliferation of municipal bylaws and programs aimed at eliminating the cultivation of marijuana.

Electrical Inspection Programs

Starting in 2005, some BC municipalities began implementing multi-partner initiatives that drew on municipal bylaws to compel entry into residences suspected of having a grow op. A pilot project of one such program, conducted in Surrey, in 2005, has become the template for other similar initiatives in British Columbia. The Electrical Fire and Safety Initiative (EFSI), piloted in Surrey in the spring of 2005, was a joint initiative between police officers, firefighters, the provincial government, the BC Safety Authority, and municipal electrical inspectors. The stated goal of the project was to reduce the number of residential grow ops in Surrey without resorting to arrest and prosecution. The project itself was an eight-step process that drew on a multifaceted interagency partnership. The process used by Surrey remains essentially the same since this pilot.

Typically, the Surrey detachment of the RCMP passes tips about residential cannabis grow ops to the EFSI Team, or possible marijuana grow ops are identified through an analysis of electricity consumption records provided by BC Hydro. The addresses of suspected residences are reviewed to ensure they are not part of a current criminal investigation. Members of the team perform a drive-by of selected homes to check for possible high-power usage issues such as hot tubs and swimming pools. Surrey officials also undertake a search of residential documents such as building permits, and police checks are performed on vehicles located at the site. Notices are then posted on homes, and couriered to residents to indicate they have 48 hours to permit an inspection. In the original pilot project, if residents refused admittance to the inspectors, they were told their electrical supply would be disconnected if they did not permit an inspection within 48 hours. As the program currently exists, residents have 48 hours to allow entry by inspectors who then search for evidence of fire, electrical, health, and other safety risks. Depending on what the inspectors find, residents can have their electrical and/or water services disconnected, and they can be ordered to undertake repairs. Some programs require residents to pay the costs of the inspection. The current program in Surrey is deemed to be a success by its team and is now ongoing; other municipalities in British Columbia have implemented a similar version of this initiative. In the original pilot project, police officers accompanied the inspection teams inside the homes. Due to court challenges (to be discussed later), officers often do not enter the homes but remain outside, parked in their cars or in the vicinity.[34]

In 2005, Surrey Fire Chief Len Garis released a report that followed this pilot project. This report echoed the public safety concerns associated with grow ops that had been freely reported in newspapers. Garis associates residential grow ops with violence, gangs, and undesirable and racialized Others. But one of the most significant methods Garis uses to demonize grow ops is linking them to "grave" public safety concerns. These "dangers" include a stock set of claims also found in police-based sources and media reports, such as house fires due to faulty wiring associated with grow lights and electrical power bypasses, weapons, and booby traps, as well as violence incited by robberies and assaults stemming from turf battles between grow operators. Media coverage of Garis' pilot program was extensive and generally positive with very little debate or disagreement about the virtues of this initiative.[35]

BC Safety Standards Amendment Act

One of the recommendations of Surrey Fire Chief Garis'[36] 2005 report was to create enabling legislation that would allow BC Hydro to release information about its customers to municipalities. In 2006, the BC Liberal government followed suit and introduced and passed the Safety Standards Amendment Act, a legislative move that allows the province's electricity producers to disclose electricity consumption information to municipal governments. The purpose of this amendment is to help identify clandestine residential cannabis grow ops on the assumption that unusually large consumption of electricity could indicate the presence of hydroponic equipment used for the indoor cultivation of cannabis. This legislation permits the disclosure of this information to safety authorities for the purposes of inspections. In addition, the amendment permits local governments to disclose electrical consumption information to police. This amendment gave impetus to the development of electrical inspection programs similar to the one in Surrey to other municipalities.

The headline and accompanying articles on the front page of an edition of the *Vancouver Sun* in 2006 (see Figure 5.2) uncritically praises the

—BRITISH COLUMBIA—

BC Hydro to report suspected pot farms under new legislation

BY CHAD SKELTON
VANCOUVER SUN

IAN LINDSAY/VANCOUVER SUN FILES

B.C. has 15,000 to 20,000 marijuana growing operations, most of them in Lower Mainland homes.

Provincial legislation introduced Thursday will require BC Hydro to hand over to municipalities a list of all addresses with unusually high power consumption — a move police say could effectively drive marijuana growers out of residential areas.

There are an estimated 15,000 to 20,000 marijuana growing operations in B.C. — the vast majority of them in private homes in the Lower Mainland.

Growing operations require massive amounts of electricity. But, citing privacy legislation, BC Hydro would only release information on a home's electricity consumption to police or municipal inspectors if they already had an address under investigation.

Under the new law, BC Hydro and other electricity providers will be required to provide to any city that asks for it a list of all addresses in their jurisdiction with unusually high consumption, plus two years' billing records for each address.

Insp. Paul Nadeau, head of the RCMP's Greater Vancouver Drug Section, said it is impossible to know exactly what effect the new law will have. But he said it could put a major dent in the province's $7-billion marijuana trade.

"I think we're going to see them move out of residential areas," he said. "They need hydro. They can't get around that. The jig is up. This idea that some of them have that, 'Because I pay my hydro, they'll leave me alone' — that's over now."

Solicitor-General John Les agreed.

"If municipalities want to use this legislation aggressively, I think they can — in very significant ways — put a run on the grow-op industry in this province," he said.

Some growers, instead of paying for their power, illegally steal it using an electrical bypass.

But because BC Hydro vigorously investigates electricity theft — and notifies police of the suspects it identifies — stealing power exposed growers in the past to far more risks than just paying their power bill on time.

The new law — the first of its kind in Canada — may encourage more growers to steal power, Nadeau acknowledged, but he said police and BC Hydro have

prepared for that.

"We're going to catch them either way," he said. "They're either going to have to pay their bills and surface on these lists, or they're going to be stealing it and surfacing in other ways."

While police will have access to the consumption lists, Les said he expects the information will be used primarily by city inspectors and fire departments to shut down growing operations without a criminal investigation.

Surrey recently spearheaded a project in which city fire inspectors put notices on the doors of suspected growing operations demanding owners allow them in to inspect their electrical work within 48 hours or have their power shut off.

By the time inspectors were let in, the marijuana had usually been removed, but the dangerous wiring remained — so a inspectors shut off the house's power until it was safe again.

The addresses Surrey targeted were those that the police didn't have time to get to.

Surrey Fire Chief Len Garis, who lobbied Victoria for the new law, said the legislation will allow his teams to work more quickly.

"Every billing period, we'll be able to get a batch of data from BC Hydro," he said. "And our goal is to be sophisticated enough that, within two to three months of a growing operation being set up, we'll be knocking on the door."

Police and fire departments have argued that marijuana growing operations pose a significant risk to neighbourhoods.

A study by the University College of the Fraser Valley last year concluded that growing operations are 24 times more likely to catch fire than a normal home.

Innocent homeowners have also been attacked in "grow rips" by criminals looking to steal pot plants who got the wrong house.

Jason Gratl, president of the B.C. Civil Liberties Association, expressed concern Thursday that the new legislation invades the privacy of homeowners while encouraging the likelihood of fires by encouraging growers to steal electricity through risky electrical bypasses.

Privacy commissioner David Loukidelis also expressed concern about the new legislation in a letter to the government Thursday.

"As a general point, such initiatives amount to a form of surveillance," he wrote.

Loukidelis asked the government to re-word the law so the consumption information can only be used by city inspectors — and not to help police launch criminal investigations.

cskelton@png.canwest.com

NEWSPAPER 🔊 VOICES
The Vancouver Sun Read Aloud
This story can be heard online
after 10:30 a.m. today at
www.vancouversun.com/readaloud

Hydro thief or Hydro hog

How BC Hydro can spot marijuana growing operations:

■ Marijuana growing operations use significantly more electricity than a typical house. Under legislation introduced Thursday, municipalities will be able to get a list of houses in their jurisdiction with unusually high electricity consumption. Police and city inspectors will then be able to use those lists to investigate and shut-down growing operations.

■ Marijuana growers who illegally steal electricity using a bypass will often show up in Hydro's records for having abnormally low electricity consumption. Such homes are investigated for electricity theft by Hydro, which then passes on the names of suspects it identifies to the local police.

Source: Vancouver Sun   VANCOUVER SUN

Is that a marijuana growing operation next door?

B.C. authorities provide this list of telltale signs that your neighbours might be sowing more than family harmony:

■ Entry to the home is usually through the garage or a back entrance to conceal activity.

■ Windows are boarded or covered and may have a layer of condensation.

■ Equipment such as large fans, lights and plastic plant containers is carried into the home.

■ Sounds of construction or electrical humming can be heard.

■ Strange odours (a skunk-like smell) emanate from the house.

■ The neighbourhood experiences localized surges or decreases in power.

Source: Government of B.C.

Figure 5.2. "BC Hydro to report suspected pot farms under new legislation." Reproduced with permission from the *Vancouver Sun*, 2006. Photo by Ian Lindsay.

new BC legislation to regulate marijuana grow ops. The oft-referenced and by now familiar claims makers comprise the bulk of the main article: Surrey Fire Chief Len Garis, Inspector Paul Nadeau (head of the RCMP's Greater Vancouver Drug Section), Solicitor General John Les, and the 2002 and 2005 RCMP-commissioned papers by Plecas and colleagues. Concern about the new legislation expressed by the BC Civil Liberties Association and the Office of the BC Information and Privacy Commissioner are given a few sentences at the end of the article. The accompanying photo to the article depicts a law enforcement agent standing behind hanging lights in an indoor grow op; she is looking down at some young and spindly marijuana plants in pots. The article ends with a picture of a marijuana leaf encased by handcuffs next to a box with the caption: "Is that a marijuana growing operation next door?" The article gives tips for identifying neighbours who grow marijuana; one of these tips advises readers to be on the lookout for neighbours who enter their homes through back entrances and garages.

BC Municipal Bylaws and Other Activities

Although some of the focus in this book is on federal drug law, especially the Controlled Drugs and Substances Act, as we noted early on, provincial laws and municipal bylaws also regulate drug use and people thought to be producing, selling, or using criminalized drugs. In Canada, the British North American Act of 1867 set up three levels of jurisdiction: federal, provincial, and municipal. Provincial and municipal initiatives are constrained by federal law and, since 1982, the Canadian Charter of Rights and Freedoms. As noted earlier, since the early 2000s, many BC municipalities have enacted new bylaws and initiated fines directed at curbing residential production of marijuana.[37] These bylaws often make homeowners financially responsible for any clean-up costs related to the cultivation of marijuana (there is no presumption of innocence as there is in the criminal justice system). The enforcement of these bylaws often draws on the electrical inspections noted previously and involves unquestioned partnerships among representatives of BC Hydro, municipal police, the RCMP, and city firefighters.

BC municipalities have been ideal locations to engage new regulatory mechanisms to govern marijuana grow op sites because of their power to enact bylaws that do not originate in criminal law.[38] BC's

Community Charter Act, as well as fire, building, and electrical codes, provide municipalities with the power to regulate issues such as fire prevention, health, and safety in private residences. This is evident in the numerous municipal bylaws that govern such matters at the local level. In addition, municipalities, and their mayors and councils, are often more easily accessible to claims makers and the media than provincial and federal governments. This accessibility makes it possible for fire and police departments to advocate for new forms of regulation. There has been a growing trend in British Columbia towards using municipal powers to regulate the production of illicit drugs. Municipalities have championed both harm reduction efforts (i.e., practical programs that focus on minimizing drug-related harms to individuals and society, such as needle exchange) as well as increased enforcement against producers and sellers of drugs. The large metropolitan City of Vancouver is the site of North America's first supervised injection facility (Insite) and is one of two Canadian cities that were recently the site of the first heroin-assisted treatment clinical trial in North America, called the North American Opiate Medication Initiative (NAOMI).

Surrey, BC, like some of its surrounding municipalities, has not embraced these harm reduction efforts, but has instead, chosen to increase enforcement against residential cannabis cultivation. Diane Watts, mayor of Surrey since 2005, and her city council developed a Crime Reduction Strategy that includes elimination of marijuana-growing operations as key to their strategy for reducing crime. As part of these efforts, in 2009, Surrey published *Responding to Marijuana Grow Operations: A Community Handbook*. The stated intent of the handbook is to assist other municipalities in and outside of British Columbia to address marijuana grow ops. While Surrey eschews harm reduction services, the handbook is not subtle in its borrowing of the language of harm reduction. In a rather innovative move discursively, it links the public safety dangers of grows ops to the language of "harms" and, in turn, defines these "harms" as fires, electrocution, unsafe renovations, mould, and children living in grow ops. The handbook refers to the 2005 pilot project in Surrey (discussed earlier) and directs municipalities to develop their own electrical inspection programs and bylaws similar to Surrey's Controlled Substances Property Bylaw, introduced in 2006. This bylaw imposes a financial penalty and a record attached to the property title of houses suspected of having a marijuana-growing operation. Another Surrey bylaw bans public displays of drug paraphernalia in businesses and the selling of drug paraphernalia to minors. This bylaw was established through amendments to an existing Business License Bylaw. Langford, BC, has also adopted a drug house bylaw that places the onus on landlords to report suspicious activities in their rental properties or absorb the costs of clean up. In this way, the bylaw enlists the aid of landlords in detecting and eliminating these operations. Other BC municipalities including Chilliwack, Surrey, Vancouver, North Vancouver District, West Vancouver, Burnaby, and Coquitlam have passed similar bylaws.[39]

As cultural geographer Kay Anderson suggests, municipal governments have long been in the business of regulating their citizens and their space in a variety of ways. Cities have been the sites of struggles over who rightfully owns or belongs in a space.[40] Valverde argues that municipalities, specifically Toronto, "rarely use their legal rights and regulatory tools to promote inclusion" or diversity.[41] To paraphrase human rights researcher Andrew Woolford, municipal policies continue to sanctify a particular form of moral order by seeing people who use or produce illegal drugs as tainted Others, perceived to be outside the supposedly moral space of the city.[42] From Woolford's perspective, spaces like municipalities take on moral as well as geographical boundaries. In turn, spokespeople draw on these moral tropes to identify marijuana grow op sites as criminal and racialized spaces that are potentially threatening to supposedly white, moral space.

Municipalities attempt to eliminate these negative "influences" by introducing new forms of regulation to restore the primacy and sanctity of "normal" space.[43] Alan Feldman describes "criminalized space" as both an ideological and economic (shaped by neo-liberal economic policy) phenomenon "through which new strategies of policing and expert knowledge ... are legitimized."[44] Marijuana grow op sites are just such kinds of criminalized spaces seen by police and municipal officials as internal threats to both the economic and moral order that must be cast out to ensure the stability of suburban living. The photograph in Figure 5.3 depicts how a criminalized space is announced to its neighbours using a large lawn sign posted by an undercover member of the police in front of a home suspected of containing a grow op. Whether or not a grow op is found, the prominent lawn sign lets other residents know and establishes the "fact" that this neighbour's home is under investigation by the police. The photo is accompanied by the headline, "Mayor wants to halt 'decay in North Delta,'" again illustrating the association that newspaper reports make between grow ops and social and economic degradation.

Figure 5.3. "Clean up North Delta." Reproduced with permission from the *Vancouver Sun* (6 March 2000). Photo by Glenn Baglo.

Surrey officials have gone even farther in their efforts to eradicate the production of marijuana. Chief of the Surrey Fire Department Len Garis has been instrumental in advocating for more regulation of marijuana grow ops, and many reports supporting this position can be found on his website.[45] In 2009, Garis et al. issued a report entitled, *Community Response to Marijuana Grow Operations: A Guide toward Promising Practices*. In 2009, Garis also made a presentation to the Senate Standing Senate Committee on Legal and Constitutional Affairs on Bill C-15, an Act to Amend the Controlled Drugs and Substances Act. Both documents reiterate the problem of grow ops reported by the media, pointing out the issues of lenient sentencing, lack of policing resources to address a growing number of cases, and public safety hazards. Both reports include an overview of Surrey's initiatives with regard to grow ops, including the above-noted bylaw and the EFSI program. The former document provides an overview of programs to curb marijuana production undertaken in Alberta and Ontario, as well as British Columbia, and urges communities to take up similar initiatives. It notes the lack of support of the BC provincial government for implementing these initiatives throughout the province despite their claimed success. It skims over the important issues raised in a court challenge to Surrey's EFSI program (to be discussed later in this chapter). However, Garis is careful to advise other municipalities to situate similar programs in the context of public safety and eschew any claims to enforcement of the federal Controlled Drugs and Substances Act. In fact, public safety is the stated raison d'être for municipal bylaws and electrical inspection programs aimed at marijuana growers. Garis, Plecas, Cohen, and McCormick's document advises other municipalities to lobby provincial and federal levels of government to obtain support for similar programs. Garis et al. also support the enactment of civil laws such as the Safer Communities and Neighbourhood Acts that have been implemented in some provinces in Canada. These Acts purportedly,

> target and shut down residential and commercial properties used for producing, selling, using illegal drugs, as well as prostitution, solvent abuse, or the unlawful sale and consumption of alcohol ... As well individuals can be prohibited from engaging in certain undesirable activities.[46]

No such law has been enacted in British Columbia, although attempts have been made through private member's bills.[47]

These authors also review the work of BC Hydro and its anticipated implementation of the "smart meter," a digital and wireless meter used to measure residential electrical consumption. They suggest that the smart meter can make the detections of grow ops easier because these units have "advanced surveillance technologies" that can detect when a grower switches electrical power on and off to match a 12-hour growing cycle.[48] No mention is given of the potential violation of privacy that this use of the smart meter could entail. Nor is it clear that such use of the meter is permitted. This document also praises the work of insurance companies and real estate associations for their attempts to eradicate marijuana grow ops.

Like the above-noted document, Garis' submission to the Standing Senate Committee promotes four additional approaches to the regulation of marijuana cultivation including stricter regulation of hydroponic shops; regulation of medical marijuana operations by municipalities; increased development and application of surveillance technology such as an electromagnet radiation analyser that can detect hydroponic equipment from a moving vehicle and long-wave hyperspectral

Figure 5.4. Headline Box: Inspections.[49]

HEADLINES: MARIJUANA GROW-OP RESIDENTIAL INSPECTIONS

Coquitlam wants hydro to help ID marijuana grow operations (2005)

Grow-op study blasted: Bias suggested – critics say police propagating hysteria (2005)

BC hydro to report suspected pot farms under new legislation (2006)

Big brother will soon be watching your hydro (2006)

Hydro use in valley raises suspicions (2007)

Over 100 pot grow-ops nipped in bud in 3 months: Municipality has been checking hydro bills for more than normal amounts of power use (2007)

Couple left "squatting" in their home: Say city wants them to pay $5,000 for search for grow-op that wasn't there (2008)

Fire chief has other tactics up his sleeve: Len Garis won't be too upset if courts nix his inspection brainchild (2008)

Unofficial grow-op searches bend the law, says lawyer: "Ruse" to gain entry violates citizens' rights, judge told (2008)

Grow-ops wilt under Surrey program (2009)

Where Surrey leads, will others follow? City's 2005 inspection initiative has been amazingly successful (2009)

Big brother alive and well in Mission: Special grow-op "safety inspection" cost innocent homeowner $5,200 (2009)

Surrey RCMP winning battle with grow-ops: Jail, property seizures follow police success in "popping two to four" pot growers a week (2009)

Figure 5.5. Headline Box: Bylaws.[50]

```
┌─────────────────────────────────────────────────────────────────┐
│                        HEADLINES: BYLAWS                          │
│                                                                   │
│   City councillor wants property owners to inspect for marijuana  │
│   operations (2004)                                               │
│                                                                   │
│     New bylaw to inform future tenants about grow-op mould,       │
│     toxins (2006)                                                 │
│                                                                   │
│     New bylaw drives 26 grow-ops out of business since last       │
│     month (2006)                                                  │
│                                                                   │
│   Drug house buyers risk health: Group seeks standardized way to  │
│   alert homebuyers about meth labs, growing operations (2008)     │
│                                                                   │
│    Lawyer fights "totalitarian" grow-op law: Act allowed          │
│    inspector to cut power to Hells Angels associate's house       │
│    (2008)                                                         │
└─────────────────────────────────────────────────────────────────┘
```

imagery to detect drug labs; and tax audits of illegal drug production income, which would require increased information sharing between Canada Revenue Agency, police, and municipalities.[51] The submission closes by supporting federal proposals for mandatory minimum sentences for grow operators, a move Garis deems to be "an important step in the efforts to reduce the public safety threats associated with growing marijuana."[52]

The authors of these documents provide very little discussion of the potential violations of privacy or of the infringement of Charter rights and due process that these initiatives may pose. Nor do they seem cognizant of the issue of public oversight of either multipartner programs or initiatives undertaken by real estate and insurance organizations. (See Figures 5.4 and 5.5.)

Until recently, newspaper reporting typically, although not exclusively, focused on the "successes" of such initiatives and praised the multipartner nature of these forms of regulation. Newspaper stories gave little consideration to a wider debate about the implications of these municipal initiatives, instead choosing to report them as an unquestioningly legitimate move towards eradication of residential growing operations.

Surrey Court Challenge to the BC Safety Standards Amendment Act

Whereas the media are most often uncritical of the new legislation and municipal efforts to regulate marijuana grow ops, by 2007, some homeowners began to question Surrey's bylaw and the establishment and practice of Surrey's Electrical and Fire Safety Inspection Team. Homeowners are challenging a number of the provisions of the bylaws related to marijuana grow op inspections, including the practice of charging all costs associated with inspections ($5,200) to the owner. Inspection fees are charged regardless of whether or not the team finds evidence of a marijuana grow op on the premises. Homeowners are also challenging the provisions of the BC Safety Standards Act that authorize warrantless entry and inspection of homes as an infringement of their rights under the Canadian Charter of Rights and Freedoms.

As we noted previously, historically, municipal bylaws have been used to manage and delineate race and identity, identify potentially criminal spaces, and protect a supposedly law-abiding, moral and safe space. To protect the rights of people, the Canadian Charter of Rights and Freedoms (1982) is a constitutional document that "guarantees the rights and freedoms set out in it subject only to such reasonable limits prescribed by law as can be demonstrably justified in a free and democratic society." The Charter outlines specific rights, including legal rights, life, liberty, and security of person.[53] Residents who are most negatively affected have also resisted these same bylaws. Resistance to municipal bylaws and federal and provincial policy in relation to marijuana grow ops is increasing, and the Charter of Rights and Freedoms has been central to these struggles.

In the following discussion of the legal case, *Arkinstall* v. *City of Surrey*, section 8 of the Canadian Charter of Rights and Freedoms is key: "Everyone has the right to be secure against unreasonable search or seizure." At the core of this legal challenge is whether or not the provisions of the BC Safety Standards Act authorizing the warrantless entry and inspection of homes for the purpose of inspecting electrical systems for safety risks related to marijuana grow ops infringe on a homeowner's Charter rights under section 8. The appellants, Jason Arkinstall and Jennifer Green, resided in a 6,800 square feet home that included an indoor pool, sauna/steam room, hot tub, greenhouse, and central air conditioning.[54] In 2005, Surrey's EFSI Team came to Arkinstall and Green's home citing unusual electricity consumption as the reason for an inspection for safety risks related to marijuana grow operations. At the time, Jason Arkinstall was not at home, but he spoke with the EFSI Team on the phone and told them that he did not object to the electrical and fire inspectors entering his home but that the police could not enter without a warrant. The EFSI Team left the premises without entering the home. Transcripts of the court case reveal that the EFSI Team had only one record of a high reading of electricity consumption, rather than a history of high consumption at this residence.[55]

In November 2006, Captain McKibbon of the Surrey Fire Department examined additional data on electricity consumption at Arkinstall and Green's home, provided by BC Hydro. Believing he saw evidence of unusual electrical consumption, he initiated another EFSI Team inspection of the home. He contacted the RCMP, but they advised him not to initiate an inspection. Although McKibbon is not a "designated safety officer or safety manager" of the BC Safety Standards Act, he flagged the house for inspection and pursued the matter. In April 2007, he again noted to the RCMP that he believed Arkinstall and Green's home had unusual electrical consumption; this time, the RCMP agreed to an inspection. It was at this point that the EFSI Team again reviewed the case file and, on 28 May 2007, they went to Arkinstall and Green's home to conduct an inspection. Arkinstall and Green refused them entry, and the EFSI Team left information in the mailbox stating that they must contact the team to set up an inspection. Similar to the EFSI visit in 2005, Arkinstall spoke with the EFSI Team and made it clear that he would permit both the electrical and fire officials to enter his home but not the RCMP. At that time, the EFSI Team told Arkinstall that the Fire Department and electrical officials could not enter his home until the RCMP had first checked it over. In fact, the EFSI Team's operational procedures mandated that its other members not enter a home until the RCMP had first inspected the premises.[56]

On 30 May 2007, the EFSI Team returned to Arkinstall and Green's home. Again, Arkinstall told the team he would permit the fire and electrical officials into his home, but not the RCMP officers of the team. McKibbon was part of the team, and he informed Arkinstall that if he did not allow the team to inspect his home his electrical power would be disconnected, which is standard procedure in these cases where a homeowner refuses entry. Arkinstall, Green, and their son moved to a hotel after their electricity was disconnected on 31 May 2007. They were able to move home again, on 5 June 2007, after their lawyer filed an interlocutory injunction. Following these events, an electrical contractor approved by the City of Surrey inspected the home and completed the EFSI Team's safety checklist. It was evident from the inspection that Arkinstall and Green's home had "never been used to house a grow-operation."[57]

Arkinstall and Green petitioned the BC Supreme Court to argue that provisions of the Safety Standards Act be declared an infringement of section 8 of the Charter. The intervener, the BC Liberties Association, supported their case. The City of Surrey, the attorney general of British Columbia, and BC Hydro and Power Authority opposed the petition.

It took a number of years for a final decision to be reached on the case. Transcripts of the hearing indicated that, since 2006, BC Hydro has forwarded the electrical consumption records of over 6,000 properties in Surrey for review, although only 1,000 of these were flagged for inspection.[58] Joseph Arvay, the defence lawyer, is reported as saying that "only one of those homes was found to have had a grow-op."[59] In May 2010, the appeal judge declared that in relation to the case "the expectation of privacy is high and the inspections are very intrusive" and do not justify regulatory warrantless entry.[60] He also found that the EFSI inspections "expose every room of an individual's home ... to the 'chilling glare of inspection.'"[61] The judge agreed that the appellants were correct in asserting that the inspections, even though conducted under the regulatory rather than criminal context, "raise the spectre of criminality." He noted that the inspections were not random nor routine; this is because high electrical energy consumers are thought to have committed a criminal offence by growing marijuana, thus giving "rise to more stigma than would be generally expected from other regulatory" types of inspections.[62] The appeal judge concluded that the provision of the Safety Standards Act that allows for "warrantless entry and inspection of residential premises for the regulatory purpose of inspecting electrical systems for safety risks that may be related to marijuana grow-operations" infringed on the appellant's rights under section 8 of the Charter of Rights and Freedoms.[63] The defence lawyer also noted that the Safety Standards Act, which allows for homes that show unusually high power consumption to be inspected "is a ruse for police to gain entry without a warrant to search for marijuana grow-ops."[64]

Mission, BC: Class Action Lawsuit

In 2009, Mission, BC, a neighbouring municipality to Surrey, initiated a Controlled Substance Property Bylaw to allow "safety inspection teams" to enter private homes solely because they believe that hydro (electricity) usage exceeds normal consumption. Safety inspection teams in Mission are also made up of BC Hydro employees, municipal police, RCMP, city fire fighters, a building inspector (and sometimes health authority and social service representatives). Municipal clerks and administrators are involved in the identification of homes to be inspected.

The enforcement of this bylaw has been met with considerable resistance from some Mission residents. On 18 January 2010, Mission residents gathered in a meeting room at the Mission Public Library to discuss joining a class action lawsuit against the city in relation to provisions of the Controlled Substances Property Bylaw. The meeting was filmed and later posted on YouTube.[65] The meeting was comprised of about 40 people, young and old and from appearances, white working-class residents predominated. Participants argued that city hall was not listening to their objections about this bylaw and they expressed the belief that the inspection program relied on "suspicions" as "valid proof" of marijuana grow ops. They also expressed worry about the "intimidation" implied in the practice of cutting off electrical power if residents denied the inspection team entry into their home. The Mission residents questioned why once a team entered their home, an inspection seemingly based on high levels of electrical consumption also targeted signs of mould as well as holes in the walls that could indicate the presence of equipment related to marijuana grow ops. One participant explained that the $5,200 inspection fee, if not paid, was attached to their taxes. Other participants objected to the practice of billing any clean-up fees for mould and any other infractions to residents, and one man indicated that he was billed $10,000. One middle-aged woman stated that she is losing her home following the inspections, partially because of the cost of water tests and the cleaning of carpets and drapes, even though she had never had a marijuana grow op in her home. Another participant described the inspection team as "very heavyhanded, they're like the Gestapo." Other participants noted that the inspections were poorly done, and they claimed that inspectors are not trained to perform these duties.

Participants also described the inspection team members as arrogant, condescending, and intimidating. One middle-aged man stated, "I really felt that I was humiliated. I had the RCMP sitting outside my house. I had these pompous asses storm into my house like they were in Nazi Germany." One participant explained that the bylaws began in Abbotsford and that he has been fighting them since 2006 when an inspection team entered a commercial building he owned in that municipality. He noted that "this is something that's going on in every community," and he argued that under the guise of public safety, "freedoms and liberties" were being lost. An elderly man came to the front of the meeting room and told the group that he had water running into his house and his yard and he could not find its source, although he suspected it originated from a creek that was covered up. When he phoned city hall, he was told, "Oh, that's not our jurisdiction." He wondered why his situation was not considered to be a public safety issue, and then questioned why the city focuses on grow operations and ignores the conditions of poor housing throughout Mission.

A woman at the meeting relayed her story of buying a home in Mission and later discovering that it was filled with mould. She recounted how she had phoned the health unit and was told it was not their problem, but that "I should move because the mould could make my kids sick. I called the municipality and they also told me that they don't deal with issues of mould, I should move. But I couldn't get anybody to go up there and check that house." The meeting ended as one of the participants stated, "These guys are eroding democracy and that is not what we pay them to do." In general, these Mission residents were distressed about the financial burden of fines, and the stigma and discrimination they experienced as a result of being suspected of a crime even though they claim to have no involvement with residential marijuana cultivation.

Since the January 2011 meeting in Mission, disturbing events have occurred. On 11 May 2011, the *Globe and Mail* reported that a recent Mission RCMP raid on one current and one former city councillor is part of an investigation into the leak of confidential information from Mission city hall related to the bylaw on inspecting marijuana grow operations. Former City Councillor Ron Taylor states that the investigation was prompted following his passing on of information to the press about a resolution passed by city councillors behind closed doors. The resolution approved the hiring of a public relations firm following the launch of the class action suit against the city. The firm's role is to influence perceptions in the community about the goals of their marijuana safety inspection teams and municipal policy and fees.[66] The outcome of this investigation has not been released. Nevertheless, this raid raises serious questions about attempts by Mission city hall and the RCMP to silence critics of municipal bylaws related to marijuana grow ops.

On 7 July 2011, Mission residents and plaintiffs Stacey Gowanlock and Mark Rees, with the support of BC Civil Liberties lawyer Micheal Vonn, initiated a class action lawsuit against the District of Mission. This lawsuit represents the 499 properties (including Gowanlock and

Rees) inspected by the Public Safety Inspection Team (PSIT) between April 2008 and December 2010 (unless they opt out). The suit seeks to address a number of concerns, including losses incurred by the costly inspections and fees charged by the city; the costs of third-party cleaning and certification processes in order to re-enter and occupy homes; and the stigma related to the inspections; in addition, they challenge the bylaw as an infringement of Charter rights. The plaintiffs allege the inspections are unconstitutional as they were an "unreasonable search and seizure" and deprive them of their right to "security of the person."[67]

The plaintiffs also allege that the PSIT dismantled and destroyed parts of their homes in order to gain access to interior walls. They allege that there was no evidence of a controlled substance in their homes. The Mission inspectors posted "large, conspicuous, and brightly coloured notices" on their homes, advertising that the occupancy permit had been "revoked because the homes contained a marijuana grow operation." Following the posting and the inspection, the plaintiffs assert that their status in the neighbourhood shifted; their neighbours viewed them negatively, and the value of their homes diminished. Following the inspection, pursuant to Mission bylaw policy, the inspection team communicated to other third parties that the plaintiffs' homes were used for marijuana grow ops, including Canada Post, the plaintiffs' mortgagee, real estate agents, prospective purchasers of their homes, and their insurers. The plaintiffs argue that no evidence of marijuana grow ops was found in their homes. Their plight is similar to the 499 other residents in Mission whose homes have been entered and inspected by the Public Safety Inspection Team.

Once the PSIT tags a home for high electrical consumption, upon entering the home, they search for evidence of violations of the Controlled Substances Property Bylaw. This "evidence" includes "unauthorized building modifications including electrical, plumbing, and mechanical system alterations, evidence of potting soil within the home, covered over windows, plant remnants, excessive soil remnants, and excessive mould/moisture damage."[68] The criteria for "evidence" is so broad that any homeowner in British Columbia can be deemed as having evidence of a grow operation in his or her home. As we complete this book, in 2013, the outcome of the class action lawsuit is still pending. Moreover, it was not until residents began to challenge these bylaws and safety inspection practices that more media stories began to appear covering these concerns.

Medical Marijuana and Organized Crime Claims

Now that BC citizens are organizing against municipal bylaws, and court decisions are ruling in their favour, a variety of institutional actors including BC fire chiefs, the RCMP, politicians, and Health Canada are setting their sights on legal medical marijuana gardens. Spokespeople for these institutions refer to medical cannabis gardens as "grow sites" and "grow ops," the same terms used to describe illegal marijuana-cultivation operations. The 2009 RCMP report, *Illicit Drug Situation in Canada*, claims that the Marihuana (sic) Medical Access Regulations (MMAR) are susceptible to exploitation by drug-trafficking organizations (DTOs).[69] In January 2009, Surrey Fire Chief Len Garis, a leading proponent of police Green Teams and harsher sentencing for marijuana cultivation, proclaimed that legal medical marijuana grow ops are prone to bad wiring that leads to fires. He argued that the addresses of growers of legal medical marijuana should be made available to "fire and electrical inspectors, especially if they are located in residential areas." These institutional spokespeople are part of an emerging trend to represent legal marijuana gardens as a threat to the public health and safety of their communities.[70]

It has long been acknowledged that marijuana has medicinal qualities that provide relief for a number of serous illnesses such as chronic pain, glaucoma, AIDS-related symptoms, seizures from epilepsy, and arthritis.[71] Marijuana is also one of the oldest known drugs and was used for medicinal purposes for thousands of years; however, it was not until the mid-nineteenth century that Western doctors began to prescribe it to their patients and wrote about its healing qualities.[72] Modern companies like GW Pharmaceuticals have developed and patented cannabis-based medicines now available by prescription in Canada for the treatment of MS-related symptoms and chronic pain.[73] As mentioned earlier, Canada criminalized marijuana in 1922 with no parliamentary debate, and as a consequence, the plant was no longer legally available for medicinal or recreational use. It was not until the 1960s, when marijuana became popular among youth and the counter-culture movement that questions about its medicinal properties began to arise again. In the late 1980s, activists and people living with HIV/AIDs in San Francisco, California, opened the first medical marijuana dispensaries.[74] These initiatives provided patients suffering from HIV/AIDS with "a safe source" of marijuana.[75] In 1996, Proposition 215 was passed in California, and legal medical marijuana dispensaries were opened throughout the state. Since then, a total of 20 US states (including California) and the District of Columbia have passed medical marijuana legislation, although, as discussed earlier, there has been an ongoing conflict between federal and state law in the United States. The US federal government and the DEA deny that cannabis has medical benefits and defy state law that has legalized medical marijuana; thus, legal medical marijuana users and suppliers are vulnerable to arrest by the DEA. However, in a groundbreaking statement in August 2013, the US Justice Department announced that it will allow states to implement their ballot initiatives to have legalized medical marijuana programs.

Like the early underground dispensaries in San Francisco, the compassion clubs in Canada provide holistic services and a safe supply of marijuana to registered patients.[76] Without a legal mandate, in 1997, Vancouver's BC Compassion Club Society (BCCCS) opened its doors. This club provides six to 12 strains of organic cannabis a day; its services also include a wellness centre providing acupuncture, counselling, nutritional advice, herbal medicine, massage therapy, and yoga at subsidized rates, including a sliding fee scale. Other compassion clubs and societies have opened in Canadian cities such as Toronto and Victoria.

Meanwhile, in response to an Ontario Court of Appeal's decision on the constitutional validity of prohibiting cannabis possession,[77] the Government of Canada initiated a medical marijuana program. However, it was not until 2001 that Health Canada created the Marihuana[78] Medical Access Division (formerly known as the Office of Cannabis Medical Access) to act as the governing body overseeing the implementation of the Marihuana Medical Access Regulations. It recognizes that marijuana is an appropriate medication for many symptoms associated with serious illnesses and that physicians are qualified to approve applications from patients for its use. However, authorized medical marijuana users did not have access to a legal supply of the plant – the growing and dispensing of marijuana for medical purposes remained illegal – and the wait time for approving applications was long. On 9 January 2003, an Ontario Supreme Court ruling stemming from a lawsuit initiated by medical marijuana users and suppliers "upheld the right for patients to have access to a safe, legal source of cannabis" and once again found the federal program unconstitutional for creating what provincial judge Lederman called the "illusion of access."'[79] The court gave the government until 9 July of the same year to recommend a legal supplier for medical users authorized under the Marihuana Medical Access Regulations.[80] Following this case, Health Canada authorized

Prairie Plant Systems (PPS) to grow marijuana in Flin Flon, Manitoba. Federally authorized and registered medical marijuana patients could purchase the dried plant from PPS via mail order.

In 2006, the federal Medical Marihuana Access Program initiated regulations that permit medical marijuana users to grow small amounts of marijuana themselves for medicinal use.[81] In recognition that seriously ill people may not be able to grow their own marijuana and that many people live in apartments and urban dwellings that are not conducive to growing the plant, Health Canada has made licences available to designated growers for people who hold an authorization to possess medical marijuana. The application process for growers is onerous and complicated; the formula to determine how many plants and how much marijuana can be grown and stored is particularly complex.

In 2009, Health Canada reported that 2,822 people were licensed to cultivate their own marijuana for medical purposes, although they may not have been actively growing their own supply at that time. During this same period, 754 people were designated growers for medical marijuana patients. In 2012, 21,986 people held an authorization to possess dried marijuana under the MMAR in Canada, yet only 13 per cent of these people had accessed dried marijuana from the federal marijuana source, Prairie Plants Systems. Thus, we can speculate that more than 85 per cent of licensed medical marijuana users obtain their cannabis from the illegal market, community-based dispensaries, or produce or grow their own medicine.[82] Although federally registered medical marijuana users could legally apply to purchase the dried plant from Prairie Plants System, the cumbersome application process, ongoing quality and safety concerns, limited choice of strains, and lack of alternate methods of ingestion such as edibles and tinctures has discouraged users from purchasing the PPS cannabis product. Canada's compassion clubs, on the other hand, provide safe, affordable, and often organically cultivated marijuana from diverse strains and using various methods of ingestion (i.e., sprays and cookies for those who cannot tolerate smoking marijuana) to an estimated "11,000 critically and chronically ill Canadians."[83] Feedback from patients suggests that the quality of the marijuana offered at compassion clubs far exceeds the medical marijuana offered by the federal government. In addition, dispensaries have been involved with or have initiated community-based research projects on the use of medical cannabis that have both empowered patients through knowledge creation and informed the medical, scientific community and policy makers about the potential benefits of community-based access and medical cannabis use in general.[84]

Until recently, politicians and the media had little to say about legal medical marijuana-growing gardens. The Canadian population at large has been overwhelmingly supportive of legal medical marijuana programs.[85] In addition, the courts have ruled – numerous times – that safe, affordable, legal marijuana should be available to medical marijuana patients in Canada.[86]

Some municipalities have, nevertheless, begun to challenge the way that medical marijuana is regulated. In 2011, the mayors of the City of Langley and the Township of Langley, BC, wrote to federal Minister of Health Leona Aglukkaq to advocate for changes to federal medical marijuana policy. In their letter, the mayors contend that current individual licences to grow marijuana should be cancelled and that any "medicinal marijuana would in the future be dispensed through licensed pharmacies by doctor's prescriptions ... and that marijuana that is dispensed be grown at a government regulated facility."[87]

The mayors' claim that the size of legal medical marijuana grow ops and the number of plants grown is "out of control," and they assert it can result in "home invasions, and other criminal related activity." They claim that the residential homes where legal medical marijuana is grown place residents at risk and "may cause long term health risks."[88] They declare that neighbourhoods "have become unsafe, individual lives have been at risk"; thus, they argue, changes in regulation are required. Similar to news media claims about the risks associated with marijuana grow ops, both mayors fail to substantiate or provide evidence in their letter to the minister of health to support their claims (see Figure 5.6).

The mayor of Surrey, Dianne Watts, a leading proponent of civil bylaws to identify and fine "recreational" marijuana growers, forwarded a resolution to the Federation of Canadian Municipalities (FCM), in June 2011, asking Health Canada to require applicants for growing medical marijuana to first obtain municipal permits; this resolution was passed. The City of Surrey also endorsed a new bylaw requiring municipal permits for those growing or using medical marijuana. The bylaw states that medical marijuana can only be grown in agriculturally zoned areas.[89]

Not all mayors or city councillors, however, agree with the mayors of Langley and Surrey. In response to the Langley mayors' letter to the minister of health, Grand Forks, BC, City Councillor Joy Davies expressed her concerns about their call for changes in regulation. Joy Davies uses medical marijuana to help moderate chronic pain from fibromyalgia,

Figure 5.6. Headline Box: Medical Marijuana.[90]

HEADLINES: MEDICAL MARIJUANA

Medical pot farm busted: Plants destroyed as compassion club leaders met with Allan Rock (2001)

Homegrown: This grow-op is legal, but its time may be running out. New federal rules will restrict users of medical marijuana to one supplier, in a mine deep underground in Manitoba. Pot fans aren't happy (2001)

Ottawa to ease rules for medical marijuana (2005)

Medical pot grower challenges law (2006)

Victoria mayor offers support to medical pot users (2006)

Ottawa must loosen medical pot rules, lawyers argue (2007)

Legal marijuana alternatives to go up in smoke: Plans to make Health Canada only purveyor of medical pot discomfit "compassion clubs" (2007)

Feds try to spark change in pot laws: Medical-marijuana users forced to rely on the black market (2008)

Compassion club seeks expansion: Nanaimo group hopes to secure a downtown location to provide marijuana to medical users across the region (2008)

Scrutiny for medical marijuana sites: Council asks where legal pot is grown to ensure homes properly modified (2009)

BC's top fire chief wants to end pot secrecy: Municipalities need to play a role in regulating legal marijuana-growing operations in residential areas, head of Fire Chiefs Association says (2009)

Medical marijuana restrictions get thumbs-down: Federal laws governing supply are ruled unconstitutional (2009)

Court loosens restrictions on medical marijuana (2009)

---

and she has received a licence from Health Canada to grow medical marijuana. She says that the information provided in the letter by the Langley mayors is not accurate, and their faulty claims will only hurt vulnerable and sick medical marijuana users. She notes that cancelling licences for legally growing medical marijuana can have negative consequences; people who need marijuana for medical purposes will not have safe and affordable access to the plant. Davies also does not believe that cancelling individual grow licences will deter crime.[91]

On 17 June 2011, Health Canada announced that it was considering improvements to the Medical Marihuana Access Program, and it launched the "Consultation of Proposed Improvements to the Marihuana Medical Access Program." Its website states that the proposed improvements are "in response to concerns heard from Canadians." Typical of news media claims, no evidence is provided to substantiate how many Canadians or what groups of people have "concerns" about the medical marijuana program.[92] The website includes a list of the concerns that support the government's call for changes in the program including "the risk of abuse and exploitation by criminal elements" and "public health and safety risks associated with the cultivation of marihuana plants in homes, including electrical and fire hazards and the presence of excess mould and poor air quality."[93] At the end of their list, Health Canada declares that "the proposed improvements would reduce the risk of abuse and exploitation by criminal elements and keep our children and communities safe."[94]

The proposed new medical cannabis access regulations were released for comment in late 2012. On 10 June 2013, citing public safety and security concerns about growing marijuana in homes, the minister of health released the new regulations that will govern access to cannabis for medical purposes in Canada.[95] The current regulations (MMAR) will be repealed on 31 March 2014. The new regulations, which come into effect on 1 April 2014, reflect some improvements in the programs – patients do not have to apply to Health Canada (nor fill out the lengthy and confusing application form) but can obtain permits to use medical cannabis from qualified prescribers including physicians and nurse practitioners. However, physicians and medical associations in Canada have made it clear that they are "resistant" to prescribing medicinal marijuana to their patients.[96] In addition, the effects of some of the claims making about marijuana cultivation are evident in these new rules. For example, the new regulations eliminate the personal licences (for individual and designated growers) to produce marijuana for medical purposes in homes. In addition, Health Canada will no longer produce or distribute marijuana. Instead, licensed commercial producers will dispense dried marijuana by courier.[97] This regulation also leaves medical cannabis dispensaries out of the distribution loop, sanctions free-market production, and may limit patient access to specific strains of marijuana (and tinctures and edibles). The omission of medical cannabis dispensaries reflects the federal government's failure to recognize the expertise about medical cannabis use available through these dispensaries. The proposed regulations admit that the cost of medical cannabis will increase significantly. These cost increases will be another hardship for patients as medical cannabis is not covered by provincial drug programs unlike other substances used for medical purposes. By removing personal licences to grow marijuana, patients are vulnerable to market prices and may be denied access to strains of cannabis they have developed that work best to alleviate their symptoms.

The safety of personal legal cannabis production sites could be easily corrected by having better guidelines, education, and monitoring of these outdoor and indoor gardens. It seems quite hypocritical to focus on safety when Canadians throughout the country have unmonitored greenhouses and outdoor gardens for other produce. In addition, given the chemicals and pesticides used for industrial food production, the focus on legal cannabis growers seems misguided and influenced by a small and vocal group of critics, rather than by the needs and constitutional rights of critically and chronically ill Canadians who could benefit from the medical use of cannabis.

Health Canada's claims that medical marijuana production sites are associated with "criminal elements" and endanger the "safety of children" suggest that the changes to the MMAR are politically motivated. There is no comprehensive scholarly and peer-reviewed research to support claims that legal medical marijuana sites are linked to criminal elements or pose safety hazards to children (see chapter 6 for a fuller examination of this topic).[98] Significantly, long-time, leading compassion club experts (BC Compassion Club Society and Vancouver Island Compassion Society), note that non-violent, peaceful, mom-and-pop growers are the norm. In all of their collective years working with compassion clubs and marijuana growers, including those who supply the clubs, not one gun or violent encounter has occurred.[99] The Canadian Association of Medical Cannabis Dispensers (CAMCD), a non-profit organization that supports the establishment of "legally permitted community-based medical cannabis dispensaries providing access to a wide range of high quality cannabis medicines to those in need and regulated in a manner consistent with the highest standard of patient care," also makes clear that compassion clubs are sites that

value compassion, harm reduction services, empowerment, dignity, affordability, and integrity.[100]

A series of policy moves including some of the changes to the MMAR,
the present federal Conservative government's National Anti-Drug
Strategy, and its resistance to moving forward on the recommendations
laid out in the *Report of the Senate Special Committee on Illegal Drugs* suggest that claims makers such as the police/RCMP are, again, the key
players shaping drug policy in Canada. This is a disappointment given
the growing body of science and social science research that recognizes
marijuana as beneficial for the relief of symptoms from many serious
diseases.[101]

Conclusion

Despite efforts by residents in Surrey and Mission, British Columbia,
to resist the regulation of marijuana cultivation by local governments,
newspaper coverage has created a persistent and resilient framework
for understanding the dangers of grow ops. Newspaper coverage has
effectively shaped perceptions that all grow ops are spaces where criminality is linked with specific public safety risks that bring issues like
fire, mould, and other property damage to unsuspecting safe neighbourhoods and innocent home buyers. It has, in turn, naturalized the
involvement of a new set of experts – fire departments, as well as real
estate and insurance company representatives, who define the problem
of grow ops. This coverage has drawn on police, fire department, and
other institutional spokespeople such as BC Hydro to make the link
between generalized threats to public safety and grow ops. Initiatives
such as Surrey's Electrical Fire and Safety Initiative draw on municipal
bylaws to compel city residents suspected (but not proven) of operating grow ops to undergo (and pay for) electrical inspections under
the auspices of municipal bylaws. The implementation of these initiatives, as well as bylaws to force landlords to keep tabs on their rental
properties, have been supported by the efforts of key claims makers.
By focusing on public safety in relation to marijuana grow ops, local
municipalities have been able to bypass foundational legal safeguards
and principles related to issues like the presumption of innocence and
warrantless entry.

The implementation of municipal initiatives and bylaws to curtail
marijuana grow ops widens the net of surveillance and regulation of

what is normally defined as criminal justice regulation. This widening net of surveillance and regulation includes the increased identification and punishment of individuals, homes, businesses, and any space suspected of housing marijuana grow ops or selling equipment for cultivation. As described above, multi-agency initiatives to identify, regulate, and curtail marijuana grow ops include police/RCMP, BC Hydro, fire departments, and electrical inspectors. This multitude of institutional players work with and overlap with traditional criminal justice in their quest to manage marijuana grow ops and, of course, the people suspected of being responsible for these operations. Municipal councils may feel "emboldened" to enact bylaws to restrict marijuana grow operations given that these institutional players officially advocate for them publicly in and outside of British Columbia with little regard for individuals' Charter rights.[102]

Ultimately, it is people, not grow ops that carry the regulatory brunt of these new municipal initiatives. As the Mission residents make clear in their class action lawsuit, they were expected to pay the price of having their home inspected, regardless of whether or not a grow op was found. Significantly, residents assert that marijuana grow ops are rarely found and that PSIT inspections and the bylaws to regulate them are unconstitutional and unlawful. Mould, moisture damage, potted soil, covered windows, electrical modifications, etc. are all treated as violations of the Controlled Substances Property Bylaw and as evidence of a marijuana grow op. The criteria are so broad that any home in British Columbia could easily be viewed as having "evidence" of a marijuana grow op. Regardless of these facts, the inspections continue in many BC municipalities, and reports from vocal spokespeople that hail the success of inspection teams do not reveal how broad the criteria for evidence are, nor how suspect the inspections are.[103] These programs pose serious questions about the public accountability of such multipartner initiatives, as well as the de facto extension of the enforcement of Canada's Criminal Code to municipalities, including fire departments. At the same time, these municipal programs represent a trend towards the proliferation of enforcement strategies aimed at the production of cannabis. For example, in March 2012, Alberta Specialized Law Enforcement Training (ASLET) with the Calgary Police Service and City of Calgary (Building Regulations) hosted a three-day "War on Grow Ops Conference" in Banff, Alberta. Conference sessions included topics such as theft of power; fire cases; drug-endangered children; authorities, permits, laws; medical marijuana; civil forfeiture; and real estate.

Inspection teams, RCMP, and BC Hydro who search for evidence of grow ops, also create and distribute tip sheets to encourage individual residents to spy on their neighbours and become police informants. In this new world, we all become complicit, then, in spying, informing, regulating, and ultimately, punishing individuals suspected of participating in an activity that is deemed a public safety risk to otherwise innocent neighbours – growing marijuana. Yet the number of individual people who have suffered through inspections because they were suspected of cultivating marijuana is growing, and until the recent class action lawsuit in Mission, their voices were rendered inaudible. These bylaws and other municipal and private initiatives target individual homeowners and operate outside the normal legal frameworks and checks and balances of criminal justice and the Charter (innocent until proven guilty, warrants to enter homes). Residents suspect that they are being targeted by inspection teams and that "imaginary grow ops" are driving municipalities to enact bylaws that fill their pockets as they collect inspection fees. It is difficult to understand how cities can contravene Charter rights and damage the reputations of homeowners and the value of their homes without recourse. The role of the media, law enforcement agents, and vocal spokespeople in shaping negative discourse about marijuana grow ops cannot be ignored.

It is debatable whether or not these municipal bylaws would have been enacted and implemented if the media had not already informed Canadians repeatedly, over many years, that grow ops are the domain of organized crime and a threat to public safety. The residents targeted by the municipalities were already viewed with prejudice. The Mission class action lawsuit counters the proliferation of misinformation produced by the media, city councils, police, and vocal spokespeople about marijuana grow ops. In this sense, a counter-discourse is emerging and challenging civil initiatives in British Columbia.

Recent amendments to the Controlled Drugs and Substances Act under the Safe Streets and Communities Act passed into law in 2012. The Act increases the maximum penalty for marijuana production from 7 to 14 years and establishes new mandatory minimum penalties to a range of drug offences. The production of more than five marijuana plants warrants a 6-month mandatory minimum sentence. Legal critics note that broadly defined aggravating factors such as growing marijuana in a rental property (or on property other than one's own) is more "likely to adversely affect poor people" who rent rather than own their homes.[104] Evidence that these claims about public safety have been effective are reflected by the addition of "potential public safety hazards in a residential area" as an aggravating factor in the revised CDSA.

6 Using Children to Promote Increased Regulation: The Representation and Regulation of Children Found at Grow Ops

Mountie Wants Parents Punished for Raising Children in a Grow-Op

Paul Nadeau, who heads the RCMP Co-ordinated Marijuana Enforcement Team, said keeping kids in a grow-op should lead to stiffer sentences for adults involved. "If we convict someone in a grow-op, and kids are in the house, whether it's his kids or someone else's, that should be taken under consideration by the judge who's sentencing," Nadeau said Friday ...

Darryl Plecas, a criminologist at the University of the Fraser Valley who heads BC's new Cent re for Criminal Justice Research, agrees that stiffer jail sentences would act as a deterrent to criminals.

"I'm amazed that the courts haven't taken an extremely strong stance," he said. "I would really question the ability of somebody to be considered an appropriate parent if they're placing their kids in that kind of situation."[1]

As the 2005 news article above demonstrates, one of the most pernicious claims made in newspapers is the oft-repeated notion that children are "found" in grow ops and their parents are unfit and criminal. In this chapter, we discuss and problematize the contentious claims made about this phenomenon: fitness to parent and the dangers to children posed by drug production. Parents of children discovered on the site of marijuana grow ops are deemed to be unfit parents and their children are seen as "at risk." Indeed, legislative changes have been proposed and implemented in British Columbia and Alberta to address this supposed problem. We locate this discussion in the increasing number of critical analyses that challenge the moralizing discourses about fitness to parent and risk environments, and the role these naturalized claims play in constructing the dangers of drugs.

Setting the Scene

In her 2005 book, *Tending the Gardens of Citizenship: Child Saving in Toronto, 1880s–1920s*, Xiaobei Chen includes a picture of a poster from the National Archives of Canada depicting head shots of a hundred or more young babies sitting inside a wooden fruit basket labelled "Our Best Crop." She notes that for most early welfare reformers, "the habitat for children, like the garden for plants, referred to where children lived, rather than broader social, economic and political structures." Undesirable spaces, such as slum streets and homes, were seen as "detrimental to children's character"[2] – thus, the slum home became the centre of reformers' energy. In contrast to slum homes, good homes were regarded as "fundamental" to making good citizens.[3] Child savers had little hope for the parents of poor children. Instead, they advocated separating children from deviant parents and toxic environments in order to avoid negative influences. Drawing on the gardening analogy, child savers believed that children could grow into productive citizens if tended properly. To illustrate how children could be cultivated to be good instead of evil, gardening imagery was used in posters to educate the public.

Whereas in the late 1880s and early 1900s, child savers viewed slum homes as potentially evil, today more affluent homes are increasingly coming to the attention of social workers. Children who live in or near marijuana grow ops are considered by social workers to be at risk for numerous evils. Homes with gardens where illicit substances are grown are certainly not regarded as appropriate contexts for good parenting and positive child rearing. Rather, domestic marijuana cultivation is depicted as a dangerous environment for children. Although a number of vocal claims makers in Canada (and the United States) have contributed to the perception of marijuana grow ops as a social problem, some of the most pernicious of these claims are directed at the racialized parents of children discovered living near or in a residence or other building containing a marijuana grow op. As we will see, in British Columbia, some members of the press and some researchers portray Vietnamese families as central to marijuana grow ops.

As we noted in earlier chapters, since the mid-1990s, vocal claims makers, including the media, representatives of firefighters, and the RCMP have used their substantial public communication resources in the form of policy directives and press releases to emphasize that

Figure 6.1. Headline Box: Children in Grow Ops.[4]

HEADLINES: CHILDREN IN GROW OPS

40 kids seized in war on drugs: In most of the cases the children are from Vietnamese families (2000)

Raids not kidding: While police swoop on grow-op homes, Ministry of Children pulls in seven kids (2000)

Grow-op parents risk losing kids (2000)

Seizing grow-operators' kids "destructive" (2001)

43 kids caught in middle of national grow-op raids: Children taken from homes as 73,000 plants pulled in 7 days (2002)

Pot raid yields 500 plants, two children (2004)

Ont. targets grow-ops, child porn (2004)

Cops find kids being kept in drug houses: Police outrage – baby found in drug bust (2005)

Infant taken from grow-op: Police investigating home invasion find 984 plants (2006)

Kids in grow-ops at risk (2006)

New Alberta law targets children exposed to drugs (2006)

Asian child slaves found in grow-ops around UK (2007)

Vancouver: Tots found in grow-ops (2007)

Children removed after grow-op found: 1,200 plants seized from basement (2009)

RCMP busts grow-op at daycare home (2009)

---

marijuana grow ops are a new social problem that requires increased public awareness, law enforcement, and legal and civil regulation. These law enforcement and municipal perspectives and concerns are regularly featured in national, provincial, and municipal newspaper articles. Since the early 2000s, these same media outlets have printed numerous articles about children in grow ops, especially in Alberta and British Columbia.

Of the 237 thematic codes that emerged from the analyses of the news articles for this project, children and health risks emerged as a prominent theme in the early 2000s. Of the 2,524 articles in our study,

101 (4%) focused almost exclusively on the issue of children (61, or 2.4%) or included mention of children in a larger article devoted to the topic of grow ops (40, or 1.58%). Of the 61 stories devoted exclusively to the topic of children in grow ops, most offer a similar perspective. With the exception of three articles, the issue of children living in or near a house with a grow up is discussed exclusively in negative terms. The majority of these articles draw on law enforcement spokespeople, and consistently overlap concerns about children with the concerns about the potential dangers of grow ops in relation to the presence of dangerous equipment, possibility of fire, mould, theft of hydro, electrocution, presence of weapons, and the possibility of violence because of burglaries and turf wars between organized crime groups. In addition, many of these articles racialize the parents of these children as Others. Similar to the earlier chapters, the analysis that follows draws on examples representative of these overall findings (see Figure 6.1).

Theoretical Framework

In this chapter, we draw extensively from feminist scholars who demonstrate how drug policy is gendered, racialized, and class based and who focus on the intersection of the regulation of women, reproduction, mothering, and the war on drugs. These scholars have been particularly adept at showing how representations of drug use and parenting focus primarily on poor and racialized parents, especially mothers. These women are sensationalized as immoral, unfit, and drug using, and in turn, used by the news media and politicians to sell newspapers and shape policy.[5] Critical race and feminist scholars show how these representations racialize the "good" white citizen as law abiding and non–drug using, in opposition to "Others" constructed as deviant, drug using, and degraded.[6]

Although there is a long history of media fascination with the children of women who use drugs and alcohol, since the 1990s, the media have also focused on children found on drug-*manufacturing* sites. Print media and other texts have introduced and contextualized the intersection of marijuana production and children as a social "problem" so terrible that it requires attention from all levels of government, enforcement agencies, and other groups. These media stories reveal how the intersection of race/ethnicity, gender, class, and culture shape a discourse that interweaves Canadian federal and provincial illicit drug policy with child protection concerns. These same news articles and texts have introduced and expanded both the scope of these issues and

notions about the appropriate modes of formal and informal regulation of these "problems."[7] News stories about marijuana grow ops
reflect particularly masculinized gendered themes, thus, the insights
of feminist studies about illegal drug use and parenting are relevant.
These studies focus on not only the gendered effects of claims about
substance use and mothering, but also on the racialized and class-based
components of these claims. We draw from these insights in feminist
scholarship to explore these same themes in Canadian newspapers.

Children at Risk

Assumptions about the dangers posed by the intersection of drug use
and parenting are not new. As early as the 1700s and 1800s, moral reformers condemned poor parents who drank distilled alcohol during
the "gin craze" in Britain. Gin consumption was blamed for poor health,
social decay, and immorality.[8] The temperance movement of the late
1800s and early 1900s also shaped opinion and policy regarding children in homes where alcohol was being consumed. Many early child
savers and temperance reformers diagnosed social inequities as fail-
ures of individual will and often focused on protecting children from
violent fathers who drank too much. Alcohol use, rather than the conditions of a rapidly expanding industrial and urbanized society, was
thought to cause poverty. Moral reformers thus positioned themselves
as defenders of the home, community, and nation.[9] The concerns of social reformers were also spatialized – slum homes, the saloon, and poor
neighbourhoods were identified as potential sites of immorality that
could place children in danger.[10] Similar concerns were voiced by anti-
opiate reformers of the time; they claimed that opium dens were sites of
immorality and corruption, where racialized men trafficked drugs and
enslaved innocent white men and women, placing the family and children (as well as the nation) at risk.[11] Although both men and women are
parents, the surveillance of poor mothers and the assessment of proper
female behaviour, especially maternal fitness, was central to early child
savers' efforts in Western nations.[12] The apprehension of children from
their parents by the state and other organizations became one of the
most powerful tools that social workers would wield over women and
families in the twentieth century and beyond.[13]

Temperance ideology and child apprehension practices still shape
child welfare policy. Following the criminalization of specific drugs like
heroin, cocaine, and marijuana in the early 1900s, social service agencies

sought to regulate mothers suspected of using these drugs. Studies conducted of heroin users in the 1950s in British Columbia illustrate that very few mothers who used these drugs were able to maintain custody of their children.[14] Social workers equated illegal drug use with unfit parenting. In the late 1950s and early 1960s, medical and legal professionals also identified maternal drug use as a risk to the developing fetus, and new ideologies about "dangerous" drug-using mothers emerged alongside new technologies (such as drug testing) and policy to regulate and punish mothers.[15] Contemporary child welfare policies also regulate the lives of mothers suspected of illegal drug use.[16]

Since the 1960s, concerns about maternal fitness have been broadened to include a host of risks to the developing fetus. In the 1980s, moral reformers and media reports in the United States focused on "out of control" crack mothers and their supposedly damaged infants. These reports reflected law-and-order sentiments and proposed criminal and civil sanctions, as well as child neglect and abuse statutes, to regulate substance-using mothers and pregnant women. Feminist researchers have shown how the press, prosecutors, and social work and medical professionals depict pregnant women as dangerous to the fetus and their children.[17] Drew Humphries,[18] for example, examined US media reports on crack and pregnancy in national television news reports between 1983 and 1994. During this period, news media reports claimed that women who used cocaine were unfit mothers and were producing a generation of crack babies who were permanently damaged and who would become future criminals and a drain on city and federal services. Mothers suspected of using crack were represented as abandoning their children for the local crack house. Media reports generally portrayed these "unfit mothers" as poor, Black, urban, and sexually immoral.[19]

As US researchers Lynn Paltrow and Jeanne Flavin observe, "at a time when evidence existed that there was no such thing as 'crack babies' and that poverty explained many of the health problems that some children were experiencing, *Time* magazine, *The New York Times*, and other leading news outlets continued to describe cocaine use during pregnancy as an epidemic destroying a generation of young people."[20] Following these claims, punitive child welfare policy and criminal law was initiated to punish pregnant women and mothers suspected of illegal drug use. Although drug use surveys note that white, Black, and Hispanic women have similar rates of drug use, social services and criminal regulation of women suspected of illegal drugs use falls on poor and racialized women.[21] Similarly, media representations of out-of-control mothers most often feature poor, racialized women. Prosecutors in the United States have charged women suspected of using illegal drugs with a criminal offence, such as "trafficking to the fetus," and civil child welfare and abuse statutes have been amended to respond to suspected maternal drug use and parents who are thought to be using illegal drugs. In a number of US states, drug testing of welfare recipients is routine. In addition, women have been tested without their consent in public hospitals when they come to deliver their children. Due to changes in federal welfare policy, civil child abuse statutes, and criminal child abuse laws, thousands of children have been apprehended by the state and placed in foster care.[22] Since the late 1990s, media reports in both Canada and the United States have focused with increased intensity on children found in drug-manufacturing sites. These reports typically emphasize the health risks and other assumed dangers related to these environments.

In Canada, the restructuring of welfare benefits in 1996 led to cutbacks, limits on eligibility, workfare programs, and increased surveillance of women.[23] The end of the Canada Assistance Program meant that Canadian provinces could create their own criteria for social assistance and refuse aid to people regardless of financial need. This period of cutbacks ushered in a renewed era of scrutiny of women's habits, especially women with children who were receiving social assistance. In the 1990s, former Ontario Premier Mike Harris defended punitive cutbacks and intrusive welfare policy by stating that all women on welfare were drug users. He also asserted that women who refused drug treatment would lose their benefits.[24] These claims illustrate the kinds of misconceptions that prevail about women who receive welfare benefits, and echo similar misinformation about drug use and parenting. These claims also reflect the emergence of a heightened level of scrutiny of any relationship between illicit drugs and parenting. It is in this context that social workers and law enforcement agencies have begun to regard marijuana grow ops as uniquely dangerous sites that must be eradicated.

Marijuana Grow Ops

Media reports analysed in this chapter, and throughout the book, typically suggest that residential and other forms of marijuana production represent a major social problem that serves as a key causal factor in drug consumption, organized crime, violence, and risk to families and communities. Newspaper reporting draws on law enforcement reports and spokespeople as key sources of information. As a consequence, media reports echo law enforcement claims that marijuana grow ops are dangerous, increasingly sophisticated, increasing in size and number, pose substantial threats to public safety in terms of fire, steal electricity, and are primarily linked to organized crime. As mentioned in earlier chapters, in its efforts to curb marijuana production, law enforcement focuses primarily on indoor cultivation, particularly in residential neighbourhoods. BC police forces have demanded and received additional resources to support "green teams" like Growbusters. In Vancouver, public awareness campaigns and Crime Stoppers, and a tip line that can be used to report marijuana grow ops, have also been initiated.

Media Representations of Children in Grow Ops

Although media reportage about marijuana grow ops has risen steadily since 1996, until the early 2000s there was little reporting about children found in these sites. In March 2000, this reporting significantly increased at the same time as a coordinated law enforcement effort to shut down these operations occurred. In March 2000, 40 children were apprehended during marijuana raids in British Columbia; of these children, it was reported that all but four were Vietnamese [25] In the press releases and news articles that accompanied the busts, police and RCMP claimed that marijuana grow ops were the domain of foreigners, motorcycle gangs, and organized crime. These articles also introduced a connection between concerns about public safety and the supposed health effects on children living at these sites.

A 2002 *Globe and Mail* article highlights emerging claims about marijuana grow ops and children and the intersecting discourses of safety, health, and risk. The article, entitled "Pot farms conceal deadly risks: Hydro stolen to run the hydroponic labs has led to fires and fears of electrocution," states that "bags of marijuana plants were hauled out of the unassuming brick house, people who live nearby were still shocked to learn a drug lab had been established on their quiet central Toronto street."[26] The article suggests that the growers of marijuana were stealing power from hydro lines for their operation, allegedly a common practice by growers who have "popped up in homes across Canada, as organized crime rings look to expand beyond the overcrowded Vancouver area."[27] The superintendent of the Peel Regional Police stated, "This is big business. It's driven by money and profit and the profit is huge." The same article claims that the police estimate that there are as many as 10,000 hydroponic marijuana grow ops in southern Ontario, a $12 million industry fuelling violence, as greedy profit-driven criminals expand their enterprises. The reporter contends:

> most are not "mom-and-pop" operations ... the mix of water, electricity and fertilizer could pose a deadly risk for unsuspecting neighbours. The scenario that disturbs police is a small child running into a nearby yard after a heavy rain. There's a live bypass cut into the underground hydro line and the child is electrocuted.[28]

In response to these concerns, the author reports, "Crown attorneys are asking for stiffer sentences. Politicians are considering tougher laws. Children's Aid agents are taking children away from parents who live in the grow houses."[29] This article is typical in that it expands the domain of the problem of grow ops to include surrounding neighbours, and it evokes images of innocent children harmed by the actions of thoughtless, criminal, and greedy grow operators.

Another news article, in the *Province* in 2002, highlights discourse related to risk, health, and safety linked to marijuana grow ops and children that are prevalent in media reportage. Entitled "43 kids caught in middle of national grow-op raids: Children taken from homes as 73,000 plants pulled in 7 days,"[30] the article begins with the claim, "Infants and children are the latest victims in the marijuana grow-op industry." Inspector Kash Heed, head of the Vancouver Police Department's drug unit, is quoted as saying, "Frequently we find young children in these operations ... Children are exposed to mould spores, carbon monoxide, pesticides, carbon dioxide, ozone exposure and electrocution ... Children's Hospital has reported an increase in respiratory problems that they believe is due to grow-ops." Heed states that the 43 children found at the grow ops were "turned over to social services or other family members." Heed's claims reiterate familiar themes in drug discourses that typically depict drug use either as already epidemic or potentially on the rise, and he uses the issue of children found at grow ops to expand on the idea that the marijuana trade is invading suburban space and bringing organized crime. He suggests that marijuana grow ops have both spread outside of British Columbia and are "moving to the suburbs and to Alberta and Ontario." He also asserts, "80 per cent of grow-ops are now controlled by organized crime, including outlaw motorcycle gangs and Asian-based crime organizations." Tim Shields

of the Surrey, BC, RCMP states in the article that police are finding mar-
ijuana-manufacturing labs in "brand-new, $400,000 homes customized
for grow-ops." He claims, "While the crime is extremely lucrative, the
punishment is small ... the vast majority are conditional sentences, no
jail time." Shields concludes that the RCMP believes "marijuana grow-
ops are a poison to our community."[31] Both Heed's and Shields' comments echo other familiar and panicked claims about drugs and their
inevitable entry into middle-class spaces.

A 2005 article in the *Province*, entitled "Mountie wants parents punished for raising children in grow-op,"[32] highlights a grow op found
by the BC Ridge Meadows RCMP Strike Force that included "four
Vietnamese adults and two boys, aged nine and 11." The article states,
"Twenty per cent of grow-ops busted by police have children living
there." Again, the key spokesperson in the article represented law enforcement; Inspector Paul Nadeau, head of the RCMP Co-ordinated
Marijuana Enforcement Team, stated, "Keeping kids in a grow-op
should lead to stiffer sentences for adults involved." Quotations from
Plecas are used to argue "that stiffer jail sentences would act as a deterrent to criminals. I'm amazed that the courts haven't taken an extremely strong stance ... I would really question the ability of somebody
to be considered an appropriate parent if they're placing their kids in
that kind of situation ... I don't see any harm whatever in taking their
kids away." Given the long record of abuse of children apprehended
by the state in British Columbia,[33] most recently raised by Mary El-
len Turpel-Lafond (the BC Representative for Children and Youth),
Plecas' comments about child apprehension and harm appear naive
and misinformed. "Naive" in thinking that the blunt instrument of
imprisonment will somehow stem the public demand for these drugs
and the ensuing profits. These comments also seem misinformed for
failing to consider what actually happens to children in government
care.[34]

This article is followed up by another in the *Province*, entitled "Cops
find kids being kept in drug houses: POLICE OUTRAGE – baby found
in drug bust."[35] This reporter again quotes Inspector Paul Nadeau of
the RCMP Co-ordinated Marijuana Enforcement Team: "It's absolutely
outrageous," he says, "that criminals are pulling (sic) their children
into dangerous situations."[36] The author, Lena Sin notes that Nadeau
claims that children found in these sites have "burn marks from touch-
ing grow-ops lights and many kids develop serious respiratory problems."[37] This article, too, draws on quotes from Plecas, "lead author of

the RCMP study of children found in grow-ops" to argue that "about 20 percent of the time, women are also involved. So as long as you have those factors, children could be involved."[38]

The assertions made by these two reporters and their informants reiterate claims about the number of children and the types of harms to children found in grow ops. Many of these claims, however, are unsubstantiated. For example, the RCMP study cited by the *Province*'s reporter Lena Sin does not exist. The RCMP has not commissioned a report on children in grow ops in Canada, and Plecas has not written a report on this subject. Rather, Plecas, Malm, and Kinney are the authors of the BC RCMP-commissioned 2005 paper, "Marijuana Growing Operations in British Columbia Revisited, 1997–2003."[39] As we noted in previous chapters, this paper is often referenced in news reporting in British Columbia, especially by police, politicians, and social workers. It is used to support demands for new child protection legislation and harsher drug laws for drug production and trafficking. Plecas et al. include about five sentences on children in their 56-page paper. They observe that most BC police records fail to note in their files the number of children present at grow ops, and they do not provide specifics about the children's living conditions.[40] This paper, however, does comment on potential health risks and public safety harms associated with indoor growing operations. The key claim made in this paper is that, in 2003, children were present in 21 per cent of marijuana grow ops in the City of Vancouver (this statistic is repeated on p. 23, p. 32, Table 3.6, and Appendix 1). No evidence is presented by Plecas et al. to support their claim, and it is difficult to know how many grow operations are included in their tally. The authors state that, in 2003, the RCMP and police in Vancouver recorded 335 cases of marijuana cultivation;[41] however, the authors do not provide the actual number of children present at these grow ops nor do they make clear if the 21 per cent figure is drawn from the sample of 335 cases or a smaller or larger sample. Readers are left to speculate. Reporters and spokespeople have extrapolated from this report to comment on the issue of children in grow ops throughout Canada, failing to reveal that their findings refer only to Vancouver in 2003.

Several news articles in BC papers uncritically describe a series of videos produced in Vancouver. The first of these public-education videos is entitled *Not Safe to Occupy: Growing Up in Grow-Ops*, produced with Chris Taulu of the Collingwood Community Policing Centre in East Vancouver. Taulu is quoted in a newspaper article as stating,

"Kids are breathing in dangerous black mould and chemicals and are at much-higher risk of electrocution and sudden fire." Taulu argues that children found at grow ops should not be cared for by their extended family and she warns, "The people you give [the child] to are also in grow-ops ... In many cases, the whole family is involved in it, so where on earth do you take them?"[42] The video includes a number of interviews with familiar spokespeople expanding on the harms of grow ops and risks to children. The video is produced by Boldfish Entertainment, a Vancouver-based company in conjunction with Chris Taulu with the help of the Public Education Society, LacViet FM 96.1, the NCPC/ CNPC, Growbusters, Vancouver Police Department, Janet Douglas with the BC Ministry of Children and Family Development, Fire and Rescue Services, City of Vancouver, Community Services, Electrical Inspection, and C. Van Nettlen with the Department of Health Care.[43]

The video begins with the following introduction: "Pesticides are toxic agents that can kill things, including children." The camera shifts to the message, "I love you Mom!" Viewers are given the option of watching the video in English or Vietnamese. The narrator of the video states that there are 7,000 marijuana grow ops run by organized crime in Vancouver, a city of 600,000 people. He claims the grow op business is booming and that most often houses containing grow ops appear to the outsider as "normal" residential homes. The camera shifts to Janet Douglas, the above-noted social worker. The narrator claims that an estimated 10,000 children are being raised in grow ops in Vancouver. In the video, spokespeople claim that grow ops present risks to children because they are "time bombs" of carbon dioxide, gas and propane leaks, black mould, fire and electrical hazards, toxic chemicals (pesticides, fertilizers), weapons, and the potential for violence because of "grow rips" (theft of marijuana plants) and organized crime.

In the video, the narrator states that, in 2002, 3,700 children were found in marijuana grow ops in Vancouver, and social workers were called to investigate by police "Growbuster" teams. The narrator and other spokespeople in the video emphasize that grow operators are motivated by profits, especially Vietnamese families who, they speculate, are addicted to gambling. Spokespeople in the video suggest that Vietnamese persons are forced into marijuana manufacturing by organized crime to pay for gambling and drug debts. These claims emphasize the "goodness" of concerned spokespeople by making it clear that the health of children should be more important than profit, at the same time as these claims reiterate the "badness" of those "willing to risk their future even their lives" by having grow ops in their homes. Furthermore, claims that there are "7,000" grow ops in Vancouver and "10,000" children on these sites are extrapolated fictions. These public-education videos include both English and Vietnamese language options (no other language options are included). The videos leave the impression that all Vietnamese families are potential criminals involved in gambling, marijuana production, and the drug trade. As Sunera Thobani observes, racialized families in Canada are constructed as inherently criminal outsiders who threaten white and supposedly moral citizens.[44]

Janet Douglas is also the author of a 2010 study, entitled *The Health and Safety of Children Living in Marijuana Grow Operations: A Child Welfare Perspective*. In this study, Douglas again, uncritically, references the Plecas et al.[45] paper, stating that the "majority of families involved in indoor marijuana grow operations in British Columbia are Vietnamese immigrants."[46] Douglas also references the Plecas et al.[47] paper following her claim that "children are estimated to be living in 21% of the grow operations in Vancouver, British Columbia."[48] These claims are problematic for a number of reasons. First, Plecas et al. point out in their paper that the majority of suspects found at grow ops (drawing from the data analysed in their study) are Caucasian males, although they note that there has been an increase in the number of Vietnamese suspects since 1997.[49] Table 4.1 in the Plecas et al. paper provides a breakdown of the ethnic group of suspects involved in the cultivation of marijuana.[50] Their Table 4.1 lists the "percentage of suspects from any minority ethnic group." In 1997, 6 per cent of suspects were identified in the Plecas et al. study as from a minority ethnic group; in 2000, the numbers rise quite dramatically, and 43 per cent of suspects are identified as from a minority ethnic group. Similar breakdowns are given for the years 2001, 2002, and 2003.[51] Appendix 2 in their paper includes a sample of the "suspect sheet" used to elicit data for the report. Ethnicity is listed and seven separate coding categories are provided: Caucasian, Oriental (except Vietnamese) (sic), East Indian, Black/African, Aboriginal, Other, and Vietnamese.[52] Although the sample "suspect sheet" provides separate coding categories for ethnicity, the report only makes the distinction between Caucasian and non-Caucasian. Plecas et al. claim that the number of Vietnamese suspects has grown over the years; however, no empirical data are provided in their paper to substantiate this claim. Instead, the statistics provided in relation to suspects involved in the cultivation of marijuana refer only to minority ethnic groups as a whole.[53] Contrary to Douglas' claim in her research study[54] that

Vietnamese immigrants make up the largest group of families involved in indoor grow ops, the Plecas et al. paper does not offer evidence to support this assertion. Furthermore, neither Plecas et al. nor Douglas problematize whether or not the increase in non-Caucasian cases is a reflection of police profiling. Nor do they problematize how both studies noted above racialize the operators of marijuana grow ops so that it appears that persons of Vietnamese descent are largely responsible not only for the increase in marijuana grow ops in Vancouver, but also for the increasing numbers of children found at these operations.

Although Janet Douglas has been a key spokesperson on the issue of grow ops and children, her comprehensive study noted above offers evidence that some of these concerns may be misplaced. Douglas examines reports of 95 grow ops involving 181 children in Vancouver and the Fraser Region who were reported to the BC Ministry of Children and Family Development for a 26-month period between 2004 and 2006.[55] Douglas observes that "there is a strong likelihood that grow operation families would be living in poverty without the income from their grow operation, so they may be balancing their ability to meet the material needs of their children against their involvement in criminal activity."[56]

Douglas contends that "the presence of mould, re-venting of gases, and the chemicals often found in grow operation homes means that resident children might well suffer from the ill effects of these environments, and could be expected to exhibit respiratory and/or dermatological ailments."[57] She examines BC PharmaNet prescription data for the children found in grow operations and compares this information with a random sample of 500 children. Her data showed "no significant difference between the grow operation children and the comparison children, with 65% of grow operation children having three or more of the above prescriptions, as compared to 72% of the comparison children who had three or more of the same categories of prescriptions."[58] So, in fact, the children from the comparison group were treated slightly more often for these ailments than children found in marijuana grow ops, which raises questions about whether or not negative health claims about children found in grow operations are valid. Douglas asserts that social workers have become the "tool for addressing the marijuana grow operation problem," and they are used by law enforcement to advance the goals of law enforcement agents.[59] She proposes, instead, that health concerns for these children should drive BC ministry policy and practice,[60] although her own data suggest that these concerns are misplaced.

A new Canadian medical study addresses the health risks to children found at drug-production sites. Responding to a request by the police and Children's Aid Society, Motherrisk Clinic at the Hospital for Sick Children in Toronto conducted a study of 75 children living in homes where drugs were being produced in the York region of Ontario from 2006 to 2010. The medical researchers accessed records indicating the health and well-being of the children found at these sites (80% of the sites were for marijuana production). None of the families in the study had been under the care of social service agencies. "Pediatricians with clinical pharmacology/toxicology backgrounds" conducted full in-clinic pediatric physical and neurological examinations of the children. Hair analysis was done, and the researchers also examined the police reports, medical history, and school reports of the children, and conducted interviews with parents and social workers. They found that the majority of the 75 children were healthy and drug free, especially those found at marijuana grow ops.[61] They conclude that the automatic removal of children found at marijuana grow ops should be reviewed and "suggest that in most cases there is no medical justification to remove" children from their parents.[62] Furthermore, they conclude that it is unlikely that growing marijuana hinders "effective parenting."[63] In fact, they note that the earnings from marijuana production may have a "favourable outcome" for the children of marijuana grow ops.[64]

Calls for Increased Regulation

One of the outcomes of these controversies has been a call for increased forms of regulation to protect children in grow ops and other illicit drug operations. In their paper, Plecas et al.[65] speculate that British Columbia might more effectively reduce the number of marijuana grow ops if Canada's Criminal Code and judicial system were amended to include harsher penalties for those convicted of this crime. This claim is reiterated in a number of earlier papers by the same authors,[66] and also in media reports by journalists and numerous spokespeople. In a 2008 newspaper article entitled "Plan targets serious drug offenders," written by former Minister of Justice Rob Nicholson,[67] the author claims that a "substantial proportion of serious drug offenders are currently not spending a single day in prison." The minister suggests this is the reason that the Conservative government is proposing mandatory minimum sentences for drug crimes, and he says that their message is clear, "If you sell or produce drugs, you'll pay with mandatory jail time." He also claims that two-thirds of the $63.8 million in additional monies that was part of Canada's new 2007 National Anti-Drug Strategy would be aimed at preventing and treating those with illegal drug dependencies. Although about two-thirds of these new monies were spent on prevention and treatment, the Canadian federal government still spent 70 per cent of its National Anti-Drug Strategy overall budget of $399.9 million on law enforcement. The National Anti-Drug Strategy's budget for prevention, treatment, and harm reduction accounted for 23 per cent, and coordination and research activities another 7 per cent.[68] Furthermore, the claims put forth by former Minister of Justice Rob Nicholson are categorically wrong. He need only acquaint himself with the government's own prison statistics to learn that a significant proportion of drug offenders in Canada are incarcerated in prison, often for lengthy periods.[69] But since the election of Canada's minority Conservative government in 2006, this government has attempted four times to implement legislation that includes mandatory minimum penalties for drug crimes (Bills C-15, C-20, S-10, and C-10). The latest version of this bill, the Safe Streets and Communities Act was passed in March 2012. This legislation includes mandatory minimum sentencing for marijuana grow ops and higher penalties for aggravating factors, such as children in the location or near the site of drug manufacturing or trafficking.[70] There is no evidence demonstrating that harsh drug laws and penalties deter marijuana production or any other type of drug offence. In fact, a growing body of scientific research reveals that drug prohibition and increases in drug law enforcement result in higher rates of drug market violence and fail to reduce the prevalence of drug use.[71]

The BC Association of Social Workers has also entered the public debates on these issues. In 2003, the BC Ministry of Children and Family Development produced the "Protocol Framework and Working Guidelines between Child Protection and Alcohol and Drug Services." It includes 23 risk factors such as alcohol and drug use and living conditions to determine whether children need protection.[72] In turn, the BC Association of Social Workers demanded an improved protocol to protect children found on the grow op sites. These demands by social workers were accompanied by a number of news articles with headings such as "Social workers worry about grow-op kids: Question criteria used to investigate"[73] and "No evidence more kids should be taken into care."[74] Unusual in our study sample, a few of these articles are critical of the assertion by social workers that children in grow ops are at risk or that new protocols are needed. Although BC ministry officials initially resisted these calls by social workers, in 2008, the ministry also developed "Fact Sheets: Child Protection Issues and Illegal Drug Manufacturing"[75] which provides detailed information for child social workers responding to "protection reports involving children found living in or frequenting illegal drug manufacturing facilities" (BCMCFD, 2008).

Critics of these moves, for example, *Vancouver Sun* reporter Ian Mulgrew, ask why the BC Association of Social Workers is "beating the bushes to have more children taken into care."[76] Mulgrew also challenges claims that all or even most grow ops are commercially sized operations. Drawing on measures of the yield of pot plants found in these sites, Mulgrew suggests that it is more likely that they are small operations used to supplement family incomes. Mulgrew also challenges the Association to provide evidence of children being electrocuted or burned to death in these sites, or to name situations where the BC Ministry of Children and Family Development has not stepped in when it had information that children were present in a grow-op. He states, "The current prohibition against marijuana is a public policy disaster that saps resources, benefits gangsters, undermines faith in the legal system and has failed miserably to stem the use of illicit drugs."[77] Mulgrew also suggests that the continued criminalization of marijuana produces a secretive underground economy that places growers and their families at risk of health and safety concerns.

On 21 September 2011, the RCMP announced their new National Marihuana Grow Initiative to "combat" marijuana grow ops. The RCMP developed a new page on their public website to educate Canadians and to act as a central database of residences where marijuana grow ops have been found. The RCMP website reiterates their claims about marijuana grow ops being the domain of organized crime groups. They also emphasize the risk of fire, explosions, violence, and safety of children. The website provides a detailed description, website address, and an information brochure about the new strategy. On the first page of the brochure, bright yellow crime-scene tape is imprinted with the words "MARIHUANA GROW INITIATIVE." On the next page of the brochure, a forlorn, and somewhat emaciated young white girl with long dark hair, dressed in a drab grey t-shirt stares out at the reader. The young girl is depicted surrounded by marijuana plants, in a dark root cellar or unfinished basement. In her hands she is holding a framed photo of what appears to be her family in happier times. The glass covering of the photo is shattered, by what looks like a bullet hole. The brochure does not include any information about children. Rather, the significance of the photo is underscored by what are by now common and familiar claims by the media and the RCMP about the public safety risks posed by marijuana grow ops. The RCMP website page claims, "When children live in grow op homes, their lives are threatened by" toxic mould, volatile chemicals, violence, abuse and neglect, greater risk of house fires, threat of electrocution and burns, increased presence of guns, and increased threat of violence. The RCMP website page concludes with: "There's no such thing as a 'safe' home when marihuana is involved. We need your help to stop organized crime. If you suspect a Marijuana Grow Operation in your neighbourhood" contact your local police. The site provides the telephone number of Crime Stoppers on the brochure and their website.[78]

Discussion

In this chapter, we argue that the circularity of claims in the Canadian media about marijuana grow ops and children found in homes that have grow ops are astonishing. We assert that the claims made by a small number of vocal spokespeople and institutional representatives who repeatedly reference one another are picked up by the media and reiterated over and over again. These findings may have relevance for critical and feminist drug researchers in and outside of Canada. We found that uncritical reiteration by the news media of claims made by law enforcement agencies and a select group of others shapes the debates, research, and policy about children and marijuana grow ops.[79] Although we do not contest claims that some grow ops may be run by organized crime or that some grow operations contribute to health risks of children residing on the site, we propose that thus far, the evidence provided by reporters and spokespeople fails to substantiate their claims. Outside of Moller et al.,[80] the current research does not take into account the diversity of both marijuana grow ops and families participating in these activities. To this end, police and other reports do not distinguish the effects on children by size of grow op, indoor versus outdoor operations, or the effects of using organic methods and proper ventilation systems as opposed to chemicals and poorly wired and ventilated grow ops. As Moller et al. point out,[81] nor is there evidence to suggest that children found in the homes where grow operations exist are at more risk for poor health outcomes than children whose families run other kinds of farms and hot houses. As noted at the beginning of this chapter, in the late 1800s and early 1900s, moral reformers in Canada sought to rescue children from slum streets and homes. Rather than examine the social, economic, and political factors that negatively shaped the home, and prospects for parents and children alike, child savers advocated separating children from deviant parents and toxic environments in order to avoid negative influences. Today, racialized parents suspected of illegal drug use in Canada and the United States are depicted by policy makers as immoral, criminal, and a danger to their children. Their homes are seen as detrimental to their children's health; thus, increased regulation and child apprehension by the state have been justified. Increasingly, similar discourse has been extended to domestic marijuana cultivation. Marijuana grow ops are depicted as dangerous environments that place children at risk. The implication of these claims is that grow operators are by definition bad parents. This implicit claim is intensified by the oft-repeated notion that grow operators are of Vietnamese origin, thus playing on racist sentiments about drug dealers, parenting, and marijuana. Similar to the news media and policy makers' claims during the 1980s crack scare in the United States, racialized parents are represented as deviant for placing their children at risk, and greedy for putting potential illicit drug profits ahead of their children's welfare. They are also depicted as unlawful Others who degrade otherwise "normal" white spaces.

Not surprisingly, reporters highlight the risk of mould and other health effects in grow ops and fail to mention poverty and lack of adequate housing for poor parents, especially in British Columbia. Federal and provincial cutbacks in social housing, provincial welfare cutbacks, and a low minimum wage negatively shape the lives of parents and children. British Columbia has the highest rate of child poverty in Canada. Inadequate housing and air-tight building envelopes, especially in rainy Vancouver, could be just as likely to contribute to the presence of mould, but no spokesperson has yet claimed that this is a risk to the health of poor children in these homes.

By tracing the discourse about children present at marijuana grow ops over a period of 15 years (1995–2009), it is evident that speculation is characteristic of many reporters' claims. These claims would not be as viable if the relationship between illicit drugs and parenting was not already criminalized and racialized by earlier attempts to regulate the lives of substance-using women in the United States and Canada.

The presumed veracity of media-based claims about children and marijuana production is established by the linking of previous discourses about child saving, drugs, and parenting, and racialized outsiders with emerging claims about BC's marijuana grow-op business. Child-saving discourse plays up the image of innocent children to generate sympathy for harsher penalties and to reiterate the essential goodness of the police and policy makers. Claims about negative effects of grow ops on children are accompanied by public safety and health concerns like fire, mould, ventilation, violence, and organized crime. These claims deflect attention away from issues like poverty and fail to address the popularity and profitability that growing marijuana may have for struggling families.[82] In turn, previously intensified media claims about parenting, drugs, and race help to solidify contemporary stereotypes about the racialized Other, the greedy and uncaring drug dealer/grow operator who threatens the morality of spaces ordinarily coded as white, including residential suburbs. Together, these discourses demonize and racialize the grow operator, an age-old rhetorical trick – with devastating consequences – that is then linked to the need for intervention from social services to protect children with harsh drug policy, laws, and penalties.

7 Alternative Perspectives

In this book, we argue that contemporary media and other claims about marijuana grow ops in Canada constitute *a drug scare fuelled by the media, RCMP, politicians, and vocal claims makers*. As Reinarman and Levine remind us, a drug scare is a phenomenon quite separate from what actually occurs. A drug scare is a "designated period" of time where individuals, groups, and media forms identify and condemn a particular drug as a new social problem requiring increased attention and regulation. We illuminate the shifting and intersecting claims reported by the media about marijuana grow ops in 2,524 articles in the *Vancouver Sun*, Vancouver *Province*, Victoria *Times Colonist*, and the national paper, the *Globe and Mail*, over a 15-year span (1995–2009). We contend that the textual and photographic claims located in both the headlines and then the actual texts of newspaper stories help to substantiate marijuana grow ops as a growing social problem. The estimated amount of marijuana thought to be produced, and the number of plants seized by law enforcement agents in Canada, are then linked to speculation about the size of the marijuana trade and the involvement of organized crime. The media and claims makers reiterate "mythical" numbers, for the evidence about marijuana production in Canada is weak (as it is in the United States and Mexico).[1] The dominant themes in these news stories include the often-unsubstantiated linking of most grow ops to organized crime and racialized criminal gangs; the linking of grow ops to public safety concerns such as fire, mould, other toxins, and shoddy electrical wiring; and the increasing participation of a number of institutionally based claims makers in the production of the "problem" of marijuana cultivation. These themes gain their potency from two interlinked processes: the articulation of these themes as linked to each other and the repetition of these claims over time. Regarding the former, newspaper reporting and policy documents about grow ops increasingly link numerous public safety risks to violence and organized crime, so much so that reporting on grow ops takes these links for granted. Canadian drug policy scholar Bruce Alexander noted more than 20 years ago:

> The biggest cost of the drug war propaganda may be the systematic reduction about people's ability to think intelligently about drugs. Society faces genuinely terrifying, immensely complex problems in the last decade of the twentieth century. The environment, educational institutions, value systems, health institutions, and economy all need urgent attention. But the obsessive concern with drug problems stirred up by incessant propaganda distracts us from these to the point of collective stupidity.[2]

By evoking fears about safety, news articles, headlines, and photographs help to substantiate rhetorical claims about the relationship among marijuana grow ops, risk, violence, and organized crime. The repetitiveness of these claims, combined with their enduring quality, helps to naturalize grow ops as a site of danger and risk to supposedly unsuspecting citizens. While photographs and headlines (of plant numbers, chemicals, grow-op fires, and weapons) effectively illustrate newspaper claims about the dangers of marijuana production, we assert that they also offer a deeper metaphorical meaning: marijuana grow ops pose an increasing risk to otherwise safe residential communities. In effect, photographs and headlines often provide evidence of a claim that the media cannot fully substantiate textually in the article: marijuana grow ops pose public safety risks to good neighbourhoods, good citizens, and good homes – meaning, in this case, the readers' own homes.

The media reports also emphasize temporal and spatial dimensions to these concerns: over time, these articles argue, more individuals will be drawn in as users and growers, and more neighbourhoods will be threatened by drug production and criminal violence. The space occupied by seemingly innocent neighbours is then recast as the site of an invasion by tainted, racialized, and mostly male criminal Others who bring violence and crime to otherwise safe residential spaces. The repeated evocation and naturalization of concerns about public safety, risk, violence, and organized crime then help to make otherwise politically debatable claims seem uncontestable because of the seeming urgency of the issue. The racialized discourses repeated in these articles have persisted over time and are rarely contested. These images of marijuana production thus provide a disturbing and frightening set of meanings about racial stereotyping, drug production, selling, and use; in turn, the reliance of newspaper reporters on institutional spokespeople such as RCMP/police means that that news reporting offers a narrow set of appropriate social responses to marijuana use and cultivation. This sense of risk and threat to otherwise moral spaces, by a supposedly out-of-control criminal activity like the cultivation of marijuana, legitimates further harsh social and legal interventions.

The coverage of marijuana grow ops, along with the policy documents we have discussed in this book, illustrate that a mostly one-sided de facto public policy debate about marijuana cultivation exists in Canada. In a sense, this coverage is classic in that it continually works to enlarge the domain of the problem by linking growing marijuana to a range of social issues. For example, by linking marijuana cultivation to public safety, the coverage has effectively drawn in a larger group of institutional claims makers including fire departments, municipalities, electricity producers, public safety authorities, real estate associations, and insurance companies.

The RCMP unveiled their new National Marihuana Grow Initiative on 21 September 2011. The initiative includes a new webpage, information site, and brochure, all of which were created through "collaboration" with "experts" around the country.[3] The RCMP initiative mirrors the dominant news reportage examined in our study period and highlights the increasing utilization of the media, including Web-based media, by the RCMP/police to communicate their position on marijuana grow ops. The RCMP webpage states that grow ops "harm communities" and are "controlled by organized crime groups." They also claim that where marijuana grow ops exist, there is a greater risk of violence, fire, explosions, and risk to children. The RCMP highlight how their new initiative is united not only with the goals of Canada's current Conservative-led federal government, but with the RCMP's business and community partners, including the Insurance Bureau of Canada and the Canadian Real Estate Association. The website provides a list of addresses from each province that allegedly contained a marijuana grow op at one time and that was dismantled by the RCMP. The list of grow operations describes the number of plants found and the date and includes information on the type of site (residence, outbuilding, and business); this information, however, does not indicate how the RCMP defines a business or outbuilding. The RCMP website includes a disclaimer that states there may be mistakes in their information, and there may be addresses on the list that did not contain a marijuana grow op. The RCMP website page, brochure, and other information about marijuana grow ops remind Canadians that they can contact Crime Stoppers and anonymously supply information if they suspect that a neighbour is engaged in growing marijuana. This new webpage and accompanying strategy highlight and reaffirm the RCMP's position that "marihuana grow operations pose a serious threat to Canadians" regardless of the diversity and actuality of growing marijuana.[4]

As a major claims maker about the gravity and scope of the problem of marijuana cultivation, the RCMP, along with municipal police forces, have a unique ability to present and circulate their views on this subject. The RCMP uses the resources of its national office and its provincial divisions, including media relations officers who issue press releases about specific drug crimes on their websites and through social media to convey their messages.[5] The BC division of the RCMP, for example, maintains a Facebook page that gives viewers opportunities to see upcoming events, post comments, read about news from the RCMP, and see videos – including ones that depict police raids on marijuana grow ops.[6] Visitors to the website for the BC division of the RCMP can also access press releases about specific drug crimes, and reporters can easily find information on how to contact media relations officers.[7] Several of the RCMP detachments in British Columbia also have their own websites. The Surrey detachment has its own Web presence accessed through the BC RCMP site.[8] The website for the RCMP in Richmond, BC, is available through the City of Richmond's website. Like the BC office, the Richmond and Surrey detachments make BC RCMP press releases available on these sites. These press releases are quite numerous; for example, there are 11 press releases in the month of August 2011 and seven in the next month.[9] These press releases seek to educate the public about RCMP concerns such as marijuana grow ops and drug trade violence and ongoing investigations. Many municipal police forces also maintain media relations units. One example is the Vancouver Police Department (VPD). Its website links visitors to a Community and Public Affairs Section that includes a Media Unit. From there, visitors can obtain contact information on media relations officers. The VPD also holds a daily press conference and issues press releases to provide the media and the public with information on a variety of issues including raids on marijuana grows ops.[10]

The Saanich Police, a municipal force on southern Vancouver Island, has found additional ways to inform the public about marijuana. In 2011, they distributed a calendar to residents' homes that promotes the work of the police. The calendar features drug law enforcement as a key component of police work and illustrates this work with a staged image of a man being apprehended ostensibly for marijuana possession by a Saanich police officer. The creation of this calendar suggests that there seems to be no end to the use of taxpayer dollars to promote particular visual and textual discourse on marijuana laws and their enforcement. In addition, press releases by the RCMP and/or municipal police are often the only sources highlighted in conventional news articles about grow ops and the marijuana trade. When an opposing voice is included in the same article, it is most often given a cursory nod and tacked on at the end. This practice of only drawing from one source about an issue becomes even more problematic against the backdrop of corporate downsizing and the amalgamation of the press, as alternative voices become even scarcer.[11]

In these claims by police, RCMP, and the media, grow operators emerge as predominately male "super-deviants," constructed through overlapping discourses as racialized, dangerous outlaws, and as unable or unwilling to operate in the best interests of public safety. In doing so, these claims makers including the media call upon familiar themes and stock characters from Canada's prohibitionist history of drug policy. At the same time, this perspective bolsters the view that a solid distinction exists between the drug producer and the normal self-regulating citizen. These binaries help to shore up the identity of these claims makers' as truth-tellers whose role it is to warn the public about dangers that exist within the social fabric.[12]

Although newspaper reporting depicts a world of organized crime and public safety dangers associated with the cultivation of marijuana, the scholarship on marijuana grow ops does not wholly support these claims. A 2011 Canadian Justice Department study, for example, disputes many of these claims, especially those related to links to organized crime. Only 5 per cent of their large sample had any possible link to organized crime (see introduction).[13] No doubt, some growers are linked to organized crime; recent scholarship has tracked the entry of large-scale cultivators with links to some form of organized crime into the arena of marijuana cultivation. But studies by scholars such as Bouchard, Potter, Weisheit and Decorte, Hammersvick, Sandberg, and Pedersen suggest that growers are a heterogeneous group characterized by differing interests and motivations for growing marijuana. Hammersvick et al., for example, found that among small-scale growers in Norway, most are "embedded in cannabis culture with an emphasis on anti-commercialism, anti-violence and ecological and community values."[14] As these authors also find, the vast number of small-scale growers, who constitute the majority of growers, only produce a supply for themselves and friends. Moreover, several of these authors suggest that prohibitionist and repressive strategies to eliminate large-scale cannabis growing will most likely harm small-scale growers who are not associated with organized crime. Hammersvick et al. argue that allowing cannabis users to legally grow a small number of plants could help curtail the participation of more serious criminals and get governments, cannabis users, and small-scale growers to "join forces" to deter "crime and large-scale operations."[15] But, for the most part, newspapers do not produce stories about these independent growers who do not have ties to organized crime; nor have they cited this peer-reviewed research published in scholarly journals, research that reveals that the majority of growers are diverse and non-violent. But media and policy construction of grow operators as "dangerous" disavows other possibilities, namely, that the reasons and realities of growing cannabis may be various and complex. This approach leaves no possibility that the responsible residential cannabis grower can coexist peaceably with neighbours.

Over the past 15 years, the conventional media in Canada could have investigated the issue of marijuana grow ops much more rigorously. The scholarly publications mentioned above and the following sources below provide alternative representations of marijuana users and growers; yet, for the most part, the news sources we examined did not include them. Alternative perspectives are mostly limited to the pages of the letters to the editors and the occasional Canadian columnist, such as Dan Gardner and Ian Mulgrew. The photo in Figure 7.1 of a marijuana grow op found in the basement of a home is accompanied by an article by Neil Boyd, a professor of criminology at Simon Fraser University. The *Vancouver Sun* headline for the article, "Back off busting BC bud" provides an alternative perspective, challenging what Neil Boyd refers to as the "scary" stories regularly highlighted in news media about marijuana grow ops.

Headlines for some other alternative articles can be found in Figure 7.1. Some of these articles decry the prohibition of marijuana and argue that its legalization could be the resolution to the underground cultivation of this plant. A few of these headlines even contradict other stories

Figure 7.1. "Back off busting BC bud." Reproduced with permission from the *Vancouver Sun*, 22 July 2000. Photo by Ward Perrin.

and themes; this is illustrated by the example headline from 2005 suggesting that firearms are rarely found during police raids of marijuana grow ops. Although these kinds of stories appear in all four newspapers included in our study, they are by far a small proportion of the overall sample. Approximately 115 stories (4.5%) out of 2,524 articles focus positively, in part or in whole, on the issue of cannabis drug law reform (see Figure 7.2).

Nor do newspapers draw on the vast number of alternative sources about the cultivation of marijuana that are easily accessible through the Internet. *Cannabis Culture*, for example, is a Canadian-based international magazine that highlights the pleasures and ritual use of marijuana and provides gardening tips for growers with images of plants and growers. This magazine focuses on the recreational, medicinal, and ritual use of cannabis. It treats both growers and users as normal

Figure 7.2. Headline Box: Alternative Views.[16]

HEADLINES: ALTERNATIVE VIEWS

Drug war vets say don't decriminalize use of marijuana, just don't police it: A cop,
a lawyer and an academic believe one letter from the attorney-general
directing police not to enforce the law of the land would diminish the
contribution of cannabis to criminal acts like gang
cultivations (1998)

Back off busting BC bud: A criminologist decries the waste and featherbedding
that accompanies the legal system's war on marijuana (2000)

Pot's fraught with perils, but prohibition is no longer an option (2001)

Enough of studies, it's time to end the war on cannabis (2001)

Life, liberty, and the pursuit of illegal drugs: In the United States, once-sacred
constitutional rights are being eroded by relentless police and military
attempts to interdict narcotics and punish users and dealers.
In Canada, the threat to civil liberties has not yet been
as extreme, but the pressures are building (2000)

Inside growing operations: A look at three of the thousands of marijuana
producers in the lower mainland, operations that police vow to
close – one at a time (2000)

Readers think there are worse crimes than selling a bit of pot (2004)

Evidence shows Harper's justice policies would exacerbate drug problem (2005)

Weapons rare in marijuana raids, Vancouver police say (2005)

Logic says legalize drugs: Reality says it won't happen (2005)

Easy money has to be removed from drugs (2009)

Legalizing drugs a better path than stiffer sentences (2009)

---

citizens, and it highlights the harms of drug regulation and the prohibi-tion of cannabis. A similar US-based magazine, *High Times*, also focuses on the recreational user and grower. Michael Poole's book, *Romancing Mary Jane: A Year in the Life of a Failed Marijuana Grower*, published in 1998, provides readers with a view of growing marijuana in British Columbia. Poole, a well-known documentary film producer (who has since passed away), tells about his attempts to grow marijuana for his own use. His story is quite hilarious, and he provides readers with in-sight into the marijuana trade. He visits other indoor and outdoor mari-juana growers, and in doing so, the reader comes to realize that this activity is not simply the purview of criminal gangs. Rather, readers meet hard-working, law-abiding families supplementing their modest incomes to support themselves and their families. Poole shows how, just like with any other crop, not all marijuana plants thrive, or grow to full maturation, and that Poole's failed attempts as a grower are often the norm.[17] Alternative city papers such as Vancouver's *Georgia Straight* also provide alternative articles about marijuana and drug prohibition. However, during our study period, articles about marijuana grow ops are rare in this paper.[18]

Medical marijuana users and growers in Canada also illustrate the diverse uses of this drug. Yet media reporting on medical marijuana is at best tepid, and more recently takes on the standpoint of fire and po-lice officials who problematize growers who have licences to produce medical marijuana. Recent media claims about these legal grow ops have suggested that these growers are linked to organized crime and pose public safety risks. As discussed earlier, in chapter 5, citing public safety and security as the impetus, on 10 June 2013, the health minister announced the new regulations that will govern access to cannabis for medical purposes in Canada. The new regulations come into effect in March 2014. The Canadian Association of Medical Cannabis Dispensers (CAMCD), a non-profit organization that represents compassion clubs in Canada, provides an alternative vision to the claims made by former Health Minister Leona Aglukkaq, media, and RCMP reports. The CAMCD highlights the diversity of growers and the wide range of high-quality cannabis medicines they provide for those in need and their consistent and high standard of patient care. As noted in chapter 5, the CAMCD also make clear that these clubs value compassion, harm reduction services, empowerment, dignity, affordability, and integrity.[19] Yet their organization is not included in media and police reports. Nor do the media cover the work of NORML, an organization working for reform of marijuana laws, with chapters around the world, including Canada. Other organizations including the Canadian Drug Policy Coalition, End Prohibition, Drugsense, Transform Drug Policy Foundation, Drug Policy Alliance, and Students for Sensible Drug Policy support drug policy reform including legally regulated markets for cannabis and other currently criminalized drugs. They are not alone. Other Canadian and international research reports and organizations have also suggested that a regulated market for cannabis would be safer than the current prohibitionist approach, yet their voices were absent from the media in our study sample.[20] They argue that the legal regulation of cannabis should encompass state licensing of small growers rather than the corporatization of cannabis production and distribution.

The alternative sources identified above question drug laws and prohibition, and they point out that prohibition contributes to the very harms that it seeks to prevent, including the illegal drug trade and drug trade violence. Although they recognize that most marijuana users and

Figure 7.3. "No such thing as standard growing operation dog." Reproduced with permission from the *Vancouver Sun*, 22 July 2000. Photo by Mark van Manen.

Figure 7.4. Bears. Reproduced with permission from the RCMP.

growers are otherwise law-abiding citizens, an unregulated market can provide ready opportunities for organized crime or criminal gangs to profit. Globally, drug trade violence, turf wars, and corrupt law officials stem from the illegal market and prohibitionist policy. They argue that the illegal drug trade would be severely limited if marijuana production and sales were legally regulated. They point out that more laws will do little to decrease drug production and selling, or drug use and addiction rates. In contrast, a legal regulated market would assure that drugs like marijuana and the production of marijuana are regulated legally, just as alcohol is.

Although our study found that the majority of articles about marijuana cultivation reiterate the perspectives of law enforcement agencies and a small group of claims makers' to the exclusion of other points of view, not all newspaper reporting about the cultivation of marijuana follows a strictly alarmist format. The newspaper headlines in Figure 7.5 illustrate some of the more humorous or odd stories that have appeared over the years. These stories often focus on the role that animals have played in the accidental discovery of marijuana grow ops and tell more lighthearted tales of cultivation incidents. The photo in Figure 7.3

Figure 7.5. Headline Box: Comic Pot News.[21]

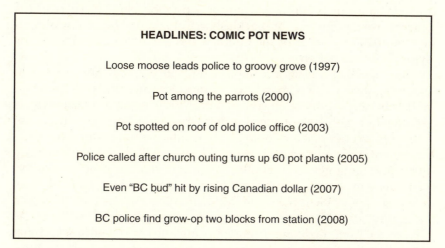

HEADLINES: COMIC POT NEWS

Loose moose leads police to groovy grove (1997)

Pot among the parrots (2000)

Pot spotted on roof of old police office (2003)

Police called after church outing turns up 60 pot plants (2005)

Even "BC bud" hit by rising Canadian dollar (2007)

BC police find grow-op two blocks from station (2008)

was a welcome reprieve from the mostly violent depictions represented in the media we examined.

Along this line, other stories describe how police have discovered grow ops after receiving accidental 911 calls from children and adults.[22] We likely do not need to remind the reader that these stories are few in number. We also found some comic relief stories that highlighted claims by the RCMP that bears had been guarding a rural grow op – claims that were later found to be untrue (see Figure 7.4).

The easy association reported by the media between grow ops, Satanism, hard-core pornography, and fighting dogs also provided much-needed comic relief. Figure 7.5 offers some headlines that exemplify comic and lighter stories.

Questions for the Future

In this book, we illuminate how the alignment of professional groups (realtors, police, RCMP, etc.) against marijuana grow ops is about more than just its stated object. We are not contesting that some marijuana-growing operations are harmful or connected to organized crime; rather, we are making clear how the movement to regulate marijuana grow ops, to enact harsher drug laws (including mandatory minimum sentencing), and civil initiatives at the municipal level (not subject to public scrutiny and due process) are all part of wider social shifts in Canada and "in political and cultural public policy."[23] These shifts emerge from a conservative backlash in Canada that holds law and order, punishment, security, the military, and law enforcement agents as symbolic of the nation.

This reporting and its accompanying policy claims are situated in emerging forms of neo-liberal rule focused less on social provision and redistribution and more on crime control, policing, and punishment as solutions to problems of social order. Drug sellers and producers are subject to a series of overlapping truth claims based on morality, criminality, outlaw status, racialization, irresponsibility, and risk; in turn, this reportage suggests that only a range of coercive and punitive interventions will stop this problem.[24] One accompanying feature of these forms of liberal rule is the proliferation of interventions that draw on a "plurality" of professions, agencies, and sites within civil society.[25] As we can see from media reporting, policing and other forms of criminal control are the site of many of these emerging partnerships, in the form of interagency connections established to control drug use and production.[26] However, as a class of male super-deviants, marijuana-growing operators also act as a lightning rod for our despair about the breakdown of sociality fostered by consumerism, neo-liberal emphasis on the entrepreneurial, cuts to social services, and demands that we become wholly self-regulating subjects. Instigating fear is the hallmark of a conservative movement tainted by neo-liberal goals and punishment is its solution. The condemnation of marijuana grow ops has served to capitalize on and advance these social and political shifts. One such example of this desire to punish is the passing into law, in March 2012, of Bill C-10 – the Safe Streets and Communities Act – which came into effect in November 2012.[27] It provides mandatory minimum sentences for drug offences, including marijuana cultivation of five or more plants and aggravating factors that are broad and vague, such as whether or not the production of marijuana constitutes a *potential* public safety hazard in a residential area.

This Act will increase an already overcrowded prison population in Canada. The Act will disproportionately impact Aboriginal peoples, the poor, and those with mental illness, and it will divert more tax dollars to prison building rather than to other social programs such as health and education. This government freely uses the media to promote its initiatives such as the National Anti-Drug Strategy. From 2007 to 2009, the Conservative-led government spent $7,261,000 to launch and advertise its new National Anti-Drug Strategy to Canadians.[28] In 2009 and 2010, the federal government spent another $4,429,091 on media promoting this strategy and its proposed legislative changes that were advertised in a variety of print media including daily and weekly newspapers and magazines across the country, television, cinema, and Internet sources.[29] The National Anti-Drug Strategy budget for the next five years (from 2012 onwards) was announced in 2012. Health Canada's budget for community initiatives has decreased by 26 per cent and funding for the Drug Treatment Program has decreased by 35 per cent in contrast to an almost 16 per cent budget increase for the RCMP Drug Enforcement Program, a 31 per cent increase to the Correctional Service of Canada for community supervision programs, a 46 per cent increase to the Parole Board of Canada, a 40 per cent increase for prosecutions, and more money to the Canada Border Services Agency. RCMP funding is earmarked to go towards investigating suspected growers of marijuana (and operators of illegal drug labs).[30]

Discourse about the link between marijuana grow ops, organized crime, and risky criminals has grown to such an extent that it becomes difficult to imagine alternatives to law-and-order discourses or other ways to respond to and understand complex social issues, including the murders at Mayerthorpe, Alberta, in March 2005. This book invites public scrutiny of events and people related to marijuana grow ops (or, more accurately, those people who cultivate and grow marijuana in indoor and outdoor gardens), and it encourages critical consideration of hasty calls for more punitive laws, prison sentencing, and civil initiatives covered in the media and reiterated in policy documents. Ultimately, we ask larger questions about the role of the media, punishment, municipal initiatives, and an expanding criminal justice system. The continuing increase in police powers that has accompanied drug laws has diminished the civil liberties of all Canadians, not merely those who use, produce, or sell marijuana. Intrusive police measures, often introduced to be used only in extraordinary circumstances, migrate to other areas of law enforcement. They become, not extraordinary, but normalized measures.[31] Intrusive municipal initiatives introduced to identify marijuana grow ops such as bylaws requiring landlords to examine rental premises for possible signs of marijuana grow ops, police "green teams," and enlisting utility providers such as BC Hydro to spy on homes when delivering services further reduce the liberties of all Canadians.

Criminologist and restorative justice advocate Elizabeth Elliot argues that punishment in the criminal justice system has not proven to be effective. She examines the scholarly literature and notes that there is no "evidence that punishment effectively deters crime or teaches moral values" to lawbreakers.[32] Increased rates of incarceration do not decrease crime or make our communities safer. She also argues that rituals of punishment weaken societies (as history demonstrates in relation to totalitarian and fascist states). Elliot argues that societies dominated by hostility may produce "legal justice" but this justice produces neither peace nor safe communities.[33] We also observe that, historically, the erosion of civil liberties and democratic civil society has often been accompanied by punishment and fear: fear of Others, fear of crime, fear of fellow citizens, expanding criminal justice, civil regulation, and incarceration, the militarization of civil society, and the erosion of vigorous investigative journalism. Thus, we caution both defenders of drug prohibition and those who seek to legally regulate cannabis to pay attention to the discourse and arguments that reduce growers of marijuana only to members of violent organized crime gangs. This reductionist perspective fuels fear of the Other and punitive responses and makes invisible the diversity of growers. In addition, it limits our understanding of cannabis growers and thus alternative policy options. Marijuana reform efforts in Canada in the 1970s and mid-1990s were stalled, in part, because oppositional claims makers focused on the dangers of marijuana and proposed to root out and punish high-level traffickers and organized crime, ignoring the fact that our drug laws and law enforcement agents consistently target visible and poor people who use/possess criminalized drugs. It is no different today.

We argue that the Canadian government led by the Conservative Party is out of step with global efforts aimed at drug policy reform. Other nations, as well as some US states, are moving away from prohibitionist law-and-order policy, are rejecting mandatory minimum prison sentencing for drug offences, and are supporting the decriminalization of cannabis and other criminalized drugs. Countries such as the Netherlands, Portugal, Mexico, the Czech Republic, Spain, Peru, Venezuela, and Colombia, as well as the state of Western Australia and 17 US states and the District of Columbia have instituted drug policy reform. Portugal decriminalized the use and possession of all illegal drugs in 2001, and the state of Western Australia introduced legislation to decriminalize cannabis. (At press, a bill is before the Uruguay Senate to create a legal regulated market for cannabis.) Neither Portugal nor Australia has experienced a rise in cannabis use nor an increase in drug-related violence.[34] In Portugal, decriminalization of use and possession of illegal drugs did not lead to major increases in drug use; in fact, the evidence indicates "reductions in problematic use, drug-related harms and criminal justice overcrowding."[35] In the United States, in defiance of federal law, 20 states and the District of Columbia have programs that allow legal medical marijuana for qualified patients. As discussed earlier in this book, in November 2012, Colorado and Washington voted to become the first two US states to legalize the possession and sale of cannabis. Adults can legally possess one ounce of cannabis, and dispensaries are being set up for the sale of the plants. In Colorado, adults can grow up to six plants in their home for personal use.

In 1998, hundreds of elected politicians, government officials, judges, barristers, professors, professionals, writers, and other prominent spokespeople from around the world (including Canada) signed an open letter featured in the *New York Times* to Secretary General of the United Nations Kofi Annan, stating, "We believe that the global war on drugs is now causing more harm than drug abuse itself."[36] They declared that the drug war impeded public health efforts, infringed on human rights, and fuelled organized crime and violence. Other open letters by other politicians followed.[37]

The 2010 Vienna Declaration endorsed by scholars and leaders around the world, launched at the XVIII International AIDS Conference in Vienna, Austria, outlines the harms that result from the criminalization of drugs and the harms of drug law enforcement on individuals and communities. These harms include HIV and Hepatitis C epidemics, overdose deaths, undermining of health services including prevention and treatment services, stigma and marginalization of illicit drug users, illicit markets and drug-related crime and violence, increased incarceration, and the individual and social costs of prison building and expanded policing.[38]

In 2011 a report entitled *War on Drugs*, by the Global Commission on Drug Policy,[39] was released by an international body composed of significant leaders such as Kofi Annan, Louise Arbour (former UN High Commissioner for Human Rights), César Gaviria (former president of Colombia), Ernesto Zedillo (former President of Mexico), and other global leaders. The report states:

> The global war on drugs has failed, with devastating consequences for individuals and societies around the world ... fundamental reforms in national and global drug control policies are urgently needed.

Vast expenditures on criminalization and repressive measures directed at producers, traffickers and consumers of illegal drugs have clearly failed to effectively curtail supply or consumption.

The Commission recommends:

End the criminalization, marginalization and stigmatization of people who use drugs but who do no harm to others. Challenge rather than reinforce common misconceptions about drug markets, drug use and drug dependence.

Encourage experimentation by governments with models of legal regulation of drugs to undermine the power of organized crime and safeguard the health and security of their citizens. *This recommendation applies especially to cannabis, but we also encourage other experiments in decriminalization and legal regulation that can accomplish these objectives and provide models for others.*[40]

In April 2012, at the Summit of Americas, attended by Canada's Prime Minister Stephen Harper and US President Barack Obama, a number of Latin American leaders vocally condemned drug prohibition and noted that the demand for illegal drugs stems from the consumption of these drugs in Canada and the United States. Similar to the conclusions of the Global Commission on Drug Policy, they asserted that drug prohibition has failed to curb the drug trade and drug-related violence in their countries. The US president and the Canadian prime minister were not swayed, although Prime Minister Harper was quoted as stating, "The current approach is not working." He later clarified his statement by affirming more enforcement efforts were needed.[41] Critics of drug policy have noted that Western intervention in Latin America is often accompanied by neo-liberal economic and social policy, privatization, and corporate expansion.[42] Thus, the intention of the war on drugs is most probably multifaceted. Critics observe that "Canada and the US have increased their support for the Mexican police and army" in their drug war interventions, at the same time that human rights violations and violence by these groups and the militarization of society are being questioned domestically.[43]

The Summit of Americas was followed up by the announcement that, in November 2012, the UN General Assembly approved a resolution presented by Mexico and co-sponsored by 95 other countries to hold a UN General Assembly Special Session on Drugs in 2016. There has not been a Special Session on Drugs since 1998. Early meetings will be held prior to the summit to discuss international concerns related to UN drug policy.

In Canada, a number of BC initiatives assert similar recommendations as the Global Commission on Drug Policy. In November 2011, four former mayors of Vancouver wrote an open letter about the ineffectiveness of marijuana prohibition. The letter states, in part, "Marijuana prohibition is – without question – a failed policy." The writers declare, "As former Mayors of the City of Vancouver, we are asking all elected leaders in British Columbia to speak out about the ineffectiveness and harms of cannabis prohibition." The mayors assert, "A regulated [legal] market would enable governments to improve community health and safety while at the same time raising millions in tax revenue."[44]

Spurred on by a campaign launched in British Columbia in 2011, Stop the Violence BC,[45] a number of politicians have endorsed the idea that cannabis should be legalized and taxed in order to reduce drug trade violence and assure safer communities.[46] In February 2012, four former BC attorneys general endorsed their campaign and called for the legalization of cannabis. Their open letter to BC Premier Christy Clark and opposition leader Adrian Dix (NDP) also called for the taxation of cannabis.[47] This letter was followed, in April 2012, by an open letter by eight current BC mayors, including the mayor of Vancouver, calling on the Liberal provincial government to legalize cannabis in an effort to reduce crime associated with the marijuana trade. The mayors also sent a letter to Premier Clark and opposition party leaders "urging them to support the regulation and taxation of cannabis."[48] In March 2012, Victoria, BC, city council voted unanimously to support Stop the Violence BC and to end cannabis prohibition and adopt a health-based strategy. In May 2012, Vancouver city council endorsed the Stop the Violence BC campaign to end cannabis prohibition and to adopt a health-based strategy.[49]

Following these events, cannabis activist Dana Larsen created the Sensible BC campaign to call for the provincial government to pass the Sensible Policing Act. This amendment to the BC Policing Act would limit police from enforcing the provisions of the Controlled Drugs and Substances Act that criminalize simple possession of cannabis by adults.[50] Sensible BC is calling upon the federal government to either remove cannabis from the Controlled Drugs and Substances Act or to provide British Columbia with a Section 56 exemption, so that cannabis can be legally taxed and sold to adults. A 2013 study estimates that it costs about $10 million annually in British Columbia alone to enforce criminal prohibition against cannabis possession.[51]

Canada has long touted its supposedly more benign approach to illegal drugs, but we now find ourselves lagging behind even the United States, which has been the key supporter of the international "war on drugs." The distinction between policy in Canada and some US states is epitomized by the fact that adults in Colorado may legally grow up to six marijuana plants in their home for personal use. In contrast, Canadians who are found to be growing six cannabis plants could be subject to a mandatory minimum sentence of 6 months in prison.

As of 2013, two Canadian federal parties, the Green Party and the Liberal Party, officially support the end of cannabis prohibition and the adoption of a strategy that includes taxation and health-based regulation. To date, the Bloc Québécois and the New Democratic Party favour decriminalization of small amounts of cannabis. The lone holdout is the Conservative Party of Canada, which as we write, has a majority government and vehemently opposes the legalization – or decriminalization of cannabis.

Even though the reform movement to end the global war on drugs is strong, it is difficult to predict what the future will hold in Canada, especially in relation to marijuana grow ops, criminal justice and civil regulation, and Canadian mainstream media. What is clear is that this is a rapidly shifting terrain and it is difficult to know the outcome. As we discussed in the beginning of this book, media, vocal claims makers, and police-fuelled drug scares shape civil and criminal laws and societal attitudes and practices. We hope that history does not repeat itself, as media-fuelled drug scares in and outside of Canada have most often led to repressive and expensive policy; negative and enduring race, class, and gendered stereotypes; misinformation about drugs and the people who use, produce, and sell them; an expansion of criminal justice and civil regulation; increased sentencing and incarceration – and terrible harms to individuals, families, and communities.

Appendix: Methodological Issues

Our analysis of marijuana grow ops emerges from a larger 3-year study, "The Media, Methamphetamine, and Marijuana Grow-op Project." Under the direction of the lead author, we collected and analysed 15 years (1995–2009) of newspaper articles in national, provincial, and local newspapers in British Columbia with a focus on how a supposedly "dire" social problem like residential marijuana cultivation is contextualized in mainstream news reporting. We sought out the context of claims about marijuana cultivation and identified the key spokespeople. We were mindful that scholars like Stuart Hall have found that the potency and longevity of media-based claims are often established through their articulation with other ideas about social and political life. Thus, we analysed how the cultivation of marijuana was articulated or linked to other "social problems" and larger themes.

We used an interpretative thematic analysis to get at the underlying concepts that structure the stories told in the newspaper articles. To analyse these articles, we repeatedly read through each one to identity patterns and recurring themes. In this process, we both noted themes that appeared repeatedly and identified ideas that were new or different. We then established a set of codes based on the themes and ideas emerging from this review of the data. We read through the articles again, and these codes were applied to all data using the qualitative data analysis software NVivo. We coded the articles in chunks using these codes to organize and retrieve examples illustrative of the main themes. While coding the articles with NVivo, we revised the initial set of codes again, to accommodate new discoveries and to create subcodes that represented a more nuanced approach to the themes in the data. We then retrieved samples of each code and compared them across a larger sample of the newspaper articles to ensure that we had used these codes in a consistent manner. At this point, we revised the coding according to the findings from the previous step.

Because more than one code can be assigned to the same chunk of data, NVivo enabled us to capture the intersection of themes and then to retrieve data that reflected these intersections. One of the disadvantages of our approach to coding was that it broke the data into small pieces, thus, potentially eliminating the connections between themes. To address this concern, we used NVivo to generate matrix tables that illustrated the relationships between analytical categories. For example, we identified 237 thematic codes in the newspaper articles about marijuana grow ops, including the following: civil liberties, crime, enforcement, arrests and charges, crop valuation, plant counts, police claims, grow-op characteristics, sentencing, violence, organized crime, and exports. Rarely did any of these themes appear alone. NVivo allowed us to capture their interrelationship and gain an overall perspective on how some themes were related to others.

In NVivo we were also able to code for geographical locations (cities, towns). We also coded for and identified 124 spokespeople. The final sample included 2,524 articles published from 1995 to 2009 in the *Globe and Mail*, the *Province*, the *Vancouver Sun*, and the *Times Colonist*.

Although there are key differences between the four newspapers, one of our key findings is that when it comes to the topic of marijuana cultivation, newspapers in our study exhibit very similar perspectives and draw on similar (or even identical) spokespeople to substantiate their claims. We specifically looked for differences between these newspapers when analysing our large database of articles. There are key differences such as format, use of photographs, and amount of information included in headlines. The *Province*, for example, used a tabloid format that relies on coloured pictures and large headlines to convey its message. The *Vancouver Sun* and the Victoria-based *Times Colonist*, along with the *Globe and Mail*, were less sensationalist in their coverage. The *Globe and Mail* contained fewer stories about the cultivation of marijuana, but those stories were often longer and more investigative, and the stories in this paper often drew on information that crossed provincial borders. The *Globe and Mail* was more likely to cover the issue of US-Canada relations especially when its reporters wrote about attempts by the federal government to decriminalize possession of small amounts of cannabis in the early 2000s. *Globe and Mail* articles were somewhat more likely to offer other perspectives than law enforcement. Nevertheless, *Globe and Mail* columnists were as likely as those writing for the *Vancouver Sun* or the *Province* to take a hard line against any attempts to change cannabis laws, and they often drew on the most egregious claims about grow ops to support their case. The *Vancouver Sun* and the Victoria *Times Colonist* included shorter articles than the *Globe and Mail*, articles that were often very similar to each other given that they were both owned by Canwest Communications at the time. The *Province* was the least likely to be comprehensive in its coverage and included much shorter stories. Although the tabloid format of this latter paper was more provocative, its photographs and information were not necessarily more extreme or controversial than the other papers when it came to information about marijuana grow ops. Despite these differences, our analysis of the themes and their overlap with each other, revealed that the underlying messages are remarkably similar. This is a key finding of our study. All three of these latter papers were more likely to focus on stories about British Columbia, but we did not discover a preference for the placement of news articles about marijuana grow ops in our sample, in terms of where articles appeared in the newspapers (front page, back page, etc.). In all four newspapers, articles appeared in front pages, inside pages, and across newspaper sections.

We were concerned that the alternative press in the lower mainland of British Columbia might have a different but important perspective on this issue. To test this theory, we analysed a sample of articles from the *Georgia Straight*, a weekly free paper available in the lower mainland of British Columbia. It has a readership of 804,000. We searched for articles on marijuana in the *Georgia Straight* from 1995 to 2009 (our study period). The majority of the articles we found in this publication were about medical marijuana, reviews of movies with content about drug use, Marc Emery (a pot activist who was extradited to the United States for selling pot seeds by mail order), Ibogaine, and Insite (Vancouver's supervised injection site). For example, for 2007, we conducted a search for articles in four separate categories: marijuana, cannabis, drug policy, and mandatory minimums. Of the 23 articles from 2007 that fit the search criteria, only one mentions growing marijuana in reference to the proposed mandatory minimum sentencing bill. There are two short notices about the documentary film, *The Union;* however, they were not film reviews (the documentary is about the marijuana-growing business). The 20 remaining 2007 *Georgia Straight* articles that fit the search criteria were about poppy for medicine (with a brief nod to marijuana as medicine), foster care children, and a brief sentence about marijuana use rates; two articles about Ibogaine for drug treatment, one of which briefly mentions marijuana as a drug treatment; an open letter about the 1907 race riots in Vancouver which are believed to have started Canada down the road to drug prohibition and the later criminalization of marijuana; drug use rates for gays and lesbians; and two mentions of marijuana in films and new music releases. The *Georgia Straight* provides alternative views about marijuana in contrast to the newspapers we analysed. It was not our intent to analyse the alternative press in our study; however, while we found that mainstream newspapers were actively reporting on marijuana grow ops, the *Georgia Straight* was rarely covering the issue in our study period. Nevertheless, the focus of our study was a systematic analysis of news stories about marijuana growing in four widely read mainstream newspapers.

Notes

Introduction

1 Gordon, 2004, p. A3.
2 Ibid.
3 Nolan & Kenny, 2003, pp. x, xi.
4 Gordon, 2004, p. A3.
5 Bennett & Bernstein, 2013, p. 4.
6 Ibid., p. 6.
7 Dhillon, 2012, p. A3.
8 Nor has domestic and global drug prohibition policy led to a decrease in drug addiction, drug use, and drug-related violence. See Room & Reuter, 2012.
9 Adlaf, Begin, & Sawka, 2005, pp. 62, 57.
10 Flight, 2007, p. 40.
11 See Caulkins & Pacula, 2006.
12 See National Anti-Drug Strategy, 2011.
13 Lucas, 2008; Nolan & Kenny, 2003.
14 Racine, Flight, & Sawka, 2008; Nolan & Kenny, 2003.
15 Ipsos Reid, 2012; Stop the Violence BC, 2012.
16 Burawoy, 2005, p. 24.
17 Fifty-two per cent of the readership of the *Province* is male, compared with 48% of the *Sun*'s readership; and 33% of the *Province*'s readers are aged 35–49 (*Sun*, 28%). Fifty per cent of the *Province*'s readers have an annual household income over $75,000 (*Sun*, 49%), and 30% of readers of the *Province* are university graduates compared with 44% of *Sun* readers (Canwest News, 2009, pp. 15 and 21). The cumulative weekly readership of both print and online versions of the *Province* is 866,800; this figure for

the *Vancouver Sun* is 841,600 (Canwest News, n.d.). The *Province* captures approximately 22% of the Vancouver readership compared with 23% for the *Sun* and 4% for the *Globe and Mail* (Canwest News, 2009, p. 10).

18 See Jiwani, 2003; Razack, 2002; Thobani, 2007b.

19 Campbell, 2000; Fraser & Kylie, 2008.

20 Boyd, 1999, 2004, 2008; Campbell, 2000; Flavin & Paltrow, 2010; Gomez, 1997; Humphries, 1999.

21 Ferrell & Websdale, 1999; Hayward & Young, 2004, p. 259.

22 Best, 1995.

23 Reinarman & Levine, 2000.

24 Altheide, 2002; Barak, 1994; Best, 1995, 1999; Cohen, 1972; Cohen & Young, 1981; Dowler, 2003; Eldridge, 1993; Ericson, Baranek, & Chan, 1991; Garofalo, 1981; Hall, 1981; Heath & Gilbert, 1996; Howitt, 1998; Lambertus, 2004; Mann & Zatz, 2002; McMullan, 2001, 2005; McMullan & McClung, 2006; Surette, 1992; Thobani, 2007b; Wykes, 2001.

25 Hall, 1981.

26 Websdale & Ferrell, 1999, p. 355.

27 McMullan, 2005, p. 18.

28 See Best, 1995; Cavender, 2004.

29 Cooke & Sturges, 2009.

30 McGovern & Lee, 2010, p. 446.

31 Kozolanka, Mazepa, & Skinner, 2012, pp. 1–9.

32 Reiner, 2000.

33 Chermak & Weiss, 2005, p. 503.

34 Chibnall, 1977; Cavender, 2004; Cooke & Sturges, 2009; Ericson et al., 1991; Hall et al., 1978; Reiner, 2000.

35 McMullan, 2005, p. 18.

36 Chermak & Weiss, 2005, p. 501; Ericson, 2007.

37 Boyd & Carter, 2010a, 2010b, 2012; Chiricos, 2006; Coomber, 2006; Coomber, Morris, & Dunn, 2000; Gomez, 1997; Goode, 2008; Greaves et al., 2002; Humphries, 1999; Manning, 2006; Reinarman & Duskin, 1999; Reinarman & Levine, 1997a, 1997b, 2000; Taylor, 2008; Young, 1981.

38 Reinarman & Levine, 1997a, 1997b, 2000.

39 Haines-Saah, et al., 2013, pp. 6, 9.

40 Ibid., pp. 7–8.

41 Ibid., p. 8.

42 Purvis & Hunt, 1993.

43 Fraser & Moore, 2008, p. 741.

44 Hall, 1981, p. 241; Huxford, 2001, p. 51.

45 Hall, 1981, p. 242; original emphasis.

46 Ibid.
47 Jenkins, 1999, p. 20.
48 Martel, 2006.
49 Woodiwess, 2001, p. 3.
50 Grinspoon & Bakalar, 1997, p. 1.
51 *Le Dain Commission Interim Report*, p. 8.
52 Ibid.
53 Grinspoon & Bakalar, 1997; Nolan & Kenny, 2003, pp. 93–94.
54 Degenhardt & Hall, 2012, p. 56. A short summary of the most recent review
    of the epidemiological literature on the negative health effects of cannabis
    use notes that although studies of the health effects of *chronic* cannabis
    use (daily or near daily use) are complicated by use of other substances
    including tobacco and alcohol, research suggests that cannabis can have
    adverse health effects on some users. This is especially the case for those
    individuals who begin cannabis use in their teenage years and use more
    than weekly during young adulthood. Data also suggest there are cases of
    cannabis dependence among heavy or chronic users.

    The risk of dependence on cannabis is about 9% among persons who
    have ever used this drug, although this statistic is lower than risk for depen-
    dence among nicotine users, at 32%, and 15% for users of alcohol. However,
    dependence to marijuana is not the same as dependence to narcotics or alco-
    hol, for on cessation of marijuana, physical withdrawal syndrome is absent.
    People who regularly smoke cannabis have more symptoms of bronchitis
    and may be more susceptible to respiratory infections and pneumonia,
    although the long-term effects of cannabis smoking on respiratory function
    are less clear. There seems to be some evidence that cannabis smoking is
    related to an increased risk in lung cancers, although uncertainty remains
    about the risk of oral and other respiratory cancers among those who smoke
    cannabis (and this is influenced by the regularity and amount smoked).

    Smoking cannabis can also increase the likelihood of experiencing
    angina in those with heart disease. Some research suggests that minor cog-
    nitive impairment might be an effect of long-term cannabis use, although
    it is difficult to determine if these effects are attributable to acute drug
    effects, abstinence effects, drug residues, or changes in the brain as a result
    of cumulative THC exposure (see chapter 2 for further discussion of THC).

    Although cannabis use is more strongly related to the use of other illicit
    drugs than tobacco or alcohol, the reasons for this remain unclear, and the
    claim that cannabis acts as a gateway drug is unfounded. It would thus
    be premature to conclude that a simple causal relationship exists between
    cannabis use and other drug use.

Some research suggests that cannabis use may trigger or amplify psychotic symptoms or disorders for those vulnerable, although the magnitude of these relationships is debatable. However, there is no evidence to date that cannabis is the cause of psychosis of schizophrenia. (See Reinarman, 2011, pp. 179–181).

55 Degenhart & Hall, 2012, p. 62.
56 Ibid., p. 63.
57 Ibid., p. 61.
58 Fischer et al., 2009; Room et al., 2008.
59 Giffen, Endicott, & Lambert, 1991, pp. 599–600.
60 Decorte et al., 2011; Manning, 2007.
61 Adlaf, Begin, & Sawka, 2005, pp. 62, 57.
62 Vancouver Coastal Health, 2007.
63 Stockwell et al., 2006.
64 Stewart et al., 2009, p. 1.
65 Ibid., p. 2.
66 Ibid., p. 35.
67 Smith et al., 2010, p. 9.
68 See Fisher et al., 2011, and Degenhardt's and Hall's 2012 discussion of the health risks related to different drugs. Although there are some documented health-related risks related to cannabis use, they are much less than adverse risks related to alcohol, tobacco, cocaine, and amphetamine use. In addition, unlike use of legal drugs such as alcohol and tobacco or criminalized drugs such as opiates and other depressants, it is nearly impossible to fatally overdose on cannabis.
69 S. Brennan, 2012, pp. 31–33; Brennan & Dauvergne, 2011, p. 17; Dauvergne, 2009, p. 5.
70 Statistics Canada, 2013a, CANSIM Table 252-0051.
71 S. Brennan, 2012, pp. 19, 31–33.
72 Statistics Canada, 2013a.
73 Statistics Canada, 2013a.
74 Brennan & Dauvergne, 2011, p. 17; Dauvergne, 2009, p. 5.
75 Brennan & Dauvergne, 2011, p. 17.
76 Brennan & Dauvergne, 2011; Dauvergne, 2009, p. 50.
77 Statistics Canada, 2013b.
78 Ibid.
79 Dauvergne, 2009, p. 5; Wallace, 2009, p. 11.
80 Brennan & Dauvergne, 2011.
81 Boyd, 2013.

82 Motiuk & Vuong, 2005, p. 24.

83 Ibid.

84 Motiuk & Vuong, 2001, 2005.

85 Bennett & Bernstein, 2013, p. 25.

86 Correctional Investigator of Canada, 2012; Office of the Correctional Investigator of Canada, 2012; Office of the Provincial Health Officer (BC), 2013.

87 Mahony, 2011, p. 22.

88 Ibid., p. 27.

89 Personal communication with Dr. Patti Janssen, UBC School of Population and Public Health, 5 July 2012.

90 Mahoney, 2011, pp. 20, 26.

91 Ibid., p. 26.

92 Dauvergne, 2009, p. 14. Historically this is not unusual; cases that are stayed, dismissed, and discharged vary for different offences. Overall, about 30% of all cases of crime reported by the police are dropped. Traffic violation cases result in the highest percentage of guilty decisions. In contrast, attempted murder accounts for only 22% of cases resulting in a guilty plea.

93 See Boyd, 1995, p. 39. In 1973, amendments to the Criminal Code provided new criminal sanctions: absolute and conditional discharges. Neil Boyd explains that "an absolute discharge involves no penalty other than courtoom appearance and a finding of guilt" and a conditional discharge "involves the completion of a condition, typically probation or community service, prior to discharge." Since the 1970s, many people charged with marijuana possession have received a discharge.

94 Bennett & Bernstein, 2013, p. 7.

95 Canadian Centre for Justice Statistics, 2011; Statistics Canada, 2013a, CANSIM Table 252-0051.

96 Canadian Centre for Justice Statistics, 2011; Dauvergne, 2009, p. 17; Statistics Canada, 2013a, CANSIM Table 252-0051.

97 S. Brennan, 2012, p. 12.

98 Drug Policy Alliance, 2012.

99 National Space Aeronautics Administration (2011), "Mission," retrieved 21 Dec. 2011 from http://www.nasa.gov/missions/science/biofarming.html.

100 E.g., UNODC, 2010a, 2010b.

101 E.g., Janson, 2002; Snitzman, Olsson, & Room, 2008; Bone & Waldron, 1997.

102 Decorte, Potter, & Bouchard, 2011.

103 See *Cannabis Culture: Marijuana Magazine*, retrieved 13 Dec. 2011 from http://www.cannabisculture.com/. For more information on this magazine, see also Boyd & Carter, 2010b; Decorte, Potter, & Bouchard, 2011; Manning, 2007.

104 We would like to point out that poppy growers do meet to advocate for legal regulation and to bring their crop to market.

105 Decorte, Potter, & Bouchard, 2011.

106 Caputo & Ostrom, 1994.

107 Wilkins & Caswell, 2004.

108 Wilkins, Bhatta, & Caswell, 2002, p. 372.

109 Ibid., p. 373.

110 Hough et al., 2003.

111 Ibid., p. viii.

112 Ibid., p. ix.

113 Weisheit, 1990, p. 124.

114 Hafley & Tewksbury, 1995.

115 Ibid., p. 203.

116 Graduate Institute of International and Development Studies – Small Arms Survey. 2011.

117 A 2012 journalistic account of outdoor cannabis growers in Marion County, Kentucky, by James Higdon, titled *The Cornbread Mafia*, claims that state marshals, police, the DEA, and the FBI have escalated the war on drugs in the United States. He also claims that the media and police in Marion County colluded in depicting the county as lawless, and nonviolent marijuana growers were represented as violent criminals. He argues that residents in Marion County have been hit hard by economic downturns, and marijuana growing is one contemporary response to these conditions.

   In addition, a 2012 journalistic account of legal outdoor medical cannabis collectives in Mendocino County, California, by Doug Fine, entitled *Too High to Fail: Cannabis and the New Green Economic Revolution*, highlights the peaceful growers he encountered and the medicinal value of cannabis. Fine recommends that cannabis be legally regulated, arguing that to do so would remedy the US economy while crippling the illegal drug trade.

118 Potter, 2010; Potter & Dann, 2005, p. 92.

119 Potter & Dann, 2005, p. 90.

120 Potter & Dann, 2005.

121 Hakkarainen & Perala, 2011.

122 Decorte, 2011.

123 Hammersvik et al., 2012, p. 1.
124 Ibid., p. 6.
125 Caulkins & Pacula, 2006.
126 E.g., Fischer et al., 2003; Hathaway & Erickson, 2003; Lucas, 2008.
127 Easton, 2004.
128 Bouchard, 2007, 2008; Bouchard, Alain, & Nguyén, 2009, Bouchard, Potter, & Decorte, 2011.
129 Bouchard, 2008, p. 304.
130 See Easton, 2004.
131 Bouchard, Alain, & Nguyen, 2009.
132 Ibid.
133 Kalacska & Bouchard, 2011, p. 424.
134 Werb, Nosyk, Kerr, Fischer, Montaner, & Wood, 2012, p. 1.
135 Ibid., pp. 6, 7.
136 Malm & Tita, 2006.
137 Ibid., p. 363. It seems evident from Figure 1 on page 363 that this is the case.
138 Plecas, Malm, & Kinney, 2005.
139 Dandurand, Plecas, Chin, & Segger, 2002.
140 Chin, Dandurand, Plecas, & Segger, 2001.
141 See Figure 3.3, which is actually an estimation, not actual numbers from seizure date/records.
142 Plecas et al., 2005, p. 32.
143 Plecas et al., 2005; Royal Canadian Mounted Police, 2011c.
144 See Table 5.2, in Plecas et al., 2005, p. 42.
145 Ibid., pp. 1, 35.
146 Ibid., p. 1.
147 Ibid.
148 Plecas et al., 2005, see Tables 2.10 and 2.ll, pp. 21–2. By using data from suspected cases, the authors claim that grow ops increased in BC by 203% between 1997 and 2003. Thus, by using "suspected cases," the problem of marijuana cultivation seems bigger than it might be.

   Curiously, the 2002 paper spends more time examining "founded cases," while the 2005 paper only discusses them briefly. For example, the 2002 paper includes a regional breakdown of founded cases; however, this information is excluded from the 2005 paper even though it would have been useful to have this type of regional comparison for suspected versus founded cases.

   The authors' claim in the 2005 paper about increases in marijuana cultivation in British Columbia is based on cases coming to the attention of the police rather than founded cases. Over the 7-year period, the authors state in Table 2.10 that 87% of the cases where a full investigation was conducted were founded cases, yet, if one looks at increases over time using only founded cases, the results are quite different. The correct number of founded cases over the 7-year period would be 58%. Therefore, over the 7-year study period, the number of founded cases increased by only 62% (in contrast to 203%). Furthermore, it appears that the number of founded cases decreased from 1997 to 2003.

149 See, e.g., City of Surrey, 2009; Garis, 2009, 4 Nov.; Garis, 2009.
150 Solecki, Burnett, & Li, 2011.
151 Beeby, 2011.
152 Department of Justice, 2011c.
153 Solecki, Burnett, & Li, 2011.
154 Ibid., p. 15.
155 Ibid., p. 17.
156 Ibid., pp. 20–2.
157 Ibid., p. 20.
158 Ibid., p. 11.
159 Ibid., p. 27.
160 Boyd, 2004; Grayson, 2008.
161 Department of Justice, 2011c; Grayson, 2008, 190.
162 Mulgrew, 2005.
163 Boyd & Carter, 2008, 2010a, 2010b, 2011; *Cannabis Culture*; Decorte et al., 2011; Poole, 1998.
164 Decorte et al., 2011.

1. A Brief Sociohistory of Drug Scares, Racialization, Nation Building, and Policy

1 Reinarman & Levine, 1997a, p. 1.
2 Best, 1995, 1999; Reinarman & Levine, 1997a, 1997b.
3 Martel, 2006, p. 14.
4 Goode, 2008, p. 539.
5 Anderson, 1991; Boyd, 1984; Comack, 1986; Boyd, 2006; Mosher, 1998.
6 In the late nineteenth and early twentieth centuries, there was considerable overlap between anti-opiate and temperance reformers, and both groups identified drugs such as opium and alcohol as the main culprit of society's ills. Reformers associated alcohol and opium with poverty, urbanization, wife beating, criminality, and the disintegration of family values.

The Women's Christian Temperance Union (WCTU) and the anti-opium movement believed that moderate use of alcohol and opium was impossible. In order to protect the family and the nation, they advocated sobriety and the criminalization of these drugs. Opium smoking was constructed as the domain of "evil Chinese men" who lured moral white women and men into a life of deprivation and crime.

Following colonization, First Nations people were seen by colonizers as "savages" unable to control their alcohol consumption (introduced to them by white settlers and fur traders).

7 Maracle, 1993.

8 Anderson, 1991; Mawani, 2002.

9 Anderson, 1991.

10 Boyd, 1984; Comack, 1986.

11 Anderson, 1991. A number of city licence fees were also initiated to profit from and curtail Chinese people from participating in numerous business ventures, including laundries and green grocers.

12 Anderson, 1991, pp. 68, 69.

13 Ibid., p. 65.

14 Yet, Ottawa was slightly tempered early on because of trade agreements with China and some industrialists and merchants who wished to continue profiting from the recruitment of Chinese labourers for contract work. In 1885, the BC government sent a resolution to Ottawa about restricting Chinese immigration.

The Anti-Chinese League in Vancouver in 1886 was made up of prominent politicians including the mayor, members of Parliament, and ex-aldermen. Politicians, law enforcement, moral reformers, and media outlets contributed to the enactment of anti-Asian discourse, and discriminatory policies and law. Thus, government representatives of the city were at the forefront of the anti-Chinese movement along with white labour unions.

The media in Vancouver also played a significant role in constructing British settlers as the rightful citizens of the new colony and demonizing Chinese men as immoral outsiders.

15 This repeated itself following entry into the Second World War with the confiscation of homes, property, and business, and the internment of thousands of Japanese citizens and residents.

16 Boyd, 1984, p. 115.

17 Boyd, 1984; Comack, 1986; Boyd, 2006.

18 Solomon & Green, 1988.

19 Barnes, 2002, p. 193.

20 Giffen, Endicott, & Lambert, 1991, pp. 74–5.

21 Ibid., p. 75.
22 Canada was not officially represented at the conference.
23 Anderson, 1991; Boyd, 2008; Martel, 2006; Valverde, 1991.
24 In the United States, a number of laws were also enacted to deport suspected agitators.
25 Musto, 1987.
26 Hewitt, 2006.
27 Anthony & Solomon, 1973, p. 3.
28 Anthony & Solomon, 1973; Carstairs, 2006.
29 Anderson, 1991, p. 115.
30 Giffen et al., 1991, pp. 594, 596.
31 BC Archives, 2008, p. 125.
32 Carstairs, 2006, p. 26.
33 Ibid., p. 27.
34 Nolan & Kenny, 2003, p. x.
35 Hewitt, 2006, p. 59.
36 Ibid., p. 43.
37 Ibid., p. 59.
38 Ibid., p. 131.
39 Ibid., p. 39.
40 Giffen et al., 1991, p. 129.
41 Ibid., p. 130.
42 Ibid., p. 127.
43 Mikuriya, 1968, pp. 269–70.
44 Ibid., p. 253.
45 However, marijuana has a long history in human societies. Marijuana is a product of the hemp plant, *cannabis sativa*, and the drug was used for medicinal purposes in China, Africa, and India for thousands of years, and was popular in medieval Europe; however, it only came to the attention of Western doctors in the mid-nineteenth century. At that time, these same doctors praised marijuana for its medicinal qualities and prescribed it for a range of ailments.
46 Said, 2001.
47 Campbell, 2000.
48 Murphy, 1973 (1922), pp. 332–3.
49 Giffen et al., 1991, pp. 599–600.
50 Musto, 1987.
51 Ibid., p. 219.
52 The WCTU also came into prominence and gained a large following in the early 1900s. These women constructed alcohol as an evil substance

threatening families and the nation. White middle-class women, unable to vote and participate in the formal political process, saw themselves as the moral defenders of the home and of Anglo-Saxon life. They regarded sobriety and morality as "innate" to the female sex, and reformers sought to "transform" immoral women and men (Hannah-Moffat, 2001).

As part of the war economy, national alcohol prohibition was enacted in Canada in 1918. It lasted for only one year, although several provinces continued to criminalize the sale of alcohol. Both temperance and anti-opiate reformers argued that moderate use of alcohol and opium (in smoking form) was impossible; thus, abstinence and self-control were advocated.

53 Anslinger & Oursler, 1961.
54 Between 1929 and 1939, the unemployment rate rose. The federal government failed to adequately provide for families and single men who could not find employment. Relief camps were set up for single men in Canada by the military. Responding to terrible conditions in the camps, unemployed men organized the Relief Camp Workers Union in 1932, and from Vancouver, BC, the "On-to-Ottawa Trek" in 1935. Public sentiment was high, supporting the thousands of unemployed men who attempted to travel to Ottawa.

When the Depression began, Mackenzie King was prime minister. He ignored the plight of the unemployed and failed to respond to the concerns of Canadians and the hardships they endured.

55 Orloff, 1988.
56 Galliher et al., 1998, p. 661.
57 Anslinger & Oursler, 1961; Anslinger & Tompkins, 1953.
58 Musto, 2002, p. 428.
59 Anslinger & Oursler, 1961; Anslinger & Tompkins, 1953; Galliher et al., 1998.
60 Galliher et al., 1998; McWilliams, 1990.
61 Anslinger & Tompkins, 1953, p. 206.
62 Ibid., pp. 206–12.
63 Anslinger & Tompkins, 1953; Giffen et al., 1991.
64 Musto, 1987.
65 *Reefer Madness* opens with the following script: "The motion picture you are about to witness may startle you. It would not have been possible, otherwise, to sufficiently emphasize the frightful tale of the new drug menace which is destroying the youth of America in alarming numbers." This foreword warns film viewers that marijuana leads to "acts of shocking

violence … ending in incurable insanity … The scenes and incidents, while fictionalized for the purposes of this story, are based upon actual research into the results of marijuana addiction."

Following these warnings, the camera shifts to a number of newspaper headlines: "Dope Peddlers Caught in High School," "Federals Aid Police in Drug War," "School-Parent Organizations Join Dope Fight." Then the film cuts to a flyer, a public notice sponsored by a school and parent association, and their guest speaker, Dr. Carroll, who has come to town to educate parents about the scourge of marijuana. In the movie, Dr. Carroll shows a short film to the parents gathered in the high school. News headlines, text, and film excerpts from the US Federal Bureau of Narcotics and police illuminate how marijuana is being grown, sold, and eventually corrupting youth in towns throughout the nation. (Boyd, 2008, pp. 47–53.)

The discussion above brings our attention to how "fictional" film and news media intersect. Myths about marijuana by moral reformers in the 1930s were communicated in both film and news media and both Americans and Canadians educated themselves about the plant through these media.

66 Coomber, 2006.
67 See Anslinger & Oursler, 1961; Anslinger & Tompkins, 1953.
68 Musto, 2002, p. 422.
69 Ibid., pp. 425–6.
70 Ibid., pp. 428–9.
71 Giffen et al., 1991, p. 599.
72 Ibid., pp. 184–6.
73 Brecher and the Editors of *Consumer Reports*, 1972, p. 452.
74 LaGuardia, 1944.
75 Musto, 2002, p. 452.
76 Boyd, 2008, p. 61.
77 Carstairs, 2006, p. 153.
78 Giffen et al., 1991; Stevenson et al., 1956.
79 Interesting to note, early on the special committee refers to an article by Dr. Stevenson, published in the *Bulletin*, where he opposes any plan to set up drug maintenance programs for people addicted to heroin or other narcotics and provides misleading information about the "British system." The committee rejects other evidence and reports.
80 Senate, 1955, p. 8.
81 Ibid., p. 509.
82 *Narcotic Control Act*, S.C. 1961, c. 35.
83 Giffen et al., 1991.

84 Room & Reuter, 2012. Canada is also a signatory of these two international conventions: 1971 Convention on Psychotropic Substances and the 1988 Convention Against Illicit Trafficking in Narcotics and Psychotropic Substances.
85 Carstairs, 2006, p. 158; Martel, 2006.
86 Brecher et al., 1972, p. 422.
87 Martel, 2006; Giffen et al., 1991, p. 492.
88 Martel, 2006, p. 3.
89 Ibid.
90 Ibid.
91 Goode, 2008, p. 539.
92 Commission of Inquiry into the Non-Medical Use of Drugs, 1973.
93 Martel, 2006, p. 3.
94 Commission of Inquiry into the Non-Medical Use of Drugs, 1973.
95 Martel, 2006.
96 Ibid., p. 195.
97 Ibid.
98 Ibid., p. 192.
99 Ibid., p. 195.
100 The schedules have expanded over the years to include an ever-increasing array of mostly synthetic drugs.
101 Fischer, 1997, p. 57.
102 Ibid.; Martel, 2006.
103 There is evidence that this discursive separation of user from dealer occurred much earlier in Canada especially with the emergence of the treatment movement in the 1950s (see Giffen et al., 1991), but these debates were not focused so specifically on the cannabis user.
104 Erickson, 1992.
105 Nolan & Kenny, 2003, p. xvii.
106 Nolan & Kenny, 2003.
107 See Health Canada, 2011a.
108 Treasury Board of Canada, Department of Justice Supplementary Tables, Horizontal Initiatives, 2007/08 and 2012/13. Data on budgets for the 2007–12 period can be found at http://www.tbs-sct.gc.ca/hidb-bdih/plan-eng.aspx?Org=37&Hi=28&Pl=164. Data for the 2012–17 period can be found at http://www.tbs-sct.gc.ca/hidb-bdih/plan-eng.aspx?Org=37&Hi=28&Pl=447.
109 Boyd & Carter, 2008, 2010b; Carter, 2009; Grayson, 2008; Stoddart, 2004.
110 Reinarman & Levine, 1997b, p. 19.

2. Problematizing Marijuana Grow Ops:
   Mayerthorpe and Beyond

1 Hagan, 2001; "Our way home," 2007; Woodcock & Vakumovic, 1968.
2 Schmidt, 1998, p. A7.
3 Ibid.
4 "Kelowna drug trade 'like,'" 1998, p. B6; "Dope-growing houses worry,"
   2000, p. B7; Hunter, 2002, p. A12; Tibbetts, 2002, p. A5; Jurock, 2003, p. E1;
   "Huge pot 'factory' no," 2004, p. A14; Skelton, 18 Jan. 2005, p. A1; "Higher
   THC levels are," 2007, p. L8; Wente, 2007, p. A7; Blatchford, 2009, p. A2.
5 Ferguson, 5 July 1998a, p. A17.
6 "Harsh pot sentence," 2000, p. A14.
7 "Almost 7,000 pot," 2000, p. B3.
8 "Pot finds fixed," 1997, p. A6.
9 Skelton, 1999, p. A1
10 "RCMP, military smoke out," 2004, p. B2.
11 "Crime: 400 marijuana plants," 1999, p. B1; Skelton, 2001, p. B1; "Almost
   7,000 pot plants found," 2004, p. B3; "Princeton: Huge grow-op," 2005,
   p. A8; "20,000 pot plants seized," 2005, p. A27; "RCMP seize 3,400 marijuana," 2006, p. B7; Little, 2007 p. A3; "Cops take 4.8m joints," 2007, p. A3;
   Mercer, 2008, p. A5; "3,000 pot plants found," 2008, p. A23; "B.C. seizes its
   biggest," 2008, p. A5; Matas, 2008, p. S3.
12 Middleton, 1997a, p. A9.
13 MacQueen, 2000, p. A1.
14 Willcocks, 2002, p. A14.
15 "Theft makes pot grower angry," 2002, p. A3.
16 Plecas et al., 2002; Plecas et al., 2005.
17 See Nuttall-Smith, 2003, p. D12.
18 Easton, 2004, p. 15.
19 Ibid.
20 Cayo, 2004, p. A4.
21 Kilmer, 2012, p. 168.
22 Jiwa, 1998, p. A12.
23 Ibid.
24 Plecas et al., 2005; Solecki, Burnett, & Li, 2011.
25 Plecas et al., 2005, p. 32.
26 Canadian Firearms Centre, 1998.
27 Hall, 2003, p. B8.
28 Skelton, 25 Sept. 2004, p. C2.
29 Colebourn, 2004, p. A6.
30 O'Brian, 2004, p. B1.

31 O'Brian, 2002, p. B7.

32 "Home invaders had wrong," 2003, p. B4.

33 Ferguson, 5 July 1998a, p. A17; Fong, 1999, p. A1; Churchill, 1999, p. A1; Jiwa, 2000, p. A12; Tibbetts, 1004, p. A14; "Tougher laws and stricter," 2005, p. E6; Fraser, 2006, p. A29; "Mandatory jail sentences will," 2007, p. A21; Hunter, 2007, p. A3; Ivens, 2008, p. A6; Bailey, 2009, p. S2; Bellet, 2009, p. A7.

34 "Pot growers keeping up," 1997, p. A24.

35 Jiwa, 2000, p. A12.

36 Ibid.

37 Gordon, 2004, p. A3.

38 Skelton, 18 Jan. 2005, p. A1.

39 Ibid.

40 Pahl, 2011.

41 Ibid.

42 Ibid., p. 3.

43 Ibid., p. 5.

44 Ibid., p. 6.

45 Ibid., p. 7.

46 Pahl, 2011.

47 Freeze & Walton, 2005, p. A10.

48 Harding & Walton, 2005, p. A1.

49 Freeze & Walton, 2005, p. A10.

50 Galloway & Curry, 2005, p. A11.

51 Blackwell, 2005, p. A25.

52 Ibid.

53 "Mountie killings are a," 2005, p. A20; Sadava, 4 March 2005a, p. A1; Sadava, 4 March 2005b, p. A1; Woods, 2005, p. A5; McMartin, 2005, p. B1.

54 "Nothing benign about grow-ops," 2005, p. A18.

55 Pahl, 2011.

56 Cormier, 5 March 2005, p. A6.

57 Loyie, & Sadava, 2005, p. A1.

58 "Nothing benign about grow-ops," 2005, p. A18.

59 Hughes, 2005, p. A14.

60 In 2010, Canadian Minister of Justice Rob Nichoson extradited Marc Emery to the United States to stand trial for selling marijuana seeds through the Internet. Emery's extradition was approved even though he had claimed income and paid Canadian taxes on his business for years.

     In Canada, his alleged crime would have been subject to a fine; however, in the United States, he was subject to a 5-year prison sentence. He is serving his prison time as we write. Critics note that the Conservative-led federal government's quest to punish marijuana offences and their law-and-order stance has led to significant and far-reaching policy shifts.

Canadians are vulnerable to extradition and harsher punishment than legally prescribed in Canada. Canadians serving time in US prisons who apply to be transferred home to serve their time are being refused by the Canadian government, ignoring the tenets of federal prison transfer treaties signed by both countries.

61 Kurt Tousaw is a well-known constitutional lawyer and critic of Canada's punitive drug policy and crime policy. He has been active in a number of significant Supreme Court Charter challenges to cannabis regulation in Canada.
62 Hunter, 2005, p. A10.
63 "For the fallen Mounties," 2005, p. C6.
64 Blackwell, 2005, p. A5.
65 Appleby & Walton, 2005, p. A10.
66 Harding & Walton, 2005, p. A1.
67 Cormier, 9 March 2005, p. A6.
68 See Etzler, 2005, p. A21. Other articles included statements by BC court judges defending their sentencing practices. See Austin, 2005, p. A10.
69 Naumetz, 2005, p. A6.
70 Ibid.
71 Theodore, 2008, p. S3.
72 Ibid.
73 Plecas et al., 2005.
74 Solecki, Burnett, & Li, 2011.
75 'Marijuana is an addictive drug,'" 2007, p. A9.
76 Skelton, 1999, p. A1. See also O'Neil, 2003, p. A1.
77 Martin, 2005, p. A18.
78 Ibid.
79 Dhillon, 2012, p. A3.
80 Spencer, 20 Sept. 2007, p. A8.
81 Bellet, 2009, p. A7.
82 Degenhardt et al., 2008.
83 Siren & Applegate, 2006.
84 "PM wants marijuana bill," 2003, p. A28.

3. Marijuana Grow Ops and Organized Crime

1 Woodiwess, 2001.
2 Brennan & Dauvergne, 2011, p. 17; Dauvergne, 2009, p. 5.
3 Brennan & Dauvergne, 2011, pp. 19, 31.
4 Statistics Canada, 2013a.

5 Dyer, 1999, p. 457.
6 Ibid.
7 Ibid., p. 458.
8 Woodiwess, 2001.
9 Haysom, 1998, p. A8; Porter, 1998, p. B4; Ward, 1999, p. B1; "BC living easy for," 1999, p. A11; Berry, 2000, p. A6; Sinclair, 2001, p. A27; Bronskill, 2002, p. A1; O'Neil, 2003, p. A1; Mofina, 2003b, p. A6; Skelton & Hall, 2004, p. C2; Skelton, 7 Oct. 2005c, p. B1.
10 Tonner, 1998, p. A20.
11 McCune, 2000, A42.
12 "Ont. targets grow-ops," 2004, p. A34.
13 Ibid.
14 Middleton, 27 July 1997b, p. A9.
15 Ferguson, 5 July 1998b, p. A16.
16 Austin, 2002, p. A4.
17 "Police seek more," 2002, p. A1.
18 Ramsey, 2007, p. A3.
19 Easton, 2004.
20 Lazaruk, 24 Aug. 2008, p. A15.
21 Bellet, 10 May 2003, p. B4.
22 Bellet, 9 May 2003, p. B1.
23 Mitrovica, 1999, p. A1.
24 Gordon, 2006, p. A4.
25 Ibid.
26 Mickleburgh, 2005; Smith, 2004.
27 Howell, 2007; Smith, 2004.
28 Global Commission on Drug Policy, 2011; Robin & Reuter, 2012; Pew Center, 2008, 2009.
29 Tu Thanh, Ha, 2002, p. 1; "Higher THC levels are," 2007, p. L8; Ferguson, 5 July 1998a, p. A17.
30 Vincent, 1998, p. A6.
31 Moore, 2002, p. B4.
32 Wente, 2007, p. A17.
33 Ibid.
34 Mehmedic, Chandra, Slade et al., 2010.
35 RCMP, 2009.
36 DEA, 2008, p. 10.
37 Ibid.
38 Room et al., 2008.
39 "UN drug report unintentionally," 2006, 28 June, p. A16.
40 Moore, 2002, p. B4.

41 Boyd, 1998; Fisher et al., 2011.
42 Whereas the 2002 Moore article above also linked THC levels with organic marijuana, critics such as Lucas (2009) note that compassion clubs (illegal medical cannabis dispensaries), which exist throughout Canada providing care for over 10,000 Canadians, advance organic cannabis because the plant is not contaminated by pesticides and other chemicals which may further hinder a patient's health. Compassion clubs also note that the only legal source of medical marijuana made available in Canada is through Prairie Plants Systems, where marijuana is grown in an abandoned mine. The plants are not grown organically.
43 Bronskill, 2001, p. A1.
44 Lunman, 2002, p. 1.
45 Matas, 2002, p. n/a.
46 Smith, 2000, p. 1.
47 Anderssen, 2002, p. 1.
48 Tibbets, 2004, p. A15.
49 Luymes, 2008, p. A8.
50 Appleby, 5 July 2008, p. A13.
51 Solecki, Burnett, & Li, 2011.
52 Sinoski & Fitzpatrick, 2007, p. A1.
53 See Decorte, Potter, & Bouchard, 2011; Hough et al., 2003; and Wilkens & Casswell, 2004.
54 Poole, 1998.
55 Ramsey, 2007, p. A3.
56 Office of National Drug Control Policy (ONDCP), 2010, p. 72.
57 Personal communication, Rielle Capler (policy analyst and research coordinator, Vancouver Compassion Club), 10 Nov. 2011.
58 Dhillon, 2012, p. A3.
59 Hall & Knox, 2004, p. A5.
60 Lavoie, 2004, p. A3.
61 Luymes, 2007, p. A19.
62 Hall & Bolan, 2007, p. A1.
63 Brennan & Dauvergne, 2011, p. 17.
64 Geddes, 23 July 2012.
65 Bellet, 2000, p. B1; "Pot house invaded by," 2001, p. A3; Bronskill, 2002, p. A4; Bohn, 2003, p. B3; Fong, 2004, p. A1; Hunter, 11 Jan. 2004, p. A9; O'Brian, 2004, p. B1; Ramsey, 2005, p. A10; Badelt, 2005, p. B1; Luba, 2006 p. A12; Tonner, 2006, p. B6; Edmonds, 2006, p. B3; Keating, 2007, p. A18; Wingrove, 2008, p. A10; Fournier, 2008, p. A11; Matas, 2009, p. A7.
66 Brethour, 2007, p. S1.
67 Hall & Bolan, 2007, p. A1.

68 Reinarman & Levine, 1997b, p. 24.
69 Campbell, 2000.
70 Bolan, 2008, p. A4.
71 Bolan, 2009, p. A10.
72 Perreault, 2013, p. 3; Statistics Canada, 2013a.
73 Brennan & Dauvergne, 2011, pp. 1, 5.
74 Ibid., p. 9.
75 Perreault, 2013, p. 14.
76 Brennan & Dauvergne, 2011, p. 8; Statistics Canada, 2013a.
77 Ibid.
78 Ibid., p. 1.
79 Mahony, 2011, p. 1.
80 Ibid., p. 24.
81 Ibid., p. 9.
82 Ibid., p. 10.
83 Brennan & Dauvergne, 2011, p. 17.
84 Plecas et al., 2005, p. 32.
85 Ibid., p. 42.
86 Solecki, Burnett, & Li, 2011.
87 Ibid.
88 Ibid., p. 11.
89 Bennett & Bernstein, 2013, p. 4.
90 Ibid., p. v.
91 Woodiwess, 1993, p. 13.
92 Ibid., pp. 24, 25.
93 Bullington, 1993, p. 41.
94 ONDCP, 2010, 2011.
95 US Department of State, 2012.
96 Pew Center on the States, 2008, 2009.
97 NACLA, 2002.
98 Criticism of Canadian drug policy by US spokespeople continually fails to acknowledge marijuana reform by US states and US domestic marijuana cultivation (as discussed above and in the introduction). Marijuana reform in 17 states has led to de facto decriminalization such as reduced penalties for first time offenders and fines rather than prison sentences are the norm. In November 2012, Washington and Colorado legalized the possession of one ounce of cannabis for personal use and the setting of dispensaries for the sale of cannabis.

  In addition, adults in Colorado can legally grow up to six plants in their home for personal use. As we write, 20 states and the District of Columbia have legal medical marijuana for qualified patients, yet Canada is framed by the United States as the culprit for allegedly being the source of high-potency marijuana, medical marijuana, for having weak laws, lenient judges, and porous borders. As disturbing as these unsubstantiated claims are, so is the readiness of Canadian politicians, the RCMP, and the media to leave them unchallenged.

Even though the media claims that the United States is troubled by Canadian drug policy, it is difficult to determine the extent to which US drug policy affects Canada, nor did we set out to answer this question in our study. Critics of US drug policy refer to the Americanization of international law, including the implementation of harsh prohibitionist drug law, throughout the world. US support and aid (including military aid) to other nations is linked to enacting US-style international law, including drug law, and economic and social policies. Ethan Nadelman notes, "Foreign governments have responded to US pressure, inducements, and examples by enacting new criminal laws, regarding drug trafficking, money laundering, insider trading, and organized crime and by changing financial and corporate secrecy laws as well as their codes of criminal procedure to better accommodate US requests for assistance." Since the war on terror following 9/11, US pressure increased.

However, Canada is not reliant on US aid, although the free flow of trade is always a concern with its more powerful southern neighbour. Since 2007, a growing number of critics point to the emulation of American-style failed drug policy by the federal Conservative government, including mandatory minimum sentencing for drug offences and prison building. The DEA and US ambassadors, and other US politicians and pundits have applied pressure to Canadian officials. However, outside of public criticism printed in the media, we are not privy to private, off the record, conversations between government officials. However, Canadian scholars on US/Canadian relations note that historically there is no solid evidence that the threat of US retaliation has ever been realized nor is it a factor in shaping policy in Canada. (See Bow, 2009; Hale, 2012.)

US politicians and bureaucrats make unofficial statements to the press complaining about Canada's supposedly more liberal approach; more often than not these statements are intended for a US audience. We note that during our study period (and later) the RCMP and Canadian Border Control appear to be very open to US training and opportunities to work together as does the Conservative federal government led by Prime Minister Harper. However, we contend that US influence on Canadian drug policy is much less than some would suggest.

The media's and Canadian officials' fear of a negative US response to drug policy reform is often self-serving rather than real. During our study period, in contrast to media reports, we saw no evidence that US/Canadian trade and relations have been negatively impacted by drug policy reform efforts in Canada. The establishment of the Canadian federal medical marijuana program and later in Vancouver, BC, the first safer injection site, Insite, and the North American Opiate Medication Initiative (NAOMI), the first contemporary heroin maintenance clinical trial, and expanded needle exchange, was not followed by a shift in trade relations.

There are also many other examples of divergent Canadian policy, such as Canada's opposition to the Vietnam War and acceptance of US draft dodgers at that time and Prime Minister Chretien's refusal to join the US-led invasion of Iraq in 2003. Events in Canada and the United States are contingent on many factors including governing political parties and global and domestic influences. Since 2007, Canadian federal drug policy is more closely aligned with US federal policy.

Prime Minister Harper's law-and-order mandate appears to be more home grown than born out of US political pressure. Moreover, Canadian federal drug policy is in direct opposition to drug policy reform efforts in Canadian provinces, cities, and towns, as well as some US states.

99 Degenhardt et al., 2008; Room & Reuter, 2012;Werb et al., 2011; Wood et al., 2010.

4. Racialization of Marijuana Grow Ops

1 Mosher, 1998, p. 6. Clayton Mosher (1999, pp. 7–11) also revealed how some contemporary reporters in Canada were prominent contributors to the racialization of crime in Ontario in the late 1980s and 1990s through his examination of news articles related to Jamaican men and crime, including Timothy Appleby, who wrote for the *Globe and Mail*.

Appleby's anecdotal observations about a crime wave perpetuated by young Black, primarily Jamaican men (no substantive evidence supported this claim) contributed to changes in the enforcement agency of the Department of Immigration to prioritize and deport Black men arrested for crimes in Canada.

In our study, we discovered that Appleby also produced a number of articles in the 2000s which contributed to the racialization of marijuana grow ops, early on linking them to Vietnamese men.

2 Reinarman & Levine, 1997b, p. 24.
3 See Mirchandani & Chan, 2002; as well as Chan & Mirchandani, 2002; Jiwani, 2002, Macklin, 2002; McCalla & Satzewich, 2002.
4 See Hall, 1997; Tator & Henry, 2006.
5 Thobani, 2007.

6 Razack, 2002, p. 3.
7 Freeze, 2006, A8; Ramsey, 2006, p. A3; "British pot grow-ops skyrocket," 2007, p. A31; Bellet & Shore, p. A1; Ramsey, 2007, p. A3; Mason, 2007, p. A7; Luymes, 2008, p. A8.
8 Royal Canadian Mounted Police, 2009, p. 17.
9 "People, drugs and money," 2003, p. B4.
10 Ibid.
11 O'Neil, 2003, p. A1.
12 Ibid.
13 Ibid.
14 Ibid.
15 Skelton, Hall, & Knox, 2004, p. A5.
16 Bolan, 2004, p. A1.
17 Culbert, 2005, p. A7.
18 Dyer, 1999; Thobani, 2007b; Razack, 2002.
19 Skelton, 11 March 2005b, p. A1.
20 "Asian 'child slaves' found," 2007, p. C27.
21 Appleby & O'Reilly, 2006, p. A21.
22 "Production of potent pot," 2007, p. A8.
23 Ibid.
24 Young, 18 Sept. 2004, p. D1.
25 Ibid.
26 Plecas et al., 2005.
27 Solecki, Burnett, & Li, 2011; Plecas et al., 2005.
28 Ibid., p. 17.
29 Ibid., p. 36.
30 Plecas et al., 2005.
31 Grayson, 2008, p. 190.
32 Mosher, 1998; Smith, 2006, p. 85.
33 Commission on Systemic Racism in the Ontario Criminal Justice System, 1995.
34 Government of Canada, 1996.
35 Bennett & Bernstein, 2013; Office of the Provincial Health Office (BC), 2013.
36 Office of the Correctional Investigator, 2012, p. 3.
37 Ibid., p. 16.
38 Ibid., p. 11.
39 Ibid.
40 Ibid., p. 31.
41 Ibid., pp. 3, 4.
42 Ibid., p. 6.

43 Ibid., p. 28.
44 Correctional Service of Canada, 2009b.
45 Correctional Service of Canada, 2009a, 2009b.
46 Motiuk & Vuong, 2001, 2005.
47 Boyd, 2006; Correctional Service of Canada, 2009b; Nellis, 2012.
48 J. Macdonnell, BC Corrections Branch, personal communication, 31 July
   2007; Office of the Provincial Health Office (BC), 2013.
49 J. Macdonnell, personal communication, 31 July 2007.
50 Office of the Provincial Health Officer (BC), 2013.
51 Personal communication, 5 July 2012 with Dr. Patricia Janssen, from
   "Doing Time" study; Cowper, 2012.
52 Cowper, 2012, p. 23.
53 Ibid., p. 26.
54 Yalkin, & Kirk, 2012.
55 Ibid., p. 1.
56 Alexander, 2010; Davis, 2003; Drucker, 2011; Mauer and the Sentencing
   Project 1999; Sullivan & Tifft, 1980.
57 Edwards, Bunting, & Garcia, 2013, p. 4.
58 Ibid.
59 Ibid., p. 75.
60 Levine, Gettman, & Siegal, 2010, pp. 5, 6.
61 Ibid., p. 5.
62 Ibid.
63 Levine & Siegal, 2011, p. 1.
64 Ibid.

5. Civil Responses to Marijuana Grow Ops

1 *Jason Arkinstall and Jennifer Green* v. *City of Surrey, British Columbia, and
   Power Authority, and Attorney General of British Columbia* (2008). Hereafter
   referred to as *Arkinstall* v. *City of Surrey.*
2 Young, 1997, p. A1.
3 "Police seek more power," 2002, p. A1.
4 Oberman, 2002, p. 1.
5 Plecas et al., 2002, 2005.
6 Pemberton & Morton, 2002, p. B8.
7 Tibbetts, 2002, p. A5.
8 Solecki, Burnett, & Li, 2011, p.14
9 For information from the RCMP, see RCMP, 2011d. See also BC Hydro,
   2011.

10 "A drug-house primer," 1999, p. A8.
11 Jurock, 2003, p. E1. This list of tips includes the following:

- Few people are seen coming and going from the home.
- People make late night or very short visits.
- There are strange smells coming from the home, often at the same time of day or night. It can smell strongly of fabric softener, or have a "skunk" smell.
- People are continually coming and going with large bulky items or garbage bags.
- There is evidence of tampering to the electric meter (damaged or broken seals) or the ground around it.
- There are water and/or electrical cords running to the basement or outbuildings.
- The home makes a humming sound or has motorized, fanlike noises.
- The property has excessive security (guard dogs, "keep out" signs, high fences, heavy chains, and locks on gates).
- The windows of the home are always covered, and have condensation on them.
- The neighbours are never seen taking groceries or furniture into the home. They put out little or no garbage.
- Outbuildings have air conditioners.

12 Sieberg, 1999, p. B1.
13 *Vancouver Sun*, 23 March 2000, p. A14.
14 "Dope-growing houses worry," 2000, p. B7.
15 Reevely, 2003, p. B1.
16 Plecas, Malm, & Kinney, 2005, p. 33.
17 Ibid., p. 8.
18 Ibid., pp. 32–34.
19 "Booby traps at pot sites," 2001, p. A15.
20 Plecas, Malm, & Kinney, 2005, p. 32.
21 Simpson, 2002, p. B5.
22 "Courts too lenient on," 2002. p. A14.
23 Dickson, 2002, p. C1.
24 Jurock, 2003, p. E1.
25 Other examples include Hume, 2004, p. A12; Weber, 2004, p. A17.
26 Bernstein & Bennett, 2013, p. 3.
27 Weber, 2004, p. A.17.
28 Hunter, 18 Jan. 2004, p. A26; Sutherland, 2007, p. C3; O'Brian, 2008, p. A3; "It's already going to pot," 2008, p. A5.
29 Dawson, Colebourn, Berry, & Tanner, 2000, p. A12.

30 Spencer, 2004, p. C10.
31 "Day 3: Series," 2006, p. A8.
32 Valverde, 2012, pp. 3, 6.
33 Bernstein & Bennett, 2013, p. 2.
34 Garis, Plecas, Cohen, & McCormick, 2009, p. 5. More information about
   this program can be obtained from the website of the Surrey Fire Chief Len
   Garis: http://www.surrey.ca/city-services/4589.aspx, retrieved 17 Nov.
   2011.
35 Garis, 2005; Carter, 2009.
36 Garis, 2005.
37 These bylaws use the capabilities of municipalities to regulate issues like
   "nuisance" and focus specifically on federally regulated substances by reiterating municipal powers to conduct inspections for electrical, fire, health,
   and other issues.
38 The Ontario Human Rights Commission (OHRC), for example, has
   recently challenged the legitimacy of some city bylaws that control the
   spacing of group homes, given that these bylaws interfere with the rights
   of people with addictions and mental health issues. See OHRC,
   2011.
39 City of Surrey, 2009; Loukedelis, 2006; e.g., City of Chilliwack, 2006.
40 Anderson, 1991. A series of discriminatory municipal bylaws were enacted
   in the late 1800s and early 1900s to exclude Chinese people from specific
   activities, especially in Vancouver, BC. These discriminatory bylaws were
   brought forward by politicians and managed by coalitions of politicians,
   police, and health and safety inspectors who came together to do so.
      Vancouver bylaws, to name only a few, were passed to restrict Chinese
   residency and ownership of businesses and homes to specific districts
   (what is now labelled "Chinatown"); to ban all white girls and women
   from working in Chinese businesses; restrictions on business licences; and
   annual licence fees for business operations. These fees and restrictions
   were not placed on white Canadians and non-Chinese immigrants.
      Racist ideology and government policy also included federal immi-
   gration policy such as the Head Tax and Chinese Exclusion legislation,
   exclusion from practising law and other professions, discriminatory pay,
   and municipal restrictions on housing, businesses, and residency in white
   neighbourhoods in Vancouver. These bylaws and provincial and federal
   policy shaped the space called Chinatown in Vancouver.
      Anderson and other critical scholars point out that Chinatown was then
   constructed by white colonists as a site of deviancy and immortality, a
   physical place as well as a cultural space that "accrued a field of meaning
   that became the context and justification for recurring rounds of government

practice in the ongoing construction of both the place and the racial category 'Chinese'" (Anderson, 1991, p. 31).

First Nations, Chinese, Japanese, South Asian, and any other group of people deemed to be categorized (by white settlers) as non-white were denied representation in government, the vote, employment in many professions, immigration, and residency and property ownership outside of designated areas, and a host of other regulations and fees.

41 Valverde, 2012, p. 210.
42 Woolford, 2001, p. 27.
43 Woolford, 2001.
44 Feldman, 2001.
45 For the Surrey Fire Chief's website see http://www.surrey.ca/city-services/8224.aspx, retrieved 17 Nov. 2011.
46 Garis et al., 2009. p. 17.
47 See Legislative Assembly of British Columbia, 2009.
48 Garis et al., 2009, p. 20.
49 Spencer, 2005, p. A15; Kari, 2005, p. A32; Skelton, 2006, p. A32; Smyth, 2006, p. A6; Skelton, 2007, p. A1; Spencer, 20 Dec. 2007a, p. A8; Lazaruk, 4 May 2008, p. A6; Lewis, 2008, p. A14; Fraser, 2008, p. A4; Mercer, 2009, p. A12; Lewis, 18 June 2009, p. A8; Lewis, 15 Feb. 2009, p. A19; Colebourn, 6 Oct. 2009, p. A4.
50 "City councillor wants property," 2004, p. B2; Spencer, 31 Jan. 2006, p. A10; Spencer, 10 March 2006, p. A11; Hogben, 2008, p. A1; Bellet, 2008, p. B2.
51 Ibid., p. 5.
52 Ibid.
53 The Canadian Charter of Rights and Freedoms says:

7. Everyone has the right to life, liberty and security of the person and the right not to be deprived thereof except in accordance with the principles of fundamental justice.
Search or seizure
8. Everyone has the right to be secure against unreasonable search or seizure.
Detention or imprisonment
9. Everyone has the right not to be arbitrarily detained or imprisoned.
10. Everyone has the right on arrest or detention
(a) to be informed promptly of the reasons therefor;
(b) to retain and instruct counsel without delay and to be informed of that right; and

(c) to have the validity of the detention determined by way of habeas corpus and to be released if the detention is not lawful. Department of Justice, 2011a.

54 *Arkinstall* v. *City of Surrey*, 2010, p. 4.
55 However, media claim that Jason Arkinstall is a "Hells Angel associate" although no proof is provided (see Bolan, 2010).
56 Ibid., p. 6.
57 Ibid.
58 Ibid., p. 11.
59 Fraser, 2008.
60 *Arkinstall* v. *City of Surrey*, 2010, p. 23.
61 Ibid., p. 26.
62 Ibid., p. 27.
63 Ibid., p. 32.
64 Fraser, 2008.
65 Mission Residents Class Action Lawsuit Meeting, 2010.
66 "Former city councillor raided after criticizing marijuana laws," *YouTube*, retrieved 17 May 2011 from http://www.youtube.com/watch?v=N49lSwOajlI.
67 Golwanlock & Rees v. *District of Mission*, 2011.
68 District of Mission, 2011.
69 RCMP, 2009.
70 Garis, 2009; Health Canada, 2011b, 2011c; RCMP, 2009.
71 Grinspoon & Bakalar, 1997; Nolan & Kenny, 2003, pp. 93–94.
72 Grinspoon & Bakalar, 1997.
73 See http://www.gwpharm.com/Sativex.aspx, retrieved 23 May 2012.
74 See Fine (2012) for a detailed journalistic account of legal medicinal cannabis cultivators in Mendocino County, California.
75 Lucas, 2008; Belle-Isle & Hathaway, 2007.
76 Belle-Isle & Hathaway, 2007; Hathaway & Rossiter, 2007; Lucas, 2008, 2009, 2010.
77 See: *R.* v. *Parker*, 2000.
78 Marihuana is the legal spelling in Canada.
79 Lucas, 2009, p. 297.
80 *Hitzig* v. *The Queen*, 2003; Lucas, 2009.
81 See Department of Justice, 2011b.
82 See *Canada Gazette*, 2012.
83 Lucas, 2008, 2009.
84 Lucas, 2010; Reiman, 2008, 2009.

85 Angus Reid Public Opinion, 2010; Capler, 2006; Lucas, 2008.
86 See *R. v. Parker*, 2000; *R. v. Hitzig et al.*, 2003; *Sfetkopoulos v. Canada*, 2008; *R. v. Mernagh*, 2011; *R. v. Wakeford*, 1999.
87 Fassbender & Green, 2011.
88 Ibid.
89 Diakiw, 2011.
90 Colebourn, 2001, p. A2; Curtis, 2001, p. A1; Greenaway, 2005, p. A4; Tibbetts, 2006, p. A8; Shaw, 2006, p. A2; Babbage, 2007, p. A9; Knox, 2007, p. A3; Kari, 2008, p. A26; Walker, 2008, p. B7; Sinoski, 2009, p. A3; Bellet, 2009, p. A8; Mulgrew, 3 Feb. 2009, p. A2; "Court loosens restrictions on," 2008, p. A6.
91 Yu, 2011.
92 Health Canada, 2011c.
93 Ibid.
94 Ibid.
95 Health Canada (10 June 2013), "Harper Government Announces New Medical Marijuana Regulations," retrieved 12 June 2013 from http://www.hc-sc.gc.ca/ahc-asc/media/nr-cp/_2013/2013-79-eng.php.
96 See Belle-Isle, Walsh, Callaway et al., 2013.
97 *Canada Gazette*, 2012.
98 See Solecki, Burnett, & Li, 2010; Moller, Koren, Karaskov, & Garcia-Bournissen, 2011.
99 Personal communication, Philippe Lucas (past director of VICs), Rielle Capler (policy analyst and research coordinator, Vancouver Compassion Club), 9 and 10 Nov. 2011.
100 See Canadian Association of Medical Cannabis Dispensaries, 2011.
101 Grinspoon & Bakalar, 1997; Nolan & Kenny, 2003, pp. 93–4. For further discussion of MAAR and the benefits of medical marijuana, see Belle-Isle & Hathaway, 2007; Hathaway & Rossiter, 2007; Lucas, 2008, 2009, 2010.
102 See Bernstein & Bennett, 2013, p. 5, for a discussion of municipal bylaws that restrict harm reduction and methadone services.
103 See Garis, Plecas, Cohen, & McCormick, 2009, p. 6.
104 Bennett & Bernstein, 2013, p. 6

6. Using Children to Promote Increased Regulation: The Representation and Regulation of Children and Parents Found at Grow Ops

1 Bermingham, 2005, p. A21.
2 Chen, 2005, p. 55.

3 Ibid.
4 Morton, 2000, p. A1; Anderson, 8 Mar. 2000, p. A22; Anderson, 19 Mar.
   2000, p. A29; Larsen, 2001, p. A31; Austin, 2002, p. A4; "Pot raids yield
   500," 2004, p. B3; "Ont. targets grow-ops," 2004, p. A34; Sin, 2005, p. A8;
   Grindlay, 2006, p. A7; Severinson, 2006, p. A12; "New Alberta law targets,"
   2006, p. A12; "Asian 'child slaves' found," 2007, p. C27; "VANCOUVER:
   Tots found in," 2006, p. A.17; Colebourn, 27 Nov. 2009, p. A17; "RCMP
   busts grow op at," 2009, p. A12.
5 Boyd, 1999, 2004; Campbell, 2000; Flavin & Paltrow, 2010; Gomez, 1997;
   Humphries, 1999; Rutman, Callahan, & Swift, 2007.
6 See Thobani (2007a) for a discussion of exalted subjects.
7 Doyle, 2006.
8 Musto, 2002; Warner, 2002.
9 Chen, 2005; Hannah-Moffat, 2001.
10 Hannah-Moffat, 2001.
11 Boyd, 2004; Carstairs, 2006; Murphy, 1973.
12 Edwards, 1988.
13 Chen, 2005; Swift, 1995; Roberts, 2002.
14 Stevenson et al., 1956.
15 Boyd, 1999, 2004; Campbell, 2000.
16 Rutman, Callahan, & Swift, 2007.
17 Beckett, 1995; Boyd, 2004; Flavin & Paltrow, 2010; Gomez, 1997; Maier,
   1992; Turnbull, 2001.
18 Humphries, 1999.
19 Boyd, 1999; Flavin & Paltrow, 2010; Humphries, 1999.
20 Flavin & Paltrow, 2010, p. 232.
21 Ibid.
22 Boyd, 2004; Flavin & Paltrow, 2010; Humphries, 1992; Noble, 1997; Roberts, 2002.
23 Chunn & Gavigan, 2004; Creese & Strong-Boag, 2005; Wallace, Klein, &
   Reitsma-Street, 2006.
24 Etsten, 2000, p. 8.
25 Culbert & Morton, 2000; Launders, 2000.
26 Oberman, 2002, p. 1.
27 Ibid.
28 Ibid.
29 Ibid.
30 Austin, 2002.
31 Ibid.
32 Bermingham, 2005.

33 Report of the Aboriginal Committee, 1992; Bennett & Sadrehashemi, 2008.
34 Bennett & Sadrehashemi, 2008; Turpel-Lafond, 2011.
35 Sin, 2005, A8.
36 Ibid.
37 Ibid.
38 Ibid.
39 Plecas et al., 2005.
40 Ibid, p. 8.
41 Ibid., p. 16.
42 Bermingham, 2005.
43 Boldfish Entertainment also produced with the Government of Canada's National Crime Prevention Strategy, *Counting the Costs: Don't Get Stuck with the Bill* (2006), a film about the risks to property owners and the nation from marijuana grow ops in British Columbia.
44 Thobani, 2007a.
45 Plecas et al., 2005.
46 Douglas, 2010, p. 44.
47 Plecas et al., 2005.
48 Douglas, 2010, p. 123.
49 Plecas et al., 2005, p. 35.
50 Ibid., p. 36.
51 Ibid.
52 Ibid., Appendix 2.
53 Plecas et al., 2005.
54 Douglas, 2010, p. 44.
55 Ibid., pp. 79–80.
56 Ibid., p. 44.
57 Ibid., p. 137.
58 Ibid.
59 Ibid., p. 151.
60 Ibid., p. 152.
61 Moller, Koren, Karaskov, & Garcia-Bournissen, 2011.
62 Ibid., p. 4.
63 Ibid.
64 Ibid.
65 Plecas et al., 2005.
66 Chin, Dandurand, Plecas, & Segger, 2001; Dandurand, Plecas, Chin, & Segger, 2002.
67 Nicholson, 2008, p. A7.
68 DeBeck, Wood, Montaner, & Kerr, 2009, p. 189.

69 Beattie, 2006; Landry & Sinha, 2008.
70 Senate of Canada, 2010.
71 Degenhardt et al., 2008; Room & Reuter, 2012; Werb et al., 2011; Wood, 2010.
72 BC Ministry of Children and Family Development, 2003.
73 Saltman, 2007, p. A14.
74 Mulgrew, 2007, p. B1. Ian Mulgrew is also the author of the 2005 book, *Bud Inc.: Inside Canada's Marijuana Industry* (Toronto: Random House Canada).
75 BC Ministry of Children and Family Development, 2008.
76 Mulgrew, 2007, p. B1.
77 Ibid.
78 See RCMP, 2011a.
79 Also see Carter, 2009.
80 Moller et al., 2011.
81 Ibid.
82 Moller et al., 2011.

7. Alternative Perspectives

 1 Kilmer, 2012.
 2 Alexander, 1990, p. 71.
 3 See Royal Canadian Mounted Police, 2011b.
 4 Ibid.
 5 Royal Canadian Mounted Police, 2011e.
 6 Royal Canadian Mounted Police, 2011f.
 7 Vancouver Police Department, 2011a.
 8 Royal Canadian Mounted Police, 2011g.
 9 City of Richmond, 2011.
10 Vancouver Police Department, 2011b.
11 Canada.com is owned and operated by Postmedia Network Inc., Canada's largest publisher by circulation of paid English-language daily newspapers. Its properties include three of the daily newspapers in our sample: the *Vancouver Sun*, *Province*, and *Times Colonist*. It also owns the *Calgary Herald*, *Edmonton Journal*, *Ottawa Citizen*, and *National Post*. See Postmedia Network's website http://www.postmedia.com/2011/10/27/about-postmedia-network/, retrieved 22 Dec. 2011.
12 Brook & Stringer, 2005, p. 320.
13 Department of Justice, 2011c.
14 Hammersvik, Sandberg, & Pedersen, 2012, p. 5. See the introduction for a fuller discussion of these researchers' work.
15 Hammersvik, Sandberg, & Pedersen, 2012, p. 6.

16 Boyd, Conroy, & Puder, 1998, p. A23; Basham, 1998, p. A17; Krause, 2004, p. C9; Jones, 2001, p. A19; Martin, 2001, p. A13; Boyd, 2000, p. A19; Gardner, 2000, p. A20; Nuttall-Smith, 2000, p. A1; "Evidence shows Harper's justice," 2005, p. A10; Bridge, 2005, p. A12; Cayo, 2005, p. A15; Mulgrew, 23 March 2009, p. A3; Nicholl, 2009, p. A10.

17 Poole, 1998. Ian Mulgrew's 2005 journalistic account of the marijuana trade in Canada, *Bud Inc.*, also introduces readers to a wide range of cultivators.

18 See the Appendix for a discussion of the *Georgia Straight*.

19 See Canadian Association of Medical Cannabis Dispensaries, 2011.

20 A report from the City of Vancouver entitled *Preventing Harm from Psychoactive Substance Use* (City of Vancouver, 2005) makes recommendations for drug policy reform. The Health Officers Council of BC has also devised a model for a regulated market for currently prohibited substances (Health Officers Council of BC, 2005, 2011). In 2007, the Canadian Public Health Association passed resolutions that speak to the harms generated by prohibitionist policy and the failure of the war on drugs to eradicate the illegal market and lower drug use rates. See also the Global Commission on Drug Policy, 2011

21 "Loose moose leads police," 1997, p. A24; "Pot among the parrots," 2000, p. A4; Davidson, 2003, p. A3; Fox, 2005, p. A13; Dowd, 2007, p. C3; "B.C. police find grow," 2008, p. A5.

22 Hunter, 2009, p. A11.

23 Reinarman, 1988.

24 Bunton, 2001, p. 234; Grayson, 2008, p. 168.

25 Dean, 2002, p. 44.

26 Garland, 2001; Fischer, Turnbull, Poland, & Haydon, 2004.

27 This bill came into force in November 2012. See http://www.justice.gc.ca/eng/news-nouv/nr-cp/2012/doc_32758.html.

28 Public Works and Government Services of Canada, 2008–9.

29 Public Works and Government Services of Canada, 2010–11.

30 Department of Justice Canada, 2012, *Supplementary Tables – Horizontal Initiatives – National Anti-Drug Strategy*, retrieved 24 Dec. 2012 from http://www.tbs-sct.gc.ca/rpp/2012-2013/inst/jus/st-ts03-eng.asp. These data can be compared with the supplementary tables for the 2007–12 period, available at http://www.tbs-sct.gc.ca/hidb-bdih/plan-eng.aspx?Org=37&Hi=28&Pl=164.

31 Oscapella & Canadian Drug Policy Coalition Policy Working Group, 2012.

32 Elliot, 2011, p. 37.

33 Ibid., p. 54.

34 Hughes & Stevens, 2010; Lenton, 2011.

35 Hughes & Stevens, 2010.
36 DrugSense, 2012.
37 Cardoso, Gaviria, & Zedillo, 2009. In 2009, three former presidents of Brazil, Colombia, and Mexico expressed in an opinion piece in the *Wall Street Journal* that the war on drugs does not work and violence and organized crime associated with the trade is a critical problem in their countries. They drew from the critical report, *Latin American Commission on Drugs and Democracy.*
38 Wood et al. (2010) states: "The criminalisation of illicit drug users is fuelling the HIV epidemic and has resulted in overwhelmingly negative health and social consequences. A full policy reorientation is needed."
39 Global Commission on Drug Policy, 2011.
40 Ibid. p. 2; emphasis added.
41 Doward, 2012; Mayer, 2012.
42 See Boyd, 2004, chapter 6; Chomsky, 2000; Nadelmann, 1993; Paley, 2012.
43 Paley, 2012.
44 Four former Vancouver mayors, 2011.
45 See their reports (Stop the Violence BC, 2011a, 2011b).
46 Stop the Violence BC is described on its website as "a coalition of academics, past/present members of law enforcement, and the general public concerned about the links between cannabis prohibition in BC and the growth of organized crime and related violence in the province." See http://stop theviolencebc.org/.
47 Mulgrew, 2012.
48 S. Brennan, 2012.
49 Bigham, 2012.
50 Sensible BC, 2012.
51 Boyd, 2013.

Newspaper References

3,000 pot plants found in Richmond warehouse. (2008, 30 Mar.). *Province*,
   p. A23.

20,000 pot plants seized. (2005, 28 Sept.). *Province*, p. A27.

A drug-house primer: RCMP booklet helps neighbours to list and report
   goings-on. (1999, 22 Sept.). *Province*, p. A8.

Almost 7,000 pot plants found at old chicken farm city's biggest marijuana
   bust. (2004, 26 Nov.). *Vancouver Sun*, p. B3.

Anderson, C. (2000, 8 Mar.). Grow-op parents risk losing kids. *Province*, p. A29.

Anderson, C. (2000, 19 Mar.). Raids not kidding: While police swoop on grow-op
   homes, ministry of children pulls in seven kids. *Province*, p. A22.

Anderssen, E. (2002, 13 July). Would softer pot law stir the wrath of the U.S.?
   The neighbours are likely to yell, but not everybody thinks that's the end of
   the world. *Globe and Mail*, p. 1.

Appleby, T. (2008, 20 June). Police raids net cash, weapons, drugs. *Globe and
   Mail*, p. A17.

Appleby, T. (2008, 5 July). Homegrown industry thrives. *Globe and Mail*, p. A13.

Appleby, T., & O'Reilly, N. (2006, 25 Nov.). Grow-op bust a snapshot of market.
   Globe and Mail, p. A21.

Appleby, T., & Saunders, J. (2004, 29 Dec.). Grow-ops too many to raid, police
   say. *Globe and Mail*, p. A13.

Appleby, T., & Walton, D. (2005, 5 Mar.). Killer had lengthy record, "fire in his
   eyes." *Globe and Mail*, p. A10.

Asian "child slaves" found in grow-ops around U.K.: Hundreds of Vietnamese children smuggled in. (2007, 15 Oct.). *Province*, p. C27.

Austin, I. (2002, 27 Nov.). 43 kids caught in middle of national grow-op raids:
   Children taken from homes as 73,000 plants pulled in 7 days. *Province*,
   p. A4.

Austin, I. (2005, 8 Mar.). Two top judges defend sentencing. *Province*, p. A10.

Babbage, M. (2007, 4 Dec.). Ottawa must loosen medical pot rules, lawyers argue. *Globe and Mail*, p. A9.

Badelt, B. (2005, 2 Aug.). Man slain at grow-op: Police find 200 marijuana plants in Coquitlam home of victim. *Vancouver Sun*, p. B1.

Bailey, I. (2009, 23 Dec.). B.C. calls on Ottawa to tighten drug laws. *Globe and Mail*, p. S2.

Basham, P. (1998, 27 Oct.). A record of failure: Re-evaluating the war on drugs: Despite police, prison and propaganda, illegal drugs are readily available. A think-tank analyst argues that drug warriors have been unable to demonstrate that social and economic benefits of prohibition outweigh the costs. *Vancouver Sun*, p. A17.

B.C. living easy for foreign thugs: Word is out around the world that province is soft on crime. (1999, 26 June). *Times Colonist*, p. A11.

B.C. seizes its biggest-yet marijuana grow-op. (2008, 21 May). *Globe and Mail*, p. A5.

Beeby, D. (2011). Only one in six convicted in grow-op cases goes to jail, study finds. *Globe and Mail*, 24 Oct. Retrieved 31 May 2013 from http://www.theglobeandmail.com/news/politics/only-one-in-six-convicted-in-grow-op-cases-goes-to-jail-study-finds/article558774/

Bellet, G. (2000, 16 May). Mayor vows to reclaim neighbourhoods: Lois Jackson says North Delta's war on marijuana growers is just a first step in improving the quality of life in older residential areas. *Vancouver Sun*, p. B1.

Bellet, G. (2003, 9 May). In every neighbourhood. Series: Crime and Consequence. *Vancouver Sun*, p. B1.

Bellet, G. (2003, 10 May). Tips on marijuana operations overwhelm Richmond police. Series: Crime and Consequence. *Vancouver Sun*, p. B4.

Bellet, G. (2008, 23 Apr.). Lawyer fights "totalitarian" grow-op law: Act allowed inspector to cut power to Hells associate's house. *Vancouver Sun*, p. B2.

Bellet, G. (2009, 19 Oct.). B.C.'s top fire chief wants to end pot secrecy: Municipalities need to play a role in regulating legal marijuana-growing operations in residential areas, head of fire chief's association says. *Vancouver Sun*, p. A8.

Bellet, G. (2009, 10 Dec.). VPD opposes Senate move to soften penalty on grow ops: Proposal would remove minimum sentence for less than 200 plants. *Vancouver Sun*, p. A7.

Bellet, G., & Shore, R. (2007, 13 Dec.). "We've chopped the head off the snake": Raids here and abroad net $168 million in drugs, 100 arrests, 5.5 tonnes of drugs, $300,000 worth of vehicles, $6 million in real estate, 17 prohibited weapons, $2.1 million in cash. *Vancouver Sun*, p. A1.

Bermingham, J. (2005, 11 Sept.). Mountie wants parents punished for raising children in a grow-op. *Province*, p. A21.

Berry, S. (2000, 20 Feb.). Gangs franchise grow-ops. *Province*, p. A6.

Bigham, S. (2012, 1 May). Vancouver city council call to end prohibition on marijuana. News1130. Retrieved 31 May 2013 from http://www.news1130.com/2012/05/01/vancouver-city-council-call-to-end-prohibition-on-marijuana/

Blackwell, T. (2005, 8 Mar.). Killings pushed buttons in U.S.: Murders of Alberta officers underline American fears. *Vancouver Sun*, p. A5.

Blatchford, C. (2009, 7 Feb.). Seeing pot through benign soft lens ignores hard realities of grow ops. *Globe and Mail*, p. A2.

Bohn, G. (2003, 25 Mar.). Neighbours cheer as police raid marijuana-growing operation. *Vancouver Sun*, p. B3.

Bolan, K. (2004, 17 Sept.). Gangster's confession: I arranged hit on boss. Series: Inside Crime Inc. *Times Colonist*, p. A1.

Bolan, K. (2006, 30 June). 46 held in raid – Seized: 3,600 kilograms of pot, 800 kilograms of cocaine, $1.5 million US. *Times Colonist*, p. A3.

Bolan, K. (2008, 12 July). Gun dealer supplied arms to UN gang: Police weren't aware of connection before huge weapons bust. *Vancouver Sun*, p. A4.

Bolan, K. (2009, 23 July). Senate delay on drug bill risks lives. *Vancouver Sun*, p. A10.

Bolan, K. (2010, 21 May). Court axes inspection law used to find pot operations: Cities need warrant to enter premises appeal court rules. *Vancouver Sun*, p. A1.

Booby traps at pot sites can be fatal. (2001, 23 Aug.). *Province*, p. A15.

Boyd, N. (2000, 22 July). Back off busting B.C. bud: A criminologist decries the waste and featherbedding that accompanies the legal system's war on marijuana. *Vancouver Sun*, p. A19.

Boyd, N., Conroy, J. & Puder, G. (1998, 13 June). Drug war vets say don't decriminalize use of marijuana, just don't police it: A cop, a lawyer and an academic believe one letter from the attorney-general directing police not to enforce the law of the land would diminish the contribution of cannabis to criminal acts like gang cultivations. *Vancouver Sun*, p. A23.

Brennan, R. (2012, 26 Apr.). B.C. mayors want marijuana legalized. *Toronto Star*. Retrieved 31 May 2013, from http://www.thestar.com/news/canada/2012/04/26/bc_mayors_want_marijuana_legalized.html

Brethour, P. (2007, 24 Oct.). Unstable gang scene unique to B.C. *Globe and Mail*, p. S1.

Bridge, M. (2005, 5 Mar.). Weapons rare in marijuana raids, Vancouver police say. *Vancouver Sun*, p. A12.

British pot grow-ops skyrocket, linked to Vietnamese. (2007, 14 Mar.). *Province*, p. A31.

Bronskill, J. (2001, 7 May). U.S. syndicates use B.C. as hub for pot smuggling. *Times Colonist*, p. A1.

Bronskill, J. (2002, 15 May). RCMP says illegal drugs fund foreign terrorists. *Vancouver Sun*, p. A4.

Cardoso, F., Gaviria, C., & Zedillo, E. (2009, 23 Feb.). *Wall Street Journal*. Retrieved 28 May 2012 from http://online.wsj.com/article/SB123535114271444981.html

Cayo, D. (2004, 10 Sept.). The money monster. *Times Colonist*, p. A4.

Cayo, D. (2005, 15 Nov.). Logic says legalize drugs: Reality says it won't happen. *Vancouver Sun*, p. A15.

Churchill, B. (1999, 22 Sept.). RCMP compiles booklet to help residents spot drug houses: The information describes what signs to look for and includes a victim-impact statement to promote stiffer penalties. *Vancouver Sun*, p. B1.

City councillor wants property owners to inspect for marijuana operations. (2004, 28 July). *Vancouver Sun*, p. B2.

Colebourn, J. (2001, 12 Apr.). Medical pot farm busted: Plants destroyed as compassion club leaders met with Allan Rock. *Province*, p. A2.

Colebourn, J. (2004, 7 Jan.). Police warn of "grow-rippers." *Province*, p. A6.

Colebourn, J. (2009, 16 Oct.). Surrey RCMP winning battle with grow-ops: Jail, property seizures follow police success in "popping two to four" pot growers a week. *Province*, p. A4.

Colebourn, J. (2009, 27 Nov.). Children removed after grow-op found: 1,200 plants seized from basement. *Province*, p. A17.

Community takes on grow-ops. (2004, 23 Nov.). *Times Colonist*, p. A6.

Cooper, S. (2009, 11 Oct.). Drug-smuggling gangs high on helicopters: Big payoffs tempt young trainee pilots to make cross-border trips. *Times Colonist*, p. A9.

Cops air video to help curb grow-ops. (2006, 26 July). *Province*, p. A22.

Cops take 4.8m joints out of circulation. (2007, 11 Oct.). *Province*, p. A16.

Cormier, R. (2005, 5 Mar.). Mounties lacked defenses against high-powered rifle. *Times Colonist*, p. A6.

Cormier, R. (2005, 9 Mar.). Searches failed to find Roszko's assault rifle. *Vancouver Sun*, p. A6.

Court loosens restrictions on medical marijuana. (2008, 11 Jan.). *Globe and Mail*, p. A6.

Courts too lenient on pot growers: Minimum fines are needed to provide a real disincentive to illegal marijuana cultivation. (2002, 28 Nov.). *Times Colonist*, p. A14.

Crime: 400 marijuana plants found in east side house. (1999, 21 Sept.). *Vancouver Sun*, p. B1.

Crime: Marijuana growth industry, police say. (1999, 24 Nov.). *Vancouver Sun*, p. B1.

Culbert, L. (2005, 30 Sept.). RCMP chronicles scope of organized crime. *Vancouver Sun*, p. A7.

Culbert, L., & Morton, B. (2000, 14 Mar.). 40 kids seized in war on drugs: In most of the cases the children are from Vietnamese families. *Vancouver Sun*, p. A1.

Curren, R. (1997, 5 May). Grass is greener north of the 49th. *Times Colonist*, p. A1.

Curtis, M. (2001, 2 Sept.). Homegrown: This grow-op is legal, but its time may be running out. New federal rules will restrict users of medical marijuana to one supplier, in a mine deep underground in Manitoba. Pot fans aren't happy. *Times Colonist*, p. A1.

Davidson, D. (2003, 3 June). Pot spotted on roof of old police office. *Province*, p. A3.

Dawson, F., Colebourn, J., Berry, S., and Tanner, A. (2000, 16 Apr.). Fighting back: Pot growers targeted. *Province*, p. A12.

Dhillon, S. (2012, 8 Nov.). Vote threatens to nip B.C. market in the bud. *Globe and Mail*, p. A3.

Dickson, L. (2002, 28 Nov.). Marijuana growers turn eye to upscale locales. *Times Colonist*, p. C1.

Dope-growing houses worry Island fire chiefs. Laments one: We're going to lose a firefighter. Says a second: Lights are bombs. *Vancouver Sun*, p. B7.

Doward, J. (2012, 7 Apr.). "War on drugs" has failed, say Latin American leaders. *Guardian*. Retrieved 23 May 2012 from http://www.guardian.co.uk/world/2012/apr/07/war-drugs-latin-american-leaders

Dowd, A. (2007, 28 Sept.). Even "B.C. bud" hit by rising Canadian dollar. *Vancouver Sun*, p. C3.

Edmonds, E. (2006, 30 June). Elderly couple victims of daylight home invasion. *Vancouver Sun*, p. B3.

Etzler, D. (2005, 8 Mar.). Deaths not related to pot. *Province*, p. A21.

Evidence shows Harper's justice policies would exacerbate drug problem. (2005, 6 Dec.). *Vancouver Sun*, p. A10.

Ferguson, A. (1998a, 5 July). B.C. pot's high potency is key to popularity. *Province*, p. A17.

Ferguson, A. (1998b, 5 July). Killer weed. *Province*, p. A16.

Ferguson, A. (1998c, 5 July). Police blame judges for surge in grow ops. *Province*, p. A17.

Ferguson, A. (1998, 23 Aug.). Pot corrupts with quick, easy cash. *Province*, p. A7.

Fitzpatrick, M. (2007, 18 Aug.). RCMP reports surge in organized crime. *Vancouver Sun*, p. A1.

Fong, P. (2004, 31 Jan.). B.C. bud buys guns for Afghans: *Vancouver Sun*, p. A1.

Fong, B.M. (1999, 19 Oct.). Traffickers "laugh" at the legal system: Following a major drug raid, a senior RCMP officer says B.C. penalties are too lenient. *Vancouver Sun*, p. A1.

For the fallen Mounties: Let's pause and grieve, but not act in haste. (2005, 5 Mar.) *Vancouver Sun*, p. C6.

Former city councillor raided after criticizing marijuana laws. (2011, 17 May). Retrieved 4 Nov. 2011 from http://www.youtube.com/watch?v=N49lSwOajlI

Four former Vancouver mayors call for end to "failed policy" of marijuana prohibition. (2011, 23 Nov.). Retrieved 5 Jan. 2012 from the *Georgia Straight*. http://www.straight.com/article-546326/vancouver/four-former-vancover-mayors-call-end-failed-policy-marijuana-prohibition

Fournier, S. (2008, 25 Nov.). Two men face charges after grow-op murder: Pot dealer was found beaten to death last Nov. 30. *Province*, p. A11.

Fox, S. (2005, 15 June). Police called after church outing turns up 60 pot plants. *Province*, p. A13.

Fraser, K. (2006, 26 Oct.). Judge pushes for tougher sentences involving grow-ops. *Province*, p. A29.

Fraser, K. (2008, 22 Apr.). Unofficial grow-op searches bend the law, says lawyer: "Ruse" to gain entry violates citizens' rights, judge told. *Province*, p. A4.

Freeze, C. (2006, 16 Nov.). U.S. officials troubled by expansion of Asian-Canadian drug gangs. *Globe and Mail*, p. A8.

Freeze, C., & Walton, D. (2005, 5 Mar.). Drug crime nourished in sleepy communities. *Globe and Mail*, p. A10.

Galloway, G., & Curry, B. (2005, 5 Mar.). McLellan presses judiciary on pot sentences. *Globe and Mail*, p. A11.

Gardner, D. (2000, 13 Sept.). Life, liberty and the pursuit of illegal drugs: In the United States, once-sacred constitutional rights are being eroded by relentless police and military attempts to interdict narcotics and punish users and dealers. In Canada, the threat to civil liberties has not yet been as extreme, but the pressures are building. Series: Part eight of a special series: How America dictates the global war on drugs. *Vancouver Sun*, p. A20.

Geddes, J. (2012, 5 July). Harper's anti-drug strategy gets a little less compassionate. *Maclean's*. Retrieved 11 Aug 2012 from http://www2.macleans.ca/2012/07/25/drug-money/

Geddes, J. (2012, 23 July). Updated: Guns at the border – on seizures and spending. *Maclean's*. Retrieved 11 Aug. 2012 from http://www2.macleans.ca/2012/07/23/guns-at-the-border-on-seizures-and-spending/

Gordon, J. (2004, 3 Nov.). Ottawa vows to wipe out pot-growing operations. *Vancouver Sun*, p. A3.

Gordon, J. (2006, 15 Mar.). Meth, ecstasy, pot production rising. *Vancouver Sun*, p. A4.

Greenaway, N. (2005, 26 June). Ottawa to ease rules for medical marijuana. *Times Colonist*, p. A4.

Grindlay, L. (2006, 11 Jan.). Infant taken from grow-op: Police investigating home invasion find 984 plants. *Province*, p. A7.

Hall, N. (2003, 15 Nov.). RCMP team dismantles 2 marijuana operations. *Vancouver Sun*, p. B8.

Hall, N. (2004, 26 Mar.). Police seize 4,300 marijuana plants worth $3.5 million. *Vancouver Sun*, p. B7.

Hall, N., & Bolan, K. (2007, 15 Sept.). Gang violence: Too close for comfort – solicitor-general urges tougher sentences for thugs who open fire in public. *Vancouver Sun*, p. A1.

Harding, K., & Walton, D. (2006, 4 Mar.). In the line of duty. *Globe and Mail*, p. A1.

Harsh pot sentence is the right direction: Large grow operations are not the victimless crimes they're made out to be. Unless the courts impose harsher sentences, neighbours and children within the houses will be danger. (2000, 23 Mar.). *Vancouver Sun*, p. A14.

Haysom, B. (1998, 21 Aug.). Police sweep massive grow op: "Sophisticated organized crime" behind pot: Police. *Province*, p. A8.

Higher THC levels are creating "pot 2.0." (2007, 26 Apr.). *Globe and Mail*, p. L8.

Hogben, D. (2008, 27 Oct.). Drug house buyers risk health: Group seeks standardized way to alert homebuyers about meth labs, growing operations. *Vancouver Sun*, p. A1.

Home invaders had wrong address. (2003, 12 Aug.). *Vancouver Sun*, p. B4.

Howell, M. (2007, 16 Feb.). The quiet Americans. *Vancouver Courier*. Retrieved 8 March 2007 from http://www.Vancourier.com/issues07/023207/news/023207nn1.html

Huge pot "factory" no ma-pa operation. (2004, 13 Jan.). *Province*, p. A14.

Hughes, B. (2005, 7 Mar.). What caused the tragedy? *Globe and Mail*, p. A14.

Hume, M. (2004, 24 Nov.). Developer plans to keep community from going to pot. *Globe and Mail*, p. A12.

Hunter, S. (2002, 13 June). Grow-ops outpacing police efforts to smoke out plants. *Province*, p. A12.

Hunter, S. (2004, 11 Jan.). Police alarmed by number of grow-rips. *Province*, p. A9.

Hunter, S. (2004, 18 Jan.). Realtors want drug declaration added to B.C. seller's disclosure. *Province*, p. A26.

Hunter, S. (2005, 8 Mar.). We're being unfairly "demonized," say B.C. pot advocates. *Province*, p. A10.

Hunter, S. (2007, 28 June). Judge wishes he could have jailed man over grow-op: Law should provide a deterrent, he says. *Province*, p. A3.

Hunter, S. (2009, 21 Jan.). Toddler's 911 call leads cops to marijuana grow operation. *Province*, p. A11.

"Island's biggest" marijuana farm was size of two football fields, police say. (2004, 24 Aug.). *Vancouver Sun*, p. B3.

It's already going to pot, home buyers discover. (2008, 10 Sept.). *Globe and Mail*, p. A5.

Ivens, A. (2008, 20 June). Police release photos of city's worst thieves: Cops blame catch-and-release court cycle. *Province*, p. A6.

Ivens, A. (2010, 8 Jan.). Call for fire services to be given addresses of legal pot growers: Bad wiring can lead to grow-blazes. *Province*, p. A25.

Jiwa, S. (1998, 24 Sept.). "Some serious hardware": Pot growers are arming themselves like commandos. *Province*, p. A12.

Jiwa, S. (2000, 1 Oct.). A conviction in Alberta for growing pot could send you to jail for four years: In B.C. you'd probably get three to six months because … judges show a soft spot for marijuana farmers. *Province*, p. A12.

Jones, D. (2001, 4 Aug.). Pot's fraught with perils, but prohibition is no longer an option. *Vancouver Sun*, p. A19.

Jurock, O. (2003, 29 Mar.). Is there a grow-op next door? *Vancouver Sun*, p. E1.

Kari, S. (2008, 21 Sept.). Feds try to spark change in pot laws: Medical-marijuana users forced to rely on the black market. *Province*, p. A26.

Keating, J. (2007, 23 Oct.). Three adults face charges after cops discover grow-op and loaded handgun. *Province*, p. A18.

Kelowna drug trade "like fast cancer." (1998, 8 Oct.). *Vancouver Sun*, p. B6.

Knox, J. (2004, 15 Aug.). The pot patrol: How spotters untangle web of B.C. bud. Series: Island's Odd Jobs. *Times Colonist*, p. C1.

Knox, J. (2007, 17 Apr.). Legal marijuana alternatives to go up in smoke: Plans to make health Canada only purveyor of medical pot discomfit "compassion clubs." *Times Colonist*, p. A3.

Krause, L. (2004, 11 Sept.). Readers think there are worse crimes than selling a bit of pot. *Vancouver Sun*, p. C9.

Larsen, D. (2001, 24 Apr.). Seizing grow-operators' kids "destructive." *Province*, p. A31.

Launders, D. (2000). Vancouver cops seize pot-kids. *Cannabis Culture*, 26, 22–3.

Lavoie, J. (2004, 7 Feb.). RCMP to take over operation of organized-crime unit. *Times Colonist*, p. A3.

Lazaruk, S. (2008, 4 May). Couple left "squatting" in their home: Say city wants them to pay $5,000 for search for grow-op that wasn't there. *Province*, p. A6.

Lazaruk, S. (2008, 24 Aug.). Organized and high-tech, Vancouver is one of Canada's three criminal hubs. *Province*, p. A15.

Let's stop grow-ops stealing power from you and me. (2008, 7 Apr.). *Province*, p. A16.

Lewis, B. (2008, 13 May). Fire chief has other tactics up his sleeve: Len Garis won't be too upset if courts nix his inspection brainchild. *Province*, p. A14.

Lewis, B. (2009, 15 Feb.). Big brother alive and well in Mission: Special grow-op "safety inspection" cost innocent homeowner $5,200. *Province*, p. A19.

Lewis, B. (2009, 18 June). Where Surrey leads, will others follow? City's 2005 inspection initiative has been amazingly successful. *Province*, p. A8.

Little, M. (2007, 31 Aug.). Island cops uncover thousands of pot plants: Police say this summer's program, the eighth, pulled in "the largest haul." *Province*, p. A3.

Loose moose leads police to groovy grove. (1997, 1 June). *Province*, p. A24.

Loyie, F., & Sadava, M. (2005, 4 Mar.). Four Mounties shot dead in Alberta grow-op raid. *Vancouver Sun*, p. A1.

Luba, F. (2006, 6 Jan.). Terrified family wrong target of grow-op rip. *Province*, p. A12.

Lunman, K. (2002, 13 Dec.). U.S. fears change in marijuana laws: Canada will pose a "dangerous threat" if it decriminalizes pot, drug czar says. *Globe and Mail*, p. 1.

Luymes, L. (2007, 19 Aug.). Organized crime loves B.C. Federal report says we are hub for drug production, distribution. *Province*, p. A19.

Luymes, G. (2008, 24 Aug.). Gangs cast shadow over Bible-belt Abbotsford: Organized crime is growing in might as the Fraser Valley city expands. But churches and the community are fighting back. *Province*, p. A8.

MacQueen, K. (2000, 12 May). Bust or back off: As growing-op busts mount, how best to deal with the province's $3-billion cannabis industry? Should we follow the U.S. get-tough approach, or consider legalizing and ease up on pot policing? Series: B.C. on Marijuana: Our Split Personality. *Vancouver Sun*, p. A1.

Mandatory jail sentences will fill up our prisons. (2007, 22 Nov.). *Province*, p. A21.

Manitoba joins the list of top marijuana producers: U.S. officials say the province has moved ahead of Colombia in pot production. (2000, 3 Apr.). *Vancouver Sun*, p. A8.

"Marijuana is an addictive drug." (2007, 11 Nov.). *Province*, p. A9.

Marc Emery's U.S. prosecutor urges pot legalization. (2012, 18 Apr.). *CBC News*. Retrieved on 6 June 2012 from http://www.cbc.ca/news/canada/british-columbia/story/2012/04/18/bc-marijuana-legalization.html

Martin, D. (2001, 6 Nov.). Enough of studies, it's time to end the war on cannabis. *Vancouver Sun*, p. A13.

Martin, J. (2005, 22 Nov.). Punishment of criminals should replace catch-and-release policy. *Province*, p. A18.

Mason, G. (2007, 25 Oct.). For gangsters, life is often cheaper than the rings on their fingers. *Globe and Mail*, p. A7.

Matas, R. (2002, 22 Nov.). Stop marijuana trade, U.S. drug czar urges: $5 billion worth of highly potent B.C. product flows south each year, director says. *Globe and Mail*, p. n/a.

Matas, R. (2008, 24 Sept.). Police seize 9,000 pot plants from grow op. *Globe and Mail*, p. S3.

Matas, R. (2009, 28 Mar.). B.C. bud's sinister role in the violent drug trade. *Globe and Mail*, p. A7.

Matas, R., & Bailey, I. (2009, 11 Apr.). "Let the war begin." *Globe and Mail*, p. S3.

Mayer, A. (2012, 13 Apr.). Drug legislation debate divides Americas. Retrieved 23 May 2012 from http://www.cbc.ca/news/world/story/2012/04/12/f-drug-legalization-americas.html

McCune, S. (2000, 30 Jan.). New crime boss declares war on grow-ops. *Province*, p. A42.

McMartin, P. (2005, 7 Mar.). RCMP deaths spark confused debate over pot issue. *Vancouver Sun*, p. B1.

Mercer, K. (2008, 26 Aug.). Greenhouse pot bust biggest ever: Six suspects tending huge crop arrested by cops acting on tip. *Province*, p. A5.

Mercer, K. (2009, 27 Sept.). Grow-ops wilt under Surrey program. *Province*, p. A12.

Mickleburgh, R. (2005, 30 July). Pot activist faces extradition. *Globe and Mail*. http://www.theglobeandmail.com/news/national/pot-activist-faces-extradition/article1122231/.

Middleton, G. (1997a, 27 July). They're pulling the profit rug out from under pot growers: Organized crime the real target of new police push. *Province*, p. A9.

Middleton, G. (1997b, 27 July). A $5,000 investment, a $70,000 income. *Province*, p. A9.

Mitrovica, A. (1999, 16 Aug.). Low funding caused U.S. drug action, B.C. says Blacklist considered, ruled out for now. *Globe and Mail*, p. A1.

Mofina, R. (2003a, 29 Apr.). Grow-op numbers overwhelming police. *Vancouver Sun*, p. A12.

Mofina, R. (2003b, 29 Apr.). Police overwhelmed by surge in organized crime's grow-ops. *Times Colonist*, p. A6.

Moore, D. (2002, 1 Oct.). Marijuana factory open for business: Pot processed into potent THC pellets from medicinal use. *Vancouver Sun*, p. B4.

Morton, L.C. (2000, 18 Mar.). 40 kids seized in war on drugs: In most of the cases the children are from Vietnamese families. *Vancouver Sun*, p. A1.

Mountie killings are a grim reminder of deadly grow-op industry dangers. (2005, 4 Mar.). *Province*, p. A20.

Mulgrew, I. (2007, 15 Jan.). No evidence more kids should be taken into care. *Vancouver Sun*, p. B1.

Mulgrew, I. (2009, 3 Feb.). Medical marijuana restrictions get thumbs-down: Federal laws governing supply are ruled unconstitutional. *Vancouver Sun*, p. A2.

Mulgrew, I. (2009, 23 Mar.). Easy money has to be removed from drugs. *Vancouver Sun*, p. A3.

Mulgrew, I. (2012, 14 Feb.). Legalize marijuana, former B.C. attorneys-general say. *Vancouver Sun*. Retrieved 28 May 2012 from http://www.vancouversun.com/news/Legalize+marijuana+former+attorneys+general/6152280/story.html

Naumetz, T. (2005, 27 Sept.). Scrap pot bill, urge slain officers' families. *Times Colonist*, p. A6.

New Alberta law targets children exposed to drugs. (2006, 2 Nov.). *Globe and Mail*, p. A12.

Nicholl, T. (2009, 18 Feb.). Legalizing drugs a better path than stiffer sentences. *Vancouver Sun*, p. A10.

Nicholson, R. (2008, 14 Jan.). Plan targets serious drug offenders. *Vancouver Sun*, p. A7.

Nothing benign about grow-ops. (2005, 5 Mar.). *Times Colonist*, p. A18.

Nuttall-Smith, C. (2000, 7 Aug.). Inside growing operations: A look at three of the thousands of marijuana producers in the lower mainland, operations that police vow to close – one at a time. *Vancouver Sun*, p. A1.

Nuttall-Smith, C. (2003, 5 Nov.). Pot now Canada's top crop. *Vancouver Sun*, p. D12.

Oberman, M. (2002, 14 June). Pot farms conceal deadly risks: Hydro stolen to run the hydroponic labs has led to fires and fears of electrocution. *Globe and Mail*, p. 1.

O'Brian, A. (2002, 29 Oct.). Two teen groups arrested during attempts to rip off marijuana harvests: Youths were "contracted" by brokers to steal pot, Surrey police allege. *Vancouver Sun*, p. B7.

O'Brian, A. (2004, 10 Jan.). Violent "grow rips" on the rise. *Vancouver Sun*, p. B1.

O'Brian, A. (2008, 28 Oct.). Homes used to grow pot pose serious mould risk: But no sure way to know if property once used as a drug house. *Vancouver Sun*, p. A3.

O'Connor, E. (2006, 28 June). Day 3: Series: The Province's Safe Streets Project. *Province*, p. A8.

O'Neil, P. (2003, 9 May). RCMP fears gang warfare over marijuana operations. *Vancouver Sun*, p. A1.

Ont. targets grow-ops, child porn. (2004, 29 June). *Province*, p. A34.

Paley, D. (2012, 4 July). Canada boosts police power in Mexico. *The Dominion: News from the Grassroots*. Retrieved 17 July 2012 from http://www.dominionpaper.ca/articles/4421

Pemberton, K., & Morton, B. (2002, 14 June). War on pot-growing "a failure": Police have failed to reduce marijuana operations, study says. *Vancouver Sun*, p. B8.

People, drugs, money, guns all part of web. Series: Crime and Consequence. (2003, 9 May). *Vancouver Sun*, p. B4.

PM wants marijuana bill passed quickly. (2003, 26 Sept.). *Province*, p. A28.

Police bust $1.7-million marijuana growing operation: Six arrested. (2004, 22 Mar.). *Vancouver Sun*, p. B3.

Police raid nets 1,000 pot plants. (2004, 19 Mar.). *Vancouver Sun*, p. B3.

Police seek more power to shut down pot houses. (2002, 27 Nov.). *Times Colonist*, p. A1.

Porter, C. (1998, 19 May). New RCMP unit specializes in busting Langley pot operations: Growing B.C. marijuana has become such a lucrative business that organized crime has moved in. *Vancouver Sun*, p. B4.

Pot among the parrots. (2000, 30 July). *Province*, p. A4.

Pot growers keeping up. (1997, 17 Oct.). *Province*, p. A24.

Pot house invaded by three men. (2001, 20 July). *Province*, p. A3.

Pot raid yields 500 plants, two children. (2004, 28 May). *Vancouver Sun*, p. B3.

Princeton: Huge grow-op found. (2005, 25 Jan.). *Province*, p. A8.

Production of potent pot flourishing and lucrative, RCMP report says. (2007, 18 Dec.). *Globe and Mail*, p. A8.

Ramsey, M. (2005, 2 Aug.). Murder linked to grow-op: Man, 51, called 911 after shooting but died in hospital. *Province*, p. A10.

Ramsey, M. (2006, 18 Oct.). Brace for gang war, police warn: Clash over drugs, guns, power. *Province*, p. A3.

Ramsey, M. (2007, 11 Feb.). B.C. exports grow-op skills. *Province*, p. A3.

RCMP seize 3,400 marijuana plants in raid on "sophisticated" growing operation. (2006, 18 Feb.). *Vancouver Sun*, p. B7.

RCMP busts grow op at daycare home. (2009, 28 Mar.). *Globe and Mail*, p. A12.

Reevely, D. (2003, 21 May). Pot-growers a risk, fireman warns. *Vancouver Sun*, p. B1.

Research needed, professor says. (2007, 7 Nov.). *Times Colonist*, p. A3.

Sadava, F.L. (2005a, 4 Mar.). Four Mounties shot dead in Alberta grow-op raid. *Vancouver Sun*, p. A1.

Sadava, F.L. (2005b, 4 Mar.). "Wicked devil" suspect in slaying of four Mounties. *Vancouver Sun*, p. A1.

Saltman, J. (2007, 28 Dec.). Social workers worry about grow-op kids: Question criteria used to investigate. *Province*, p. A14.

Schmidt, S. (1998, 3 Nov.). B.C. towns high on huge cannabis harvest. Illegal crop a bumper for growers who see it as engine of communities' economies, but a bummer for law enforcement. *Globe and Mail* (Western edition), p. A7.

Severinson, P. (2006, 25 May). Kids in grow-ops at risk. *Province*, p. A12.

Shaw, R. (2006, 27 Mar.). Victoria mayor offers support to medical pot users. *Times Colonist*, p. A2.

Sieberg, D. (1999, 27 July). Frustration grows over pot production. *Vancouver Sun*, p. B1.

Simpson, S. (2002, 31 Jan.). Sweep nets 20 marijuana-growing operations: Vancouver raids part of national blitz on homes used by drug dealers. *Vancouver Sun*, p. B5.

Sin, L. (2005, 1 May). Cops find kids being kept in drug houses: POLICE OUTRAGE. Baby found in drug bust. *Province*, p. A8.

Sinclair, D. (2001, 29 June). Organized crime controls it. *Province*, p. A27.

Sinoski, K. (2009, 14 Sept.). Scrutiny for medical marijuana sites: Council asks where legal pot is grown to ensure homes properly modified. *Vancouver Sun*, p. A3.

Sinokski, K., & Fitzpatrick, M. (2007, 18 Dec.). Illegal drug industry booming with potent new products. *Vancouver Sun*, p. A1.

Skelton, C. (1999, 4 Oct.). Marijuana growers get off with lenience in the courts: A Vancouver Sun investigation shows some growers pay no fines and serve no time. *Vancouver Sun*, p. A1.

Skelton, C. (2001, 10 Sept.). Massive pot operation raided: Police suspect city's biggest marijuana warehouse was set to expand. *Vancouver Sun*, p. B1.

Skelton, C. (2004, 25 Sept.). Pot thieves bring terror in the night. Series: Inside Crime Inc.: How organized crime has infiltrated our communities. *Vancouver Sun*, p. C2.

Skelton, C. (2005, 18 Jan.). B.C. jails one in 7 pot growers: Vancouver jails only one in 13. *Vancouver Sun*, p. A1.

Skelton, C. (2005, 11 Mar.). Out of control: Criminal justice system "on the brink of imploding." Series: B.C.'s Failing War against Marijuana Grow-ops. *Vancouver Sun*, p. A1.

Skelton, C. (2005c, 7 Oct.). Marijuana bankrolling other crimes. Series: The Future of Organized Crime. *Vancouver Sun*, p. B1.

Skelton, C. (2006, 7 Apr.). BC hydro to report suspected pot farms under new legislation. *Vancouver Sun*, p. A3.

Skelton, C. (2007, 11 Jan.). Hydro use in valley raises suspicions. *Vancouver Sun*, p. A1.

Skelton, C., & Hall, N. (2004, 25 Sept.). Police fear gang war over pot: Price drop expected to ignite violence between crime groups Series: Inside Crime Inc.: How organized crime has infiltrated our communities. *Vancouver Sun*, p. C2.

Skelton, C., & Morton, B. (1999, 5 Oct.). Marijuana growers thrive on B.C.'s lenient court penalties. *Vancouver Sun*, p. A1.

Skelton, C., Hall, N., & Knox, J. (2004, 25 Sept.). Police brace for nasty turf war: Series: Inside Crime Inc. *Vancouver Sun*, p. A5.

Smith, A. (2004, 27 Oct.). Why are U.S. drug cops in Vancouver. *TheTyee. ca*. Retrieved 5 Dec. 2011 from http://thetyee.ca/News/2004/10/27/WhyUSDrugCopVan/

Smith, G. (2002, 13 Sept.). Canada's pot policy under fire from U.S. *Globe and Mail*, p. 1.

Smyth, M. (2006, 11 May). Big brother will soon be watching your hydro: *Province*, p. A6.

Spencer, K. (2004, 3 Aug.). Chilliwack cracks down on budding grow-ops. *Times Colonist*, p. C10.

Spencer, K. (2005, 22 Mar.). Coquitlam wants hydro to help ID marijuana grow operations. *Province*, p. A15.

Spencer, K. (2006, 31 Jan.). New bylaw to inform future tenants about grow-op mould, toxins. *Province*, p. A10.

Spencer, K. (2006, 10 Mar.). New bylaw drives 26 grow-ops out of business since last month. *Province*, p. A11.

Spencer, K. (2007, 20 Sept.). Over 100 pot grow-ops nipped in bud in 3 months: Municipality has been checking hydro bills for more than normal amounts of power use. *Province*, p. A8.

Spencer, K. (2007, 20 Dec.). Grow-ops growing bigger, going rural. Hidden from view and guarded against ripoffs. *Province*, p. A8.

Sutherland, B. (2007, 18 Aug.). Clues that your dream home might have been a grow-op. *Vancouver Sun*, p. C3.

Theft makes pot grower angry, dopey. (2002, 16 July). *Times Colonist*, p. A3.

Theodore, T. (2008, 8 Feb.). Marijuana ruling riles solicitor general. *Globe and Mail*, p. S3.

Tibbetts, J. (2002, 27 Nov.). 50,000 "grow" houses, police say: Law enforcement officers losing battle against illegal marijuana cultivators. *Vancouver Sun*, p. A5.

Tibbetts, J. (2004, 18 Sept.). Our slack drug penalties lure major crime: U.S. *Vancouver Sun*, p. A15.

Tibbetts, J. (2006, 12 Jan.). Medical pot grower challenges law. *Vancouver Sun*, p. A8.

Tonner, M. (2006, 8 Jan.). A finger that's in jail can't pull a trigger. *Province*, p. B6.

Tonner, M. (1998, 6 Nov.). Pot smokers paying Hells Angels' bills. *Province*, p. A20.

Tougher laws and stricter enforcement needed to stop grow-ops. (2005, 12 Mar.). *Vancouver Sun*, p. E6.

Tu Thanh, Ha. (2002, 24 Sept.). Don't make pot legal, UN Official Warns. *Globe and Mail*, p. 1.

UN drug report unintentionally argues against prohibition. (2006, 28 June). *Vancouver Sun*, p. A16.

Vancouver: Tots found in grow-ops. (2006, 26 Feb.). *Province*, p. A17.

Vallis, M. (2000, 7 Mar.). Vancouver cops on sniff alert to weed out grow ops. *Province*, p. A3.

Vincent, I. (1998, 6 Apr.). Enforcers challenge cannabis liberation movement: Activists who want lawmakers to take lighter view on the use of marijuana face police who maintain the drug is dangerous. *Globe and Mail*, p. A6.

Ward, D. (1999, 11 June). 39 charged, drugs and cash seized in major cross-border crackdown: After a month-long surveillance operation along the border from Langley to Chilliwack, a team of Canadian and U.S. officers strikes against the trade of B.C.-grown marijuana for cocaine and cash. *Vancouver Sun*, p. B1.

Walker, D. (2008, 21 May). Compassion club seeks expansion: Nanaimo group hopes to secure a downtown location to provide marijuana to medical users across the region. *Vancouver Sun*, p. B7.

Walton, D., & Harding. K. (2005, 8 Mar.). Questions multiply in RCMP slayings: Did someone help the gunman? Probe looks at why his truck was found far from scene. *Globe and Mail*, p. A1.

Weber, B. (2004, 8 May). Marijuana grow-ops booming in suburbs. *Globe and Mail*, p. A17.

Wente, M. (2007, 26 June). Not the groovy '60s: Today's cannabis is harder and meaner. *Globe and Mail*, p. A17.

Willcocks, P. (2002, 7 Aug.). Police, BC ferries went off the deep end. *Vancouver Sun*, p. A14.

Wingrove, J. (2008, 31 Oct.). Missing woman's body found at grow-op. *Globe and Mail*, p. A10.

Woods, A. (2005, 8 Mar.). Canada's top policeman backtracks on RCMP deaths. *Vancouver Sun*, p. A5.

Young, G. (1998, 19 Apr.). Pot deathtraps' growing. *Times Colonist*, p. A1.

Young, G. (2004, 18 Sept.). Gang violence hits home: Series: Inside Crime Inc. *Times Colonist*, p. D1.

Young, M.L. (2004, 10 June). The lucrative business of pot. *Globe and Mail*, p. B2.

General References

41st Parliament, 1st session. *Edited Hansard, Number 060, Monday, Dec. 5, 2011*. Retrieved 13 Jan. 2011 from http://www.parl.gc.ca/HousePublications/Publication.aspx?Pub=Hansard&Doc=60&Parl=41&Ses=1&Language=E&Mode=1#SOB-5160265

Adlaf, E., Begin, P., & Sawka, E. (Eds.). (2005). Canadian addiction survey (CAS): A national survey of Canadians' use of alcohol and other drugs. Prevalence of use and related harms: Detailed report. Ottawa: Canadian Centre on Substance Abuse & Health Canada.

Alexander, B. (1990). *Peaceful measures: Canada's way out of the "War on Drugs."* Toronto: University of Toronto Press.

Alexander, M. (2010). *The new Jim Crow: Mass incarceration in the age of color-blindness*. New York: New Press.

Altheide, D.L. (2002). *Creating fear: News and the construction of crisis*. New York: Aldine de Gruyter.

Anderson, K. (1991). *Vancouver's Chinatown: Racial discourse in Canada, 1875–1980*. Montreal: McGill-Queen's University Press.

Angus Reid Public Opinion. (2010). *Half of Canadians support legalization of marijuana*. Retrieved 8 Dec. 2011 from http://www.angus-reid.com/polls/43593/half-of-canadians-support-the-legalization-of-marijuana/

Anslinger, H., & Oursler, W. (1961). *The murderers*. New York: Farrar, Straus, and Cudahy.

Anslinger, H., & Tompkins, W. (1953). *The traffic in narcotics*. New York: Funk and Wagnalls.

Anthony, B., & Solomon, R. (1973). Introduction. In E. Murphy, *The black candle*. Toronto: Coles.

Arkinstall and Green v. *City of Surrey*. (2008, 24 Oct.). BCSC 1419. Docket S073785.

Arkinstall v. *City of Surrey*. (2010, 20 May). BCCA 250. Docket CA036620.

Barak, G. (Ed.). (1994). *Media, process, and the social construction of crime: Studies in newsmaking criminology*. New York: Garland Press.

Barnes, A. (2002). Dangerous duality: The "net effect" of immigration and deportation on Jamaicans in Canada. In W. Chan & I. Mirchandani (Eds.), *Crimes of colour: Racialization and the criminal justice system in Canada* (pp. 191–203). Peterborough, ON: Broadview Press.

BC Archives. (2008). *Newspapers on Microfilm*. Retrieved 6 Oct. 2011 from http://www.bcarchives.gov.bc.ca/library/newspapr/bcarch/arch_v.htm

BC Hydro. (2011). *Electrical theft*. Retrieved 13 Dec. 2011 from http://www.bchydro.com/safety/marijuana_grow_ops.html

Beattie, K. (2006). Adult correctional services in Canada, 2004/2005. *Statistics Canada, 26*(5), 1–33.

Beckett, K. (1995). Fetal rights and "crack moms": Pregnant women in the war on drugs. *Contemporary Drug Problems, 22*(4), 587–612.

Belle-Isle, L., & Hathaway, A. (2007, Apr.). Barriers to access to medical cannabis for Canadians living with HIV/AIDS. *AIDS Care, 19*(4), 500–506. http://dx.doi.org/10.1080/09540120701207833 Medline:17453590

Belle-Isle, L., Walsh, Z., Callaway, R., Lucas, P., Capler, R., Kay, B., Stratton, T., Holtzman, S., Marshall, J., & Woodworth, M. (2013). Cannabis Access for Medical Purposes Survey (CAMPS): Preliminary findings on barriers to access in Canada. Presented in a meeting on Cannabis for Therapeutic Purposes: Health Services and Health Policy Research Priorities, BC Ministry of Health, 15 Jan. 2013.

Bennett, D., & Bernstein, S. (2013). *Throwing away the keys: The human and social cost of mandatory minimum sentencing*. Vancouver, BC: Pivot Legal Society.

Bennett, D., & Sadrehashemi, L. (2008). *Broken promises: Parents speak about B.C.'s child welfare system*. Vancouver: Pivot Legal Society and the Law Foundation of BC.

Bernstein, S., & Bennett, D. (2013). Zoned out: "NIMBYism," addiction services and municipal governance in British Columbia. *International Journal of Drug Policy*. Retrieved 30 May 2013 from http://dx.doi.org/10.1016/j.drugpo.2013.04.001

Berridge, V., & Edwards, G. (1981). *Opium and the people: Opiate use in nineteenth-century England*. London: Allan Lane.

Best, J. (1995). *Random violence: How we talk about new crimes and new victims*. Berkeley: University of California Press.

Best, J. (Ed.). (1999). *Images of issues: Typifying contemporary social problems*. New York: Aldine de Gruyter.

Boldfish Entertainment. (2004). *Not safe to occupy: Growing up in grow-ops.* Vancouver: Author.

Bone, C., & Waldron, S.J. (1997). *New trends in illicit marijuana cultivation in the United Kingdom of Great Britain and Northern Ireland.* Bulletin on Narcotics (UNODC). Retrieved 31 Oct. 2011 from http://www.unodc.org/unodc/en/data-and-analysis/bulletin/bulletin_1997-01-01_1_page006.html

British Columbia Ministry of Children and Family Development (BMCFD). (2003). *Protocol framework and working guidelines between child protection and alcohol and drug services.* Victoria, BC: Author.

British Columbia Ministry of Children and Family Development (BCMCFD). (2008). *Fact sheets: Child protection issues and illegal drug manufacturing.* Victoria, BC. Author.

Bouchard, M. (2007). A capture-recapture model to estimate the size of criminal populations and the risks of detection in a marijuana cultivation industry. *Journal of Quantitative Criminology, 23*(3), 221–241. http://dx.doi.org/10.1007/s10940-007-9027-1

Bouchard, M. (2008). Towards a realistic method to estimate cannabis production in industrialized countries. *Contemporary Drug Problems, 35*, 291–320.

Bouchard, M., Alain, M., & Nguyen, H. (2009, Nov.). Convenient labour: The prevalence and nature of youth involvement in the marijuana cultivation industry. *International Journal on Drug Policy, 20*(6), 467–474. http://dx.doi.org/10.1016/j.drugpo.2009.02.006 Medline:19345079

Bouchard, M., Potter, G., & Decorte, T. (2011). Emerging trends in cannabis cultivation – and the way forward. In T. Decorte, G. Potter, & M. Bouchard (Eds.), *World wide weed: Global trends in cannabis cultivation and its control* (pp. 273–286). Farnham: Ashgate.

Bow, B. (2009). Introduction: The question of independence, then and now. In B. Bow & P. Lennox (Eds.), *An independent foreign policy for Canada?* (pp. 3–21). Toronto: University of Toronto Press.

Boyd, N. (1984). The origins of Canadian narcotics legislation: The process of criminalization in historical context. *Dalhousie Law Journal, 8*(1), 102–136.

Boyd, N. (1995). *Canadian law: An introduction.* Toronto: Harcourt Brace.

Boyd, N. (1998). Rethinking our policy on cannabis. *Policy Options, 19*(8), 31–33.

Boyd, N. (2013). *The Enforcement of Marijuana Possession Offences in British Columbia: A Blueprint for Change.* Retrieved 2 June 2013 from http://sensiblebc.ca/wp-content/uploads/2013/02/Blueprint-for-Change.pdf

Boyd, S. (1999). *Mothers and illicit drugs: Transcending the myths.* Toronto: University of Toronto Press.

Boyd, S. (2004). *From witches to crack moms: Women, drug law, and policy*. Durham, NC: Carolina Academic Press.

Boyd, S. (2006). Representations of women in the drug trade. In G. Balfour & E. Comack (Eds.), *Criminalizing women* (pp. 131–151). Halifax: Fernwood.

Boyd, S. (2008). *Hooked: Drug war films in Britain, Canada, and the United States*. New York: Routledge.

Boyd, S., & Carter, C. (2008). *Hegemonic struggles: Mayerthorpe, marijuana grow operations and the media*. Presentation at Society for Socialist Studies Congress. The Canadian Federation for the Humanities and Social Sciences Annual Congress, University of British Columbia, 5 June.

Boyd, S., & Carter, C. (2010a). Methamphetamine discourse: Media, law, and policy. *Canadian Journal of Communication, 35*(2), 219–237.

Boyd, S., & Carter, C. (2010b). *Obstacles to harm reduction and drug policy reform: Representations of marijuana grow-operations*. Poster presentation. 21st International Conference on Harm Reduction, Liverpool, 25–29 April 2010.

Boyd, S., and Carter, C. (2012). Using children: Marijuana grow ops, media, and policy. *Critical Studies in Media Communication, 29*(3), 238–257.

Brecher, E., & Editors of Consumer Reports. (1972). *Licit & illicit drugs*. Boston: Little, Brown.

Brennan, S. (2012). Police-reported crime statistics in Canada. 2011. *Juristat*, (85–002-X). Ottawa: Statistics Canada.

Brennan, S., & Dauvergne, M. (2011). Police-reported crime statistics in Canada, 2010. *Juristat*, (85–002-X). Ottawa: Statistics Canada.

Bunton, R. (2001). Knowledge, embodiment and neo-liberal drug policy. *Contemporary Drug Problems, 28*, 221–243.

British Columbia Ministry of Children and Family Development. (2003). *Protocol framework and working guidelines between Child Protection and Alcohol and Drug Services*. Victoria: Author.

British Columbia Ministry of Children and Family Development. (2008). *Fact Sheets: child protection issues and illegal drug manufacturing*. Victoria: Author.

Brook, H., & Stringer, R. (2005). Users, using, used: A beginner's guide to deconstructing drugs discourse. *International Journal on Drug Policy, 16*(5), 316–325. http://dx.doi.org/10.1016/j.drugpo.2005.05.002

Bullington, B. (1993). All about Eve: The many faces of United States drug policy. In F. Pearce & M. Woodiwess (Eds.), *Global crime connections: Dynamics and control* (pp. 32–71). Toronto: University of Toronto Press.

Burawoy, M. (2005, June). 2004 American Sociological Association Presidential address: for public sociology. *American Sociological Review, 56*(2), 259–294. http://dx.doi.org/10.1111/j.1468-4446.2005.00059.x

Campbell, N. (2000). *Using women: Gender, drug policy, and social justice*. New York: Routledge.

Canada Gazette. (2012). *Marihuana for medical purposes regulations.* Retrieved 24 Dec. 2012 from http://www.gazette.gc.ca/rp-pr/p1/2012/2012-12-15/html/reg4-eng.html

Canadian Association of Medical Cannabis Dispensaries. (2011). Retrieved 8 Dec. 2011 from http://www.camcd-acdcm.ca/

Canadian Centre for Justice Statistics. (2011). *Cannabis violations, Canada and provinces 1998 to 2010.* Ottawa: Statistics Canada. Personal Communication, Information Officer, 29 Nov.

Canadian Firearms Centre. (1998). *Firearms, accidental deaths, suicides and violent crime: An updated review of the literature with special reference to the Canadian situation.* Retrieved 3 Mar. 2013 from http://www.justice.gc.ca/eng/pi/rs/rep-rap/1998/wd98_4-dt98_4/wd98_4.pdf

Canwest News. (2009). *Advertising plan book 2009.* Vancouver: Author.

Canwest News. n.d. *Advertising information: Audience reach.* Vancouver: Author. Retrieved 19 April 2010 from http://www.png.canwest.com/readership.html

Capler, R. (2006). *Federal marijuana policy primer.* BC Compassion Club Society & Canadians for Safe Access.

Caputo, M.R., & Ostrom, B.J. (1994). Potential tax revenue from a regulated marijuana market. *American Journal of Economics and Sociology, 53*(4), 475–490. http://dx.doi.org/10.1111/j.1536-7150.1994.tb02619.x

Carter, C. (2009, July). Making residential cannabis growing operations actionable: A critical policy analysis. *International Journal on Drug Policy, 20*(4), 371–376. http://dx.doi.org/10.1016/j.drugpo.2008.11.001 Medline: 19111455

Carstairs, C. (2006). *Jailed for possession: Illegal drug use, regulation, and power in Canada, 1920–1961.* Toronto: University of Toronto Press.

Caulkins, J., & Pacula, R. (2006). Marijuana markets: Inferences from reports by the household population. *Journal of Drug Issues, 36*(1), 173–200. http://dx.doi.org/10.1177/002204260603600108, 6(3), 335–348. http://dx.doi.org/10.1177/1462474504043636

Chan, W., & Mirchandani, K. (Eds.). (2002). *Crimes of Colour: Racialization and the criminal justice system in Canada.* Peterborough, ON: Broadview Press.

Chen, X. (2005). *Tending the gardens of citizenship: Child saving in Toronto from 1880–1920.* Toronto: University of Toronto Press.

Chermak, S. (1995). Image control: How police affect the presentation of crime news. *American Journal of Police, 14*(2), 21–43. http://dx.doi.org/10.1108/07358549510102730

Chermak, S., & Weiss, A. (2005). Maintaining legitimacy using external communications strategies: An analysis of police-media relations.

Journal of Criminal Justice, 33(5), 501–512. http://dx.doi.org/10.1016/j. jcrimjus.2005.06.001

Chibnall, S. (1977). *Law-and-order news: An analysis of crime reporting in the British press*. London: Tavistock.

Chin, V., Dandurand, Y., Plecas, D., & Segger, T. (2001). *The criminal justice response to marihuana growing operations in B.C.* Abbotsford, BC: Department of Criminology and Criminal Justice, University College of the Fraser Valley; Vancouver: International Centre for Criminal Law Reform and Criminal Justice Policy.

Chiricos, T. (2006). Moral panic as ideology: Drugs, violence, race and punishment in America. In C. Critcher (Ed.), *Critical readings: Moral panics and media* (pp. 103–123). Maidenhead: Open University Press.

Chomsky, N. (2000). *Rogue states: The rule of force in world affairs*. Cambridge, MA: South End Press.

Chunn, D.E., & Gavigan, S. (2004). Welfare law, welfare fraud, and the moral regulation of the "never deserving" poor. *Social & Legal Studies, 13*(2), 219–243. http://dx.doi.org/10.1177/0964663904042552

City of Chilliwack. (2006). *Bylaw # 3223: A Bylaw to Regulate Hydroponics Equipment and Drug Paraphernalia Dealers*. Retrieved 21 April 2006 from http://www.gov.chilliwack.bc.ca/main/attachments/files/1191/BL%203223%20%20Hydroponics%20and%20Drug%20Paraphernalia%20Bylaw.pdf

City of Richmond. (2011). *About Richmond RCMP*. Retrieved 22 Dec. 2011 from http://www.richmond.ca/safety/police/about.htm

City of Surrey. (2009). *Responding to Marijuana Grow Operations: A Community Handbook*. Retrieved 18 April 2010 from www.crimereduction.surrey.ca/.../SurreyMGOLeadersHandbookWeb.pdfommunity

City of Vancouver. (2005). *Preventing Harm from Psychoactive Substance Use*. Retrieved 12 Dec. 2011 from http://vancouver.ca/fourpillars/research.htm

Cohen, S. (1972). *Folk devils and moral panics: The creation of the mods and rockers*. Oxford: Martin Robertson.

Cohen, S., & Young, J. (Eds.). (1981). *The manufacture of news: Social problems, deviance and the mass media*. London: Constable.

Comack, E. (1986). We will get some good out of this riot yet: The Canadian state, drug legislation and class conflict. In S. Brickey & E. Comack (Eds.), *The social basis of law: Critical readings in the sociology of law* (pp. 48–70). Toronto: Garamond.

Commission of Inquiry into the Non-Medical Use of Drugs. (1973). *Final Report*. Ottawa: Information Canada.

Commission on Systemic Racism in the Ontario Criminal Justice System. (1995). *Report of the Commission on Systemic Racism in the Ontario Criminal Justice System: A community summary*. Toronto: Queen's Printer for Ontario.

Cooke, L., & Sturges, P. (2009). Police and media relations in an era of freedom of information. *Policing and Society, 19*(4), 406–424. http://dx.doi.org/10.1080/10439460903281513

Coomber, R. (2006). *Pusher myths: Re-situating the drug dealer*. London: Free Association Books.

Coomber, R., Morris, C., & Dunn, L. (2000, 1 May). How the media do drugs: Quality control and the reporting of drug issues in the UK print media. *International Journal on Drug Policy, 11*(3), 217–225. http://dx.doi.org/10.1016/S0955-3959(00)00046-3 Medline:10927199

Correctional Service of Canada. (2009a). *The changing federal offender population – Aboriginal offender highlights 2009*. Retrieved 14 June 2012 from http://www.csc-scc.gc.ca/text/rsrch-eng.shtml

Correctional Service of Canada. (2009b). *The changing federal offender population – highlights 2009*. Retrieved 14 June 2012 from http://www.csc-scc.gc.ca/text/rsrch/special_reports/sr2009/sr-2009-eng.shtml

Cowper, G. (2012). *A criminal justice system for the 21st century*. Final Report to the Minister of Justice and Attorney General Hon. Shirley Bond. BC Justice Reform Initiative.

Cresse, G., & Strong-Boag, V. (2005). *Losing ground: The effects of government cutbacks on women in British Columbia, 2001–2005*. Prepared for the BC Coalition of Women's Centres, the University of British Columbia Centre for research in Women's Studies and Gender Relations, and the BC Federation of Labour.

Dandurand, Y., Plecas, D., Chin, V., & Segger, T. (2002). Marijuana trafficking incidents in British Columbia: An empirical survey (1997–2000). Unpublished paper. Abbotsford, BC: Department of Criminology and Criminal Justice, University College of the Fraser Valley; Vancouver: International Centre for Criminal Law Reform and Criminal Justice Policy.

Dauvergne, M. (2009). Trends in police-reported drug offences in Canada. *Juristat, 29*(2), 1–25.

Davis, A. (2003). *Are prisons obsolete?* New York: Seven Stories Press.

DeBeck, K., Wood, E., Montaner, J., & Kerr, T. (2006). Canada's 2003 renewed drug strategy – an evidence-based review. Canadian HIV/AIDS Legal Network. *HIV/AIDS Policy & Law Review, 11*(2/3), 1–12.

DeBeck, K., Wood, E., Montaner, J., & Kerr, T. (2009, Mar.). Canada's new federal "National Anti-Drug Strategy": An informal audit of reported funding allocation. *International Journal on Drug Policy, 20*(2), 188–191. http://dx.doi.org/10.1016/j.drugpo.2008.04.004 Medline:18571396

Decorte, T. (2010a). Small-scale domestic cannabis cultivation: An anonymous Web survey among 659 cannabis cultivators in Belgium. *Contemporary Drug Problems, 37*(2), 341–370.

Decorte, T. (2010b, July). The case for small-scale domestic cannabis cultivation. *International Journal on Drug Policy, 21*(4), 271–275. http://dx.doi.
org/10.1016/j.drugpo.2010.01.009 Medline:20176465

Decorte, T., Potter, F., & Bouchard, M. (2011). *World wide weed: Global trends in
cannabis cultivation and its control*. Farnham: Ashgate.

Degenhardt, L., Chiu, W.T., Sampson, N., Kessler, R.C., Anthony, J.C., Anger-
meyer, M., ..., & Wells, J.E. (2008, 1 July). Toward a global view of alcohol,
tobacco, cannabis, and cocaine use: Findings from the WHO World Mental
Health Surveys. *PLoS Medicine, 5*(7), e141. http://dx.doi.org/10.1371/
journal.pmed.0050141 Medline:18597549

Degenhardt, L., & Hall, W. (2012, 7 Jan.). Extent of illicit drug use and dependence, and their contribution to the global burden of disease. *Lancet,
379*(9810), 55–70. http://dx.doi.org/10.1016/S0140-6736(11)61138-0
Medline:22225671

Department of Justice. (2011a). *Canadian Charter of Rights and Freedoms*. Retrieved 8 Dec. 2011 from http://laws.justice.gc.ca/eng/charter/.

Department of Justice. (2011b). *Medical Marihuana Consolidated Regulations*.
Retrieved 8 Nov. 2011 from http://laws-lois.justice.gc.ca/eng/regulations/
SOR-2001-227/section-25-20060322.html.

Department of Justice. (2011c). *Government of Canada introduces the Safe Streets
and Communities Act*. Retrieved 13 Dec. 2011 from http://www.justice.
gc.ca/eng/news-nouv/nr-cp/2011/doc_32631.html.

Dean, M. (2002). Liberal government and authoritarianism. *Economy and
Society, 31*(1), 37–61. http://dx.doi.org/10.1080/03085140120109240

Diakiw, K. (2011, 30 May). Surrey clamps down on medical marijuana users,
growers. *Surrey Leader*. Retrieved 12 Nov. 2011 from http://www.bclocalnews.
com/surrey_area/surreyleader/news/122872599.htm.

District of Mission. (2011). *Public safety inspection team*. Retrieved 17 Nov.
2011 from http://www.mission.ca/municipal-hall/departments/
public-safety-inspection-team/.

Douglas, J. (2010). The health and safety of children living in marijuana grow
operations: A child welfare perspective. (Unpublished doctoral thesis.)
Department of Social Work, University of British Columbia, Vancouver.

Dowler, K. (2003). Media consumption and public attitudes toward crime
and justice: The relationship between fear of crime, punitive attitudes, and
perceived police effectiveness. *Journal of Criminal Justice and Popular Culture,
10*(2), 109–126.

Doyle, A. (2006). How not to think about crime in the media. *Canadian
Journal of Criminology and Criminal Justice, 48*(6), 867–885. http://dx.doi.
org/10.3138/cjccj.48.6.867

Drucker, E. (2011). *A plague of prisons: The epidemiology of mass incarceration in America*. New York: New Press.

Drug Enforcement Administration (DEA). (2008). *United States – Canada border drug threat assessment 2007*. Washington, DC: Author.

DrugSense. (2012). Open letter to Mr. Kofi Annan. Retrieved 28 May 2012, from http://www.csdp.org/edcs/figure25.htm

Dyer, R. (1999). White. In J. Evans & S. Hall (Eds.), *Visual culture: The reader* (pp. 457–467). London: Sage.

Drug Policy Alliance. (2012). *Raising the stakes: 2011 annual report*. New York: Author.

Easton, S. (2004). *Marijuana growth in British Columbia*. Vancouver: Fraser Institute. Retrieved 21 June 2011 from http://www.fraserinstitute.org/publicationdisplay.aspx?id=13187&terms=marijuana.

Edwards, A. (1988). *Regulation and repression*. Sydney, Australia: Allen & Unwin.

Edwards, E., Bunting, W., & Garcia, L. (2013). *The war on marijuana in black and white*. New York: American Civil Liberties Union.

Eldridge, J. (Ed.). (1993). *News, truth and power*. London: Routledge. http://dx.doi.org/10.4324/9780203397404.

Elliot, E. (2011). *Security, with care: Restorative justice and healthy societies*. Halifax: Fernwood.

Erickson, P. (1992). Recent trends in Canadian drug policy: The decline and resurgence of prohibitionism. *Daedalus, 121*(3A), 247–266.

Ericson, R. (2007). Rules in policing: Five perspectives. *Theoretical Criminology, 11*(3), 367–401. http://dx.doi.org/10.1177/1362480607079583

Ericson, R., Baranek, R., & Chan, J. (1991). *Representing order: Crime, law and justice in the news media*. Toronto: University of Toronto Press.

Etsten, D. (2000). Controversial proposed legislation heightens stigma. *Journal of Addiction and Mental Health, 3*(6), 8.

Fassbender, P., & Green, R. (2011, March 8). Letter to Hon. Leona Aglukkaq, minister of health re medicinal marijuana dispensary. Retrieved 28 June 2011 from http://www.scribd.com/doc/53571952/Letter-to-HonLeona-Aglukkaq-Minister-of-Health-Re-Medicinal-Marijuana-Dispensary 3archive.

Feldman, A. (2001). Philoctetes revisited: White public space and the political geography of public safety. *Social Text 68, 19*(3), 57–89. http://dx.doi.org/10.1215/01642472-19-3_68-57

Ferrell, J., & Websdale, N. (1999). Materials for making trouble. In J. Ferrell & N. Websdale (Eds.), *Making trouble: Cultural constructions of crime, deviance, and control* (pp. 3–21). New York: Aldine de Gruyter.

Fine, D. (2012). *Too high to fail: Cannabis and the new green economic revolution*. New York: Gotham Books.

Fischer, B. (1997). "The battle for a new Canadian drug law: Legal basis for harm reduction, or new rhetoric for prohibition? In P. Erickson, D. Riley, Y. Cheung, & P. O'Hare (Eds.), *Harm reduction: A new direction for policies and programs*. Toronto: University of Toronto Press.

Fischer, B., Ala-Leppilampi, K., Single, E., & Robins, A. (2003). Cannabis law reform in Canada: Is the "saga of promise, hesitations and retreat" coming to an end? *Canadian Journal of Criminology and Criminal Justice, 45*(3), 265–298. http://dx.doi.org/10.3138/cjccj.45.3.265

Fischer, B., Jeffries, V., Hall, W., Room, R., Goldner, E., & Rehm, J. (2011, Sept.–Oct.). Lower risk cannabis use guidelines for Canada (LRCUG): A narrative review of evidence and recommendations. *Canadian Journal of Public Health, 102*(5), 324–327. Medline:22032094

Fischer, B., Rehm, J., & Hall, W. (2009). Cannabis use in Canada: The need for a "public health" approach. *Canadian Journal of Public Health, 100*(2), 101–103.

Fischer, B., Turnbull, S., Poland, B., & Haydon, E. (2004). Drug use, risk and urban order: Examining supervised injection sites (SISs) as "governmentality." *International Journal on Drug Policy, 15*(5-6), 357–365. http://dx.doi.org/10.1016/j.drugpo.2004.04.002

Flavin, J., & Paltrow, L.M. (2010, Apr.). Punishing pregnant drug-using women: Defying law, medicine, and common sense. *Journal of Addictive Diseases, 29*(2), 231–244. http://dx.doi.org/10.1080/10550881003684830 Medline:20407979

Flight, J. (2007). *Substance use by Canadian youth, a national survey of Canadians' use of alcohol and other drugs*. Ottawa: Canadian Centre on Substance Abuse & Health Canada.

Former city councillor raided after criticizing marijuana laws, *YouTube*, Retrieved 17 May 2011 from http://www.youtube.com/watch?v=N49lSwOajlI.

Fraser, S., & Moore, D. (2008, Feb.). Dazzled by unity? Order and chaos in public discourse on illicit drug use. *Social Science & Medicine, 66*(3), 740–752. http://dx.doi.org/10.1016/j.socscimed.2007.10.012 Medline:18006200

Fraser, S., & Valentine, K. (2008). *Substance & substitution: Methadone subjects in liberal societies*. New York: Palgrave MacMillan. http://dx.doi.org/10.1057/9780230582569

Galliher, J., Keys, D., & Elsner, M. (1998). *Lindesmith* v. *Anslinger*: An early government victory in the failed war on drugs. *Journal of Law & Criminology, 88*(3), 661–682.

Garis, L. (2005). *Eliminating residential marijuana grow operations: An alternative approach, a report on Surrey, British Columbia's electrical fire and safety investigation initiative.* Retrieved 16 Aug. 2010 from http://www.llbc.leg.bc.ca/public/PubDocs/docs/378581/marijuana_grow_op.pdf.

Garis, L. (2009, 4 Nov.). *Combating Canada's marijuana grow industry: Stronger penalties and other deterrents. Submission to the Standing Senate Committee on Legal and Constitutional Affairs on Bill C-15, an Act to Amend the Controlled Drugs and Substances Act.* Retrieved 5 Dec. 2011 from http://www.parl.gc.ca/Content/SEN/Committee/402/lega/images/18ap-e.pdf.

Garis, L., Plecas, D., Cohen, I.M., & McCormick, A. (2009). *Community response to marijuana grow operations: A guide to promising practices.* Retrieved 8 Dec. 2011 from http://www.surrey.ca/city-services/8224.aspx.

Garland, D. (2001). *The culture of control: Crime and social order in contemporary society.* Chicago: University of Chicago Press.

Garofalo, J. (1981). Crime and the mass media: A selective review of research. *Journal of Research in Crime and Delinquency, 18*(2), 319–350. http://dx.doi.org/10.1177/002242788101800207

Giffen, P., Endicott, S., & Lambert, S. (1991). *Panic and indifference: The politics of Canada's drug laws.* Ottawa: Canadian Centre on Substance Abuse.

Global Commission on Drug Policy. (2011). *War on drugs.* Retrieved 17 Nov. 2011 from http://www.globalcommissionondrugs.org/

Golden, J. (2000, June). "A tempest in a cocktail glass": Mothers, alcohol, and television, 1977–1996. *Journal of Health Politics, Policy and Law, 25*(3), 473–498. http://dx.doi.org/10.1215/03616878-25-3-473 Medline:10946386

Gomez, L. (1997). *Misconceiving mothers: Legislators, prosecutors, and the politics of prenatal drug exposure.* Philadelphia: Temple University Press.

Goode, T. (2008). Moral panics and disproportionality: The case of LSD use in the sixties. *Deviant Behavior, 29*(6), 533–543. http://dx.doi.org/10.1080/01639620701839377

Government of Canada. (1996). *Bridging the cultural divide: A report on Aboriginal people and criminal justice.* Ottawa: Author.

Graduate Institute of International and Development Studies – Small Arms Survey. (2011). *Estimating civilian owned firearms. Research notes (9).* Geneva, Switzerland. Retrieved 18 Nov. 2011 from http://www.smallarmssurvey.org/about-us/mission.html

Grayson, K. (2008). *Chasing dragons: Security, identity, and illicit drugs in Canada.* Toronto: University of Toronto Press.

Greaves, L., Varcoe, C., Poole, N., Morrow, M., Johnson, J., Pederson, A., & Irwin, L. (2002). *A motherhood issue: Discourses on mothering under duress.* Ottawa: Status of Women in Canada.

Grinspoon, L., & Bakalar, J. (1997). *Marihuana, the forbidden medicine*. New Haven: Yale University Press.

Hafley, S.R., & Tewksbury, R. (1995). The rural Kentucky marijuana industry: Organization and community involvement. *Deviant Behavior, 16*(3), 201–221. http://dx.doi.org/10.1080/01639625.1995.9967999

Hagan, J. (2001). *Northern passage: American Vietnam resisters in Canada*. Cambridge: Harvard University Press.

Haines-Saah, R., Johnson, J., Repta, R., Ostry, A., Young, M., Shoveller, J., et al. (2013). The privileged normalization of marijuana use – an analysis of Canadian newspaper reporting, 1997–2007. *Critical Public Health*. DOI:10.1080/09581596.2013.771812.

Hakkarainen, P., & Perala, J. (2011). With a little help from my friends – Justifications of small-scale cannabis growers. In T. Decorte, G. Potter, & M. Bouchard (Eds.), *World wild weed: Global trends in cannabis cultivation and its control* (pp. 75–90). Farnham: Ashgate.

Hale, G. (2012). *So near yet so far: The public and hidden worlds of Canadian-US relations*. Vancouver: UBC press.

Hall, S. (1981). The determination of news photographs. In S. Cohen & J. Young (Eds.), *The manufacture of news: Social problems, deviance and the mass media*. (Rev. ed., pp. 226–243). London: Constable.

Hall, S. (1997). *Representations: Cultural representations and signifying practices*. London: Sage.

Hall, S., Cricher, C., Jefferson, T., Clarke, J., & Roberts, B. (1978). *Policing the crisis: Mugging, the state, and law and order*. Houndmills, UK: MacMillan.

Hammersvik, E., Sandberg, S., & Pedersen, W. (2012, Nov.). Why small-scale cannabis growers stay small: Five mechanisms that prevent small-scale growers from going large scale. *International Journal on Drug Policy, 23*(6), 458–464. http://dx.doi.org/10.1016/j.drugpo.2012.08.001 Medline:23036648

Hannah-Moffat, K. (2001). *Punishment in disguise*. Toronto: University of Toronto Press.

Hathaway, A., & Erickson, P. (2003). Drug reform principles and policy debates: Harm reduction prospects for cannabis in Canada. *Journal of Drug Issues, 33*(2), 465–495. http://dx.doi.org/10.1177/002204260303300209

Hathaway, A., & Rossiter, K. (2007). Medical marijuana, community building, and Canada's compassionate Societies. *Contemporary Justice Review, 10*(3), 283–296. http://dx.doi.org/10.1080/10282580701526088

Hayward, K.J., & Young, J. (2004). Cultural criminology: Some notes on the script. *Theoretical Criminology, 8*(3), 259–273. http://dx.doi.org/10.1177/1362480604044608

Health Canada. (2010). *Marihuana for medical purposes – statistics*. Retrieved 31 May 2013 from http://www.hc-sc.gc.ca/dhp-mps/marihuana/stat/index-eng.php

Health Canada. (2011a). *Medical use of marihuana*. Retrieved 13 Dec. 2011 from http://www.hc-sc.gc.ca/dhp-mps/marihuana/index-eng.php

Health Canada. (2011b, 11 June). *Proposed improvements to Health Canada's Marijuana Medical Access Program*. Retrieved 11 July 2011 from http://www. hc-sc.gc.ca/dhp-mps/consultation/marihuana/_2011/program/ consult-eng.php

Health Canada. (2011c). *Consultation on proposed improvements to the Marihuana Medical Access Program*. Retrieved 8 Dec. 2011 from http://www.hc-sc. gc.ca/dhp-mps/consultation/marihuana/_2011/program/index-eng.php

Health Officers Council of British Columbia. (2005). *A public health approach to drug control in Canada*. Retrieved 31 May 2013 from http://www.phabc.org/ modules.php?name=Contentpub&pa=showpage&pid=29

Health Officers Council of British Columbia. (2011). *Public health perspectives for regulating psychoactive substances: What we can do about alcohol, tobacco, and other drugs, for discussion and feedback*. Retrieved 31 May 2013 from http:// drugpolicy.ca/solutions/publications/hocreport/.

Heath, L., & Gilbert, K. (1996). Mass media and fear of crime. *American Behavioral Scientist, 39*(4), 379–386. http://dx.doi.org/10.1177/ 0002764296039004003

Henault, C. (1971). *Survey of newspapers and magazines for the Le Dain Commission*. Ottawa: National Archives of Canada.

Hewitt, S. (2006). *Riding to the rescue: The transformation of the RCMP in Alberta and Saskatchewan, 1914–1939*. Toronto: University of Toronto Press.

Higdon, J. (2012). *Cornbread mafia: A homegrown syndicate's code of silence and the biggest marijuana bust in American history*. Guilford, CT: Lyons Press.

Hitzig et al. v. *Her Majesty the Queen; Parker* v. *Her Majesty the Queen;* and *Paquette and Turmel* v. *Her Majesty the Queen* (2003,10//07), ONCA C39532; C39738; C39740.

Hough, M., Warburton, H., Few, B., May, T., Man, L., Witton, J., et al. (2003). *A growing market: The domestic cultivation of cannabis*. Layerthorpe, York: Joseph Rowntree Foundation.

Howitt, D. (1998). *Crime, the media and the law*. West Sussex: Wiley.

Hughes, C., & Stevens, A. (2010). What can we learn from the Portuguese decriminalization of illicit drugs? *British Journal of Criminology, 50*(6), 999–1022. http://dx.doi.org/10.1093/bjc/azq038

Humphries, D. (1999). *Crack mothers: Pregnancy, drugs, and the media*. Columbus: Ohio State University Press.

Huxford, J. (2001). Beyond the referential: Uses of visual symbolism in the press. *Journalism, 2*(1), 45–71. http://dx.doi.org/10.1177/146488490100200102

Ipsos Reid. (2012, 2 July). *Seven in ten (66%) Canadians support decriminalization of marijuana in small amounts.* Retrieved 18 Dec. 2012 from http://www.ipsos-na.com/news-polls/pressrelease.aspx?id=5687

Jackson, M., & Stewart, G. (2009, Sept.). *A flawed compass: A human rights analysis of the roadmap to strengthening public safety.* Retrieved 5 Dec. 2011 from http://www.justicebehindthewalls.net/resources/news/flawed_Compass.pdf

Janson, A.C.M. (2002). The economics of cannabis cultivation in Europe. Paper presented at the 2nd European Conference on Drug Trafficking and Law Enforcement, Paris, 26 and 27 Sept. 2002. Retrieved 31 Oct. 2011 from http://www.cedro-uva.org/lib/jansen.economics.html.

Jenkins, P. (1999). *Synthetic panics: The symbolic politics of designer drugs.* New York: New York University Press.

Jiwani, Y. (2003). The criminalization of "race," the racialization of crime. In W. Chan & K. Mirchandani (Eds.), *Crimes of colour: Racialization and the criminal justice system in Canada* (pp. 67–86). Peterborough, ON: Broadview Press.

Kalacska, M., & Bouchard, M. (2011). Using police seizure data and hyperspectral imagery to estimate the size of an outdoor cannabis industry. *Police Practice and Reearch: An International Journal, 12*(5), 424–434. http://dx.doi.org/10.1080/15614263.2010.536722

Kilmer, B. (2012). Debunking the mythical numbers about marijuana production in Mexico and the United States. In E. Zedillo & H. Wheeler (Eds.), *Rethinking the "War on Drugs" through the US-Mexico prism* (pp. 168–175). New Haven, CT: Yale Center for the Study of Globalization. Retrieved 19 July 2012 from http://www.ycsg.yale.edu/center/ebook.html

Kozolanka, K., Mazepa, P., & Skinner, D. (2012). Considering alternative media in Canada: Structure, participation, activism. In K. Kozolanka, P. Mazepa, & D. Skinner (Eds.), *Alternative media in Canada* (pp. 1–24). Vancouver: UBC Press.

LaGuardia, F. (1944). Sociological Study. The LaGuardia Report. Retrieved 16 May 2012 from http://www.druglibrary.org/schaffer/library/studies/lag/foreword.htm

Lambertus, S. (2004). *Wartime images, peacetime wounds.* Toronto: University of Toronto Press.

Landry, L., & Sinha, M. (2008). Adult correctional services in Canada, 2005/2007. *Statistics Canada, 28*(6), 1–25.

Latin American Commission on Drugs and Democracy. (2009). Drugs and democracy: Towards a paradigm shift. Statement by the Latin

American Commission on Drugs and Democracy. Retrieved October 14, 2013 from: www.drogasedemocracia.org/Arquivos/declaracao_ingles_site.pdf?.

Legislative Assembly of British Columbia. (2009). *Safer Communities and Neighbourhoods Act, Bill M203–2009*. Retrieved 15 Nov. 2011 from http://www.leg.bc.ca/38th5th/1st_read/m203-1.htm.

Lenton, S. (2011). Reforming laws applying to domestic cannabis production as a harm reduction strategy – a case study. In T. Decorte, G. Potter, & M. Bouchard (Eds.), *World wide weed: Global trends in cannabis cultivation and its control* (pp. 197–214). Surrey: Ashgate.

Levine, H., Gettman, J., & Siegal, L. (2010). *Arresting blacks for marijuana in California: Possession arrests, 2006–08*. Retrieved 14 June 2012 from http://www.drugpolicy.org/resource/arresting-blacks-marijuana-california-possession-arrests-2006-08

Levine, H., & Siegal, L. (2011). *$75 million a year: The cost of New York City's marijuana possession arrests*. Retrieved 14 June 2012 from http://www.drugpolicy.org/resource/75-million-year-cost-new-york-citys-marijuana-possession-arrests

Loukedelis, D. (2006). *Local governments and the growth of surveillance* (Discussion Paper). Victoria, BC: Office of the Information and Privacy Commissioner. Retrieved 15 Oct. 2008 from http://www.oipc.bc.ca/.

Lucas, P. (2008). Regulating compassion: An overview of Canada's federal medical cannabis policy and practice. *Harm Reduction Journal, 5*(5). Retrieved from http://www.harmreductionjournal.com/content/5/1/5. http://dx.doi.org/10.1186/1477-7517-5-5 Medline:18226254

Lucas, P. (2009, July). Moral regulation and the presumption of guilt in Health Canada's medical cannabis policy and practice. *International Journal on Drug Policy, 20*(4), 296–303. http://dx.doi.org/10.1016/j.drugpo.2008.09.007 Medline:19124233

Lucas, P. (2010). Patient-centered strategies to counter stigma, oppression and forced incarceration in the C/S/X and medical cannabis movements. *Interface: A journal for and about social movements, 2*(2), 149–167.

Macklin, A. (2003). Looking at law through the lens of culture: A provocative case. In W. Chan & K. Mirchandani (Eds.), *Crimes of colour: Racialization and the criminal justice system in Canada* (pp. 87–99). Peterborough, ON: Broadview Press.

Mahony, T. (2011). Homicide in Canada, 2010. *Juristat*, (80–002-X), 1–29. Ottawa: Statistics Canada.

Mahony, T. (2011). *Women and the criminal justice system*. Ottawa: Statistics Canada, Social and Aboriginal Statistics Division, 89-503-X.

Maier, K. (1992). *Forced cesarean section as reproductive control and violence: A feminist social work perspective on the "Baby R" Case*. Unpublished master's thesis, Simon Fraser University, Burnaby, BC.

Mallea, P. (2010, Nov.). The fear factor: Stephen Harper's "Tough on Crime" agenda. Ottawa: Canadian Centre for Policy Alternatives. Retrieved 5 Dec. 2011, from http://www.policyalternatives.ca

Malm, A.E., & Tita, G.E. (2007). A spatial analysis of green teams: A tactical response to marijuana production in British Columbia. *Policy Sciences, 39*(4), 361–377. http://dx.doi.org/10.1007/s11077-006-9029-0

Mann, C., & Zatz, M. (2002). *Images of color, images of crime: Readings*. Los Angeles: Roxbury Publishing.

Manning, P. (2006). There's no glamour in glue: News and the symbolic framing of substance misuse. *Crime, Media, Culture, 2*(1), 49–66. http://dx.doi.org/10.1177/1741659006061711

Manning, P. (Ed.). (2007). Drugs and popular culture: Drugs, media and identity in contemporary society. Cullomption, Devon, UK: Willan Publishing.

Martel, M. (2006). *Not this time: Canadians, public policy, and the marijuana question 1961–1975*. Toronto: University of Toronto Press.

Mauer, M., and The Sentencing Project. (1999). *Race to incarcerate*. New York: New Press.

Mawani, R. (2002). In between and out of place: Mixed-race identity, liquor, and the law in British Columbia, 1850–1913. In S. Razack (Ed.), *Race, space, and the law: Unmapping a settler society* (pp. 47–69). Toronto: Between the Lines.

McCalla, A., & Satzewich, V. (2003). Settler capitalism and the construction of immigrants and "Indians" as racialized others. In W. Chan & K. Mirchandani (Eds.), *Crimes of colour: Racialization and the criminal justice system in Canada* (pp. 25–44). Peterborough, ON: Broadview Press.

McCormack, T. (1999, Fall). Fetal syndromes and the charter: The Winnipeg glue-sniffing case. *Canadian Journal of Law and Society, 14*(2), 77–99. Medline:12449975

McGovern, A., & Lee, M. (2010). "Copy[ing] it sweet": Police media units and the making of news. *Australian and New Zealand Journal of Criminology, 43*(3), 444–464. http://dx.doi.org/10.1375/acri.43.3.444

McMullan, J. (2001). Westray and after: Power, truth and news reporting of the Westray mine disaster. In S. Boyd, D. Chunn, & R. Menzies (Eds.), *[Ab]using power: The Canadian experience* (pp. 130–145). Halifax: Fernwood.

McMullan, J. (2005). *News, truth and crime: The Westray disaster and its aftermath*. Halifax: Fernwood.

McMullan, J., & McClung, M. (2006). The media, the politics of truth, and the coverage of corporate violence: The Westray disaster and the public inquiry. *Critical Criminology, 14*(1), 67–86.

McWilliams, J. (1990). *The protectors: Harry J. Anslinger and the Federal Bureau of Narcotics, 1930–1962*. Newark: University of Delaware Press.

Mehmedic, Z., Chandra, S., Slade, D., Denham, H., Foster, S., Patel, A.S., ..., & ElSohly, M.A. (2010, Sept.). Potency trends of Δ⁹-THC and other cannabinoids in confiscated cannabis preparations from 1993 to 2008. *Journal of Forensic Sciences*, 55(5), 1209–1217. http://dx.doi.org/10.1111/j.1556-4029.2010.01441.x Medline:20487147

Mikuriya, T. (1968). Physical, mental, and moral effects of marijuana: The Indian Hemp Drugs Commission Report. *International Journal of the Addictions*, 3(2), 253–270.

Mirchandani, K., & Chan, W. (2002). From race and crime to racialization and criminalization. In W. Chan & K. Mirchandani (Eds.), *Crimes of colour: Racialization and the criminal justice system in Canada* (pp. 9–22). Peterborough, ON: Broadview Press.

Mission Resident Class Action Lawsuit Meeting. (2010). Retrieved 12 Mar. 2010 from http://www.youtube.com/watch?v=ZDDcOV6Od_A http://www.youtube.com/watch?v=IKypKDGRuGs&feature=related http://www.youtube.com/watch?v=DA1a5W505Qc&feature=related http://www.youtube.com/watch?v=9KQvwWuV-J0&feature=related http://www.youtube.com/watch?v=Qq1zddkht3A&feature=related http://www.youtube.com/watch?v=z0JpPkH8Lhs&feature=related http://www.youtube.com/watch?v=JhpGhFd1z-U&feature=related http://www.youtube.com/watch?v=Jz9_O70P8Ew&feature=related http://www.youtube.com/watch?v=Sw9n6OHjiBY&feature=related

Moller, M., Koren, G., Karaskov, T., & Garcia-Bournissen, F. (2011, Nov.). Examining the health and drug exposures among Canadian children residing in drug-producing homes. *Journal of Pediatrics*, 159(5), 766–770, e1. http://dx.doi.org/10.1016/j.jpeds.2011.05.044 Medline:21784455

Mosher, C.J. (1998). *Discrimination and denial: Systemic racism in Ontario's legal and criminal justice systems, 1892–1961*. Toronto: University of Toronto Press.

Motiuk, L., & B. Vuong, B. (2001). *Statistical profiles of homicide, sex, robbery and drug offenders in federal corrections: An end-of-2000 review*. Ottawa: Correctional Service Canada.

Motiuk, L., & B. Vuong, B.. (2005). *Homicide, sex, robbery and drug offenders in federal corrections: An end-of-2004 review*. Ottawa: Correctional Service of Canada.

Mulgrew, I. (2005). *Bud Inc.: Inside Canada's marijuana industry*. Toronto: Random House Canada.

Murphy, E. (1973). *The black candle*. Toronto: Coles. (Originally published in 1922).

Musto, D. (1987). *The American disease: Origins of narcotic control* (expanded ed.). New York: Oxford University Press.

Musto, D. (Ed.). (2002). *Drugs in America: A documentary history*. New York: Routledge.

Nadelmann, E. (1993). *Cops across borders: The internationalization of U.S. criminal law enforcement*. University Park: Pennsylvania State University Press.

Narcotic Control Act, S.C. 1961, c. 35.

National Anti-Drug Strategy. (2011). *Drugsnot4me*. Retrieved 13 Dec. 2011 from http://www.hc-sc.gc.ca/hc-ps/drugs-drogues/youth-jeunes/index-eng.php.

Nellis, A. (2012). *Trends in U.S. corrections*. Washington, DC: The Sentencing Project. Retrieved 14 June 2012 from http://www.sentencingproject.org/template/page.cfm?id=120

Nolin, P., & Kenny, C. (2003). *Cannabis: Report of the Senate Special Committee of Illegal Drugs* (abridged ed.). Toronto: University of Toronto Press.

North American Congress of Latin America (NACLA). (2002). Profile Colombia: Drug economies of the Americas. *Report of the Americas*, 36(2), 13.

Office of National Drug Control Policy (ONDCP). (2010). *National Drug Control Strategy 2010*. Retrieved 20 June 2011 from http://www.white housedrugpolicy.gov/druggeddriving/index.html

Office of National Drug Control Policy (ONDCP). (2011). *National Drug Control Strategy*. Retrieved 14 Dec. 2011 from http://www.whitehouse.gov/ondcp/2011-national-drug-control-strategy

Office of the Correctional Investigator. (2012). *Spirit matters: Aboriginal people and the Corrections and Conditional Release Act*. Retrieved 28 May 2013 from http://www.oci-bec.gc.ca/rpt/pdf/oth-aut20121022-eng.pdf

Office of the Provincial Health Officer (BC). (2013). *Health, crime and doing time: Potential impacts of the Safe Streets and Communities Act (Former Bill C10) on the health and well-being of Aboriginal people in BC*. Retrieved 28 May 2013 from http://www.helath.gov.bc.ca/pho/pdf/health-crime-2013.pdf

Ontario Human Rights Commission. (2011). Public consultation paper: Human rights mental health strategy. Retrieved 8 Nov. 2011 from http://www.ohrc.on.ca/en/resources/discussion_consultation/mentalhealth?page=mentalhealth-Contents.html

Orloff, A.S. (1988). The political origins of America's belated welfare state. In M. Weir, A.S. Orloff, & T. Skocpol (Eds.), *The politics of social policy in the United States* (pp. 37–80). Princeton, NJ: Princeton University Press.

Oscapella, E., & Canadian Drug Policy Coalition Policy Working Group. (2012, Feb.). *Changing the frame: A new approach to drug policy in Canada*. Vancouver: CDPC. Retrieved 10 Feb. 2012 from http://drugpolicy.ca

Our way home reunion. (2007). Retrieved 17 May 2012 from http://www.ourwayhomereunion.com/home.php

Pahl, D. (2011, 3 Mar.). Report to the Minister of Justice and Attorney General Public Fatality Inquiry. Provincial Court of Alberta. Retrieved 13 Dec. 2011

from http://justice.alberta.ca/programs_services/fatality/Documents/
fatality-report-mayerthorpe.pdf.

Paltrow, L. (1992). *Criminal prosecutions against pregnant women: Reproductive freedom project*. New York: American Civil Liberties Union Foundation.

Perreault, S. (2013). Police-reported crime statistics in Canada, 2012. *Juristat*, no. 85-002-X, 1–45.

Pew Center on the States. (2008). *One in 100: Behind Bars in America 2008*. Washington, DC: Pew Charitable Trusts.

Pew Center on the States. (2009). *One in 31: The long reach of American corrections*. Washington, DC: Pew Charitable Trusts.

Plecas, D., Chaisson, K., Garis, L., & Snow, A. (2011). The nature and extent of marijuana growing operations in Mission, British Columbia: A 14-year review (1997–2011). University of the Fraser Valley. Retrieved 13 Dec. 2011 from http://www.ufv.ca/Assets/CCJR/Reports+and+Publications/Grow_Ops_in_Mission_14_Year_Review_-_2011.pdf.

Plecas, D., Dandurand, Y., Chin, V., & Segger, T. (2002). Marihuana growing operations in British Columbia: An empirical survey (1997–2000). Unpublished paper. Department of Criminology and Criminal Justice, University College of the Fraser Valley and International Centre for Criminal Law Reform and Criminal Justice Policy.

Plecas, D., Diplock, J., Garis, L., Carlisle, B., Neal, P., & Landry, S. (undated). The marihuana indoor production calculator: A tool for estimating domestic and export production levels and values. Abbortsford, BC: Centre for Criminal Justice Research, Department of Criminology and Criminal Justice, University College of the Fraser Valley.

Plecas, D., Malm, A., & Kinney, B. (2005). Marijuana growing operations in British Columbia revisited (1997–2003). Unpublished paper. Abbotsford, BC: Department of Criminology and Criminal Justice and International Centre for Urban Research Studies, University College of the Fraser Valley.

Poole, M. (1998). *Romancing Mary Jane: A year in the life of a failed marijuana grower*. Vancouver: Greystone Books.

Potter, G.R. (2010). *Weed, need and greed: A study of domestic cannabis cultivation*. London: Free Association Books.

Potter, G.R., & Dann, S.L. (2005). Urban crop circles: Urban cannabis growers in the north of England. In W.R. Palacios (Ed.), *Cocktails and dreams: Perspectives on drug and alcohol use* (pp. 89–109). Upper Saddle River, NJ: Pearson Prentice Hall.

Public Works and Government Services of Canada. *2009–2010 Annual Report on Government of Canada Advertising Activities*. Public Works and Government Services Canada. Retrieved 31 May 2013 from http://www.tpsgc-pwgsc.gc.ca/pub-adv/rapports-reports/2009-2010/tdm-toc-eng.html

Public Works and Government Services of Canada. Connecting Canadians
    with government – annual report of Government of Canada advertising
    activities 2008-2009. Retrieved 31 May 2013 from http://www.tpsgc-pwgsc.
    gc.ca/pub-adv/rapports-reports/2008-2009/tdm-toc-eng.html
Purvis, T., & Hunt, A. (1993). Discourse, ideology, discourse, ideology, dis-
    course, ideology. ... *British Journal of Sociology, 44*(3), 473–499.
R. v. Mernagh (2011). ONSC 2121. No. 1640/09.
R. v. Parker. (2000). O.J. No. 2787 (Ont. C.A.).
Racine, S., Flight, J., & Sawka, E. (2008). *Canadian Addiction Survey (CAS):
    A national survey of Canadians' use of alcohol and other drugs, public opinion,
    attitudes and opinions.* Ottawa: Health Canada.
Razack, S. (2002). Gendered racial violence and spatialized justice: The murder
    of Pamela George. In S. Razack (Ed.), *Race, space, and the law: Unmapping a
    white settler society* (pp. 121–156). Toronto: Between the Lines.
Reiman, A. (2008, Jan.). Self-efficacy, social support and service integration at
    medical cannabis facilities in the San Francisco Bay area of California.
    Health & Social Care in the Community, 16(1), 31–41. http://dx.doi.org/
    10.1111/j.1365-2524.2007.00722.x Medline:18181813
Reiman, A. (2009). Cannabis as a substitute for alcohol and other drugs.
    Harm Reduction Journal, 6(35). http://dx.doi.org/10.1186/1477-7517-6-35
    Medline:19958538
Reinarman, C. (1988). The social construction of an alcohol problem: The case
    of Mothers against Drug Drivers and social control in the 1980s. *Theory and
    Society, 17*(1), 91–120
Reinarman, C. (2011). Cannabis in cultural and legal limbo: Criminalization,
    legalization and the mixed blessing of medicalization in the USA. In S. Fra-
    ser & D. Moore (Eds.), *The drug effect: Health, crime and society* (pp. 171–188).
    New York: Cambridge University Press.
Reinarman, C., & Duskin, C. (1999). Dominant ideology and drugs in the me-
    dia. In J. Ferrell & N. Websdale (Eds.), *Making trouble: Cultural constructions
    of crime, deviance, and control* (pp. 73–87). New York: Aldine de Gruyter.
Reinarman, C., & Levine, H. (1997a). Crack in context: America's latest demon
    drug. In C. Reinarman & H. Levine (Eds.), *Crack in America: Demon drugs
    and social justice* (pp. 1–17). Berkeley: University of California Press.
Reinarman, C., & Levine, H. (1997b). The crack attack. In C. Reinarman &
    H. Levine (Eds.), *Crack in America: Demon drugs and social justice* (pp. 18–51).
    Berkeley: University of California Press.
Reinarman, C., & Levine, H. (2000). Crack in context: Politics and media in the
    making of a drug scare. In R. Crutchfield, G. Bridges, J. Weis, & C. Kubrin
    (Eds.), *Crime readings* (2nd ed., pp. 47–53). Thousand Oaks, CA: Sage.
Reiner, R. (2000). *The politics of police.* (3rd ed.). Oxford: Oxford University Press.

Report of the Aboriginal Committee. (1992). *Liberating our children, liberating our nations*. Victoria: BC: Ministry of Social Services.

Roberts, D. (2002). *Shattered bonds: The color of child welfare*. New York: Basic Civitas Books. http://dx.doi.org/10.1016/S0190-7409(02)00238-4

Room, R., Fischer, B., Hall, W., Lenton, S., & Reuter, P. (2008). *Cannabis policy: Moving beyond stalemate*. Oxford: Beckley Foundation.

Room, R., & Reuter, P. (2012, 7 Jan.). How well do international drug conventions protect public health? *Lancet, 379*(9810), 84–91. http://dx.doi.org/10.1016/S0140-6736(11)61423-2 Medline:22225673

Royal Canadian Mounted Police. (2009). *Report on the illicit drug situation in Canada, 2009*. Retrieved 31 May 2013 from http://www.rcmp-grc.gc.ca/drugs-drogues/2009/index-eng.htm

Royal Canadian Mounted Police. (2010). *Report on the illicit drug situation in Canada*. Ottawa: Her Majesty the Queen in Right of Canada.

Royal Canadian Mounted Police. (2011a). *What is the Marijuana Grow Initiative?* Retrieved 8 Dec. 2011 from http://www.Rcmp-grc.gc.ca/drugs-drogues/mgi-ircm/brochure-eng.htm.

Royal Canadian Mounted Police. (2011b). *RCMP's New National Marihuana Grow Strategy*. Retrieved 12 Dec. 2011 from http://www.rcmp-grc.gc.ca/news-nouvelles/2011/09-21-mgi-ircm-eng.htm

Royal Canadian Mounted Police. (2011c) *Canadian Firearm Program. Facts and Figures, July to September 2011*. Retrieved 18 Nov. 2011 from http://www.rcmp-grc.gc.ca/cfp-pcaf/facts-faits/archives/quick_facts/2011/se-eng.htm

Royal Canadian Mounted Police. (2011d). Marihuana grow operations. Retrieved 13 Dec. 2011 from http://www.rcmp-grc.gc.ca/fio-ofi/grow-ops-culture-eng.htm

Royal Canadian Mounted Police. (2011e). Newsroom of the BC RCMP. Retrieved 19 Dec. 2011, from http://bc.rcmp.ca/ViewPage.action?siteNodeId=28&languageId=1&contentId=-1

Royal Canadian Mounted Police. (2011f). BC RCMP News. Retrieved 19 Dec. 2011 from http://www.facebook.com/BCRCMPnews?sk=wall

Royal Canadian Mounted Police. (2011g). *RCMP in Surrey E Division*. Retrieved 22 Dec. 2011 from http://bc.rcmp.ca/ViewPage.action?siteNodeId=67&languageId=1&contentId=-1

Rutman, D., Callahan, M., & Swift, K. (2007). Risk assessment and mothers who use substances: Contradictions in child welfare practice and policy. In N. Poole & L. Greaves (Eds.), *Highs & Lows: Canadian Perspectives on Women and Substance Use* (pp. 282–288). Toronto: Centre for Addiction and Mental Health.

Said, E. (2001). *Orientalism* (25th anniversary ed.). New York: Vintage Books.

Senate of Canada. (1955). *Proceedings of the Special Committee on the Traffic in Narcotic Drugs in Canada.* Ottawa: Queen's Printer.

Senate of Canada. (5 May 2010, First Reading). Bill S.10. Third Session, Fortieth Parliament, 59, Elizabeth II. Ottawa.

Sensible BC. (2012). *Sensible BC: Decriminalize cannabis for a safer province.* Retrieved 20 Nov. 2012 from http://sensiblebc.ca/the-sensible-policing-act/

Sfetkopoulos v. *Canada* (2008, 10 Jan.) (Attorney General) (F.C.), 2008 FC 33, [2008] 3 F.C.R. 399, T-1415–0.

Siren, A.H., & Applegate, B.K. (2006). Intentions to offend: Examining the effects of personal and vicarious experiences with punishment avoidance. *Journal of Criminal Justice, 29*(20), 25–50.

Smith, A., Stewart, D., Poon, C., Saewyc, E., & the McCreary Centre Society. (2010). *What a difference a year can make: Early alcohol and marijuana use among 16- to 18-year-old BC students.* Vancouver, BC: McCreary Centre Society.

Smith, C. (2006). Racial profiling in Canada, the United States, and the United Kingdom. In C. Tator & F. Henry (Eds.), *Racial profiling in Canada* (pp. 55–91). Toronto: University of Toronto Press.

Snitzman, S.R., Olsson, B., & Room, R. (2008). *A cannabis reader: Global issues and experiences.* Lisbon: European Monitoring Centre for Drugs and Drug Addiction.

Solecki, A., Burnett, K., & Li, K. (2011). *Drug production cases in selected Canadian jurisdictions: A study of case file characteristics 1997–2005.* Ottawa: Department of Justice. Released under the Access to Information Act.

Solomon, R., & Green, M. (1988). The first century: The history of nonmedical opiate use and control policies in Canada, 1870–1970. In J. Blackwell & P. Erickson (Eds.), *Illicit drugs in Canada* (pre-publication ed., pp. 88–116). Toronto: Methuen.

Stacey Gowanlock and Mark Rees v. *District of Mission.* Supreme Court of Canada (2011, 7 July). Chilliwack, BC. Registry no. S0230558.

Statistics Canada. (2006). *Community Profiles.* Retrieved 31 May 2013, from http://www12.statcan.gc.ca/census-recensement/2006/dp-pd/prof/92-591/details/page.cfm?Lang=E&Geo1=CSD&Code1=5915022&Geo2=PR&Code2=59&Data=Count&SearchText=VAncouver&SearchType=Begins&SearchPR=01&B1=All&Custom=

Statistics Canada. (2013a). CANSIM Table 252-0051. Incident-based crime statistics, by detailed violations, annual. Retrieved 7 Oct. 2013, from http://www5.statcan.gc.ca/cansim/

Statistics Canada. (2013b). *Police reported drug offences, by gender of accused, Canada, 2009 and 2011.* Special data request. Cansim table. Canadian Centre for Justice Statistics: Uniform Crime Reporting Survey.

Stewart, D., Vallance, K., Stockwell, T., Reimer, B., Smith, A., Reist, D., & Saewye, E. (2009). *Adolescent substance use and related harm in BC*. (CARBC and McCreary Centre Society Statistical Bulletin). Victoria, BC: University of Victoria.

Stockwell, T., Sturge, J., Jones, W., Fischer, B., Carter, C. (2006). *Cannabis use in British Columbia: Patterns of use, perceptions, and public opinion as assessed in the 2004 Canadian Addiction Survey*. Victoria, BC: Centre for Addictions Research of BC.

Stop the Violence BC. (2011a). *Breaking the silence: Cannabis prohibition, organized crime and gang violence in British Columbia*. Vancouver: Author. Retrieved 28 May 2012 from http://www.Stoptheviolencebc.org

Stop the Violence BC. (2011b). *How not to protect community health and safety: What the government's own data say about the effects of cannabis prohibition*. Vancouver: Author. Retrieved 28 May 2012 from http://www.Stoptheviolencebc.org

Stop the Violence BC. (2012). *Poll: British Columbians Support Regulation, Ready for Change*. Vancouver: Stop the Violence BC. Retrieved 31 May 2013 from http://stoptheviolencebc.org/2012/11/01/poll-british-columbians-support-regulation-ready-for-change/

Stevenson, G., Lingley, L., Trasov, G., & Stansfield, H. (1956). *Drug addiction in British Columbia: A research survey*. Unpublished manuscript. Vancouver: University of British Columbia.

Stevenson, K. (no date available). An analysis of Surrey's medical marijuana grow-ops. British Columbia Institution of Technology. Retrieved 5 Dec. 2011 from City of Surrey, BC. http://www.surrey.ca/files/DCT_Medical_Marijuana_Grows_STUDY_Stevenson_BCIT.PDF

Stoddart, M. (2004). The marijuana economy, public safety and power/knowledge in the *Vancouver Sun. Brock Review, 8*(1), 45–60.

Surette, R. (1992/2007). *Media, crime, and criminal justice: Images and realities* (3rd ed.). Florence, KY: Wadsworth/Cengage Learning.

Sullivan, D., & Tifft, L. (1980). *The mask of love: Corrections in America*. New York: Kennikat Press.

Swift, K. (1995). *Manufacturing "bad mothers": A critical perspective on child neglect*. Toronto: University of Toronto Press.

Tator, C., & Henry, F. (2006). *Racial profiling in Canada: Challenging the myth of "a few bad apples."* Toronto: University of Toronto Press.

Taylor, S. (2008). Outside the outsiders: Media representations of drug use. *Probation Journal, 55*(4), 369–387. http://dx.doi.org/10.1177/0264550508096493

Terry, C., & Pellens, M. (1970). *The opium problem*. Montclair, NJ: Patterson Smith.

Thobani, S. (2007a). *Exalted subjects: Studies in the making of race and nation in Canada*. Toronto: University of Toronto Press.

Thobani, S. (2007b). Imperial longings, feminist responses: Print media and the imagining of Canadian nationhood after 9/11. In D. Chunn, S.B. Boyd, & H. Lessard (Eds.), *Reaction and resistance: Feminism, law and social change* (pp. 98–123). Vancouver: UBC Press.

Thomas, J. (2010, Summer). Adult criminal court statistics, 2008/2009. *Juristat, 30*(2), 1–38.

Turnbull, L. (2001). *Double jeopardy: Motherwork and the law*. Toronto: Sumach Press.

Turpel-Lafond, M. (2011, 17 Jan.). *Fragile lives, fragmented systems: Strengthening supports for vulnerable infants*. Victoria, BC: Representative for Children and Youth.

United Nations Office of Drugs and Crime. (2010a). *Afghanistan: Cannabis survey 2010*. Retrieved 31 Oct. 2011 from www.unodc.org/documents/crop-monitoring/Afghanistan/Afghanistan_Cannabis_Survey_Report_2010_smallwcover.pdf

United Nations Office of Drugs and Crime. (2010b). *World drug report 2010: Cannabis* Retrieved 31 Oct. 2011 from www.unodc.org/documents/wdr/WDR_2010/2.4_Cannabis.pdf

US Department of State. (2012, Mar.). *International narcotics control strategy report*. US Department of State: Bureau for International Narcotics and Law Enforcement Affairs.

Valverde, M. (1991). *The age of light, soap, and water: Moral reform in English Canada 1885–1925*. Toronto: McClelland and Stewart.

Valverde, M. (2012). *Everyday law on the street: City governance in an age of diversity*. Chicago: University of Chicago Press.

Vancouver Coastal Health. (2007). *This is not a test: 2006 Vancouver drug survey results*. Vancouver: Author.

Vancouver Police Department. (2011a). Media relations officers contact list. Retrieved 19 Dec. 2011 from http://bc.rcmp.ca/ViewPage.action?siteNodeId=446&languageId=1&contentId=-1

Vancouver Police Department. (2011b). Media and community affairs division. Retrieved 19 Dec. 2011 from http://vancouver.ca/police/organization/public-affairs/index.html.

Wakeford v. The Queen (1999). O.J. No. 1574 (Ont. S.C.J.).

Wallace, B., Klein, S., & Reitsma-Street, M. (2006). *Denied assistance: Closing the front door on welfare in BC*. Vancouver: Canadian Centre for Policy Alternatives.

Wallace, M. (2009). Police-reported crime statistics in Canada, 2008. *Juristat, 29*(3), 1–37.

Warner, J. (2002). *Craze: Gin and debauchery in an age of reason*. New York: Four Walls Eight Windows.

Websdale, N., & Ferrell, J. (1999). Taking the trouble: Concluding remarks and future directions. In J. Ferrell & N. Websdale (Eds.), *Making trouble: Cultural constructions of crime, deviance, and control* (pp. 349–364). New York: Aldine de Gruyter.

Weisheit, R.A. (1990). Domestic marijuana growers: Mainstreaming deviance. *Deviant Behavior, 11*(2), 107–129. http://dx.doi.org/10.1080/01639625.1990.9967837

Weisheit, R.A. (1991). The intangible rewards from crime: The case of domestic marijuana cultivation. *Crime and Delinquency, 37*(4), 506–527. http://dx.doi.org/10.1177/0011128791037004006

Weisheit, R.A. (1992). *Domestic marijuana: A neglected industry*. New York: Greenwood Press.

Werb, D., Nosyk, B., Kerr, T., Fischer, B., Montaner, J., & Wood, E. (2012, Nov.). Estimating the economic value of British Columbia's domestic cannabis market: Implications for provincial cannabis policy. *International Journal on Drug Policy, 23*(6), 436–441. http://dx.doi.org/10.1016/j.drugpo.2012.05.003 Medline:23085258

Werb, D., Rowell, G., Guyatt, G., Kerr, T., Montaner, J., & Wood, E. (2011, Mar.). Effect of drug law enforcement on drug market violence: A systematic review. *International Journal on Drug Policy, 22*(2), 87–94. http://dx.doi.org/10.1016/j.drugpo.2011.02.002 Medline:21392957

Werb, D., Rowell, G., Kerr, T., Guyatt, G., Montaner, J., & Wood, E. (2010). *Effect of drug law enforcement on drug-related violence: Evidence from a scientific review*. Vancouver: Urban Health Research Initiative, BC Centre for Excellence in HIV/AIDS.

Wilkins, C., Bhatta, K., & Casswell, S. (2002). The effectiveness of cannabis crop eradication operations in New Zealand. *Drug and Alcohol Review, 21*(4), 369–374.

Wilkins, C., & Caswell, S. (2004). Organized crime in cannabis cultivation in New Zealand: An economic analysis. *Contemporary Drug Problems, 30*, 757–777.

Winnipeg Child and Family Services [Northwest Area] v. G. (D.F.) [1997] 3 S.C.R. 925. Retrieved 31 May 2013 from http://csc.lexum.org/decisia-scc-csc/scc-csc/scc-csc/en/item/1562/index.do.html

Wood, E., et al. (2010). *The Vienna Declaration*. Retrieved 19 Aug. 2010 from http://www.viennadeclaration.com

Woodiwiss, M. (1993). Crime's global reach. In F. Pearce & M. Woodiwess (Eds.), *Global crime connections: Dynamics and control* (pp. 1–31). Toronto: University of Toronto Press.

Woodiwiss, M. (2001). *Organized crime and American power*. Toronto: University of Toronto Press.

Woodcock, G., & Vakumovic, I. (1968). *The Doukhobors*. Toronto: Oxford University Press.

Woolford, A. (2001). Tainted space: Representations of injection-drug use and HIV/AIDS in Vancouver's Downtown Eastside. *BC Studies, 129*, 27–50.

Wykes, M. (2001). *News, crime and culture*. London: Pluto Press.

Yalkin, T., & Kirk, M. (2012). *The fiscal impact of changes to eligibility for conditional sentences of imprisonment in Canada*. Ottawa: Office of the Parliamentary Budget Officer. Retrieved 29 May 2013 from http://www.parl.gc.ca/pbo-dpb

Young, J. (1981). The myth of drug takers in the mass media. In S. Cohen & J. Young (Eds.), *The manufacture of news: Social problems, deviance and the mass media* (pp. 326–334). London: Constable.

Yu, K. (2011, 20 Apr.). City councillor advocates change to medical marijuana laws. *Grand Forks Gazette*. Retrieved 28 June 2011 from http://www.bclocalnews.com/kootenay_rockies/grandforksgazette/news/120295284.html

Index